Developing Strategies for Competitive Advantage

Revised Edition

THE BEST OF LONG RANGE PLANNING—FIRST SERIES

THE BEST OF LONG RANGE PLANNING—SECOND SERIES

LONG RANGE PLANNING–The International Journal of Strategic Management*
The leading international journal in the field of strategic planning, providing authoritative information to senior managers, administrators, and academics on the concepts and techniques involved in the development and implementation of strategies and plans.

*Free sample copy gladly sent on request to:
Elsevier Science Ltd, The Boulevard, Langford Lane, Kidlington, Oxford OX5 1GB, UK

Developing Strategies for Competitive Advantage
Revised Edition

Edited by

Patrick McNamee

1999

Pergamon
An imprint of Elsevier Science

Amsterdam - Lausanne - New York - Oxford - Shannon - Singapore - Tokyo

ELSEVIER SCIENCE LTD
The Boulevard, Langford Lane
Kidlington, Oxford OX5 1GB, UK

Revised edition 1999

Library of Congress Cataloging in Publication Data:
A catalog record from the Library of Congress has been applied for.

British Library Cataloguing in Publication Data:
A catalogue record from the British Library has been applied for.

ISBN: 0-08-043574-2

∞ The paper used in this publication meets the requirements of ANSI/NISO Z39.48-1992 (Permanence of Paper).

Printed in The Netherlands.

Contents

PART II: WHAT HAS NOT CHANGED?

Developing missions, benchmarking strategic performance, managing mature businesses and the benefits of adroit strategic planning

Introduction

The first edition of "Developing Strategies for Competitive Advantage" in the Best of Long Range Planning Series was published in 1990 and when asked to edit a second edition my initial reaction was to ask two fundamental questions which were, since 1990:

- What has changed?
- What has not changed?

My own answers to each of these are set out below and then fleshed out with supporting articles.

PART I: WHAT HAS CHANGED?

What appears to have changed could be described as the 'rules of the game', i.e. today those enduring strategic truths or rules which needed to be followed to guarantee strategic success no longer *seem* to apply as universally as they did then. The changes in the rules of the game are considered to be those major developments which appear to have had profound strategic effects on all areas of strategic planning.

Although there has been a myriad of events which have had some impact upon strategic management there seem to be a number of categories that have been significantly important. These include:

- The dramatic rise in the strategic importance of information technology.
- The transformation of industries and the changes in the rules for success.
- The continuing rise in strategic and industrial importance of South East Asia.

The Dramatic Rise in the Strategic Importance of Information Technology

Perhaps the change that is most visible is that of the influence of the personal computer and the attendant information technology revolution. Just two indicators illustrate the immensity of this change, namely.

- The price, power and pervasiveness of personal computers in business in particular and life in general.

■ The development of information superhighways. The Internet and other information superhighways did not exist in 1990 and even today the future influence that they will have upon strategy and operations cannot be forecast with any degree of certainty.

Competitive advantage is being increasingly influenced by the opportunities offered by information technology. Indeed, for many organisations today, it could be argued that Chandler's views on the strategic roles of the railways is analogously and almost perfectly aligned with the current role of the information revolution. Thus Chandler wrote:

> *By the 1880s nearly every existing manufacturing enterprise could reach by railroad a large rural and even more swiftly growing industrial and urban markets. To meet these opportunities (successfully)[1], industrial enterprises began to enlarge their productive facilities, labour force and trained supervisory personnel.* [2]

Today, for firms taking advantage of the information revolution, Chandler could be paraphrased as follows:

> *By the late 1990s nearly every existing enterprise could reach by information superhighway large global and even more swiftly growing world markets. To meet these opportunities successfully industrial enterprises began to enlarge their information technology facilities and knowledge-trained personnel.*

In many industries the strategic effects that information technology has had upon access to markets, production methods and subsequent unit costs have been profound. This can be seen quite clearly in the ability of firms to change their value chains and hence their cost structures through outsourcing those differentiating activities which information technology has transformed into remote commodities.

Two articles illustrate these structural changes particularly well. *Outsourcing IT: The Strategic Implications* by Leslie Willcocks, Guy Fitzgerald and David Feeny highlights the key issues that ought to be considered when such a major change is contemplated. The second article: *Innovation in Banking: New Structures and Systems*, by Robert E. Morgan, Eileen Cronin and Mark A. Severn is a case study on how immense strategic change, of which one of the agents is information technology, is transforming the UK clearing banks as key decision makers wrestle with the twin problems of how to compete with electronic providers and how to reduce their fixed costs.

---

[1] Author's parenthesis.
[2] Source: Chandler, A.D. Jr., Strategy and Structure, Cambridge, Massachusetts and London, England: The MIT Press, 1962 and reprinted in Strage, H.M., Milestones in Management, Basil Blackwell, 1992, page 62.

The Transformation of Industries and the Changes in the 'Rules for Success'

In many industries the established rules seem no longer to apply, i.e. playing in the future using the rules of today will lead to failure. This type of industry transformation can occur in two main ways. The first and generally most dramatic is when 'one industry species jumps' from its own industry into another industry and in so doing ruptures the competitive rules of both its own industry and perhaps the industry which it has entered. For example, currently there exists confusion about industry rules in the previously unrelated industries of telecommunications, television, banking and computer software. Thus, through the development of personal computers and global digital networks:

- Cable television companies have entered the telecommunications industry by offering telephone services. Their presumed agenda is loading their networks with additional traffic. It seems that the established rules of the telecommunications industry are being fractured by this event.
- Similarly, it is possible that telecommunications companies may enter the high street banking industry with, once again, the agenda of loading their networks with additional traffic. Such developments are likely to have immense repercussions for traditional high street banks which are locked into very expensive high fixed cost, and perhaps redundant, branch networks.
- Threatening to complicate these rules even further is the role of companies such as Microsoft which, through their software, may come to act as electronic gatekeepers and control access to these emergent global channels.

Transformation can also occur when one or more incumbent players determine that some strategic feature of the industry has changed or can be changed and through their strategies utterly change the rules of the game. Even those incumbent firms who appear to have unassailable positions of strength will fail if such positions continue to be based upon the past rules of the game. For example IBM appeared to have achieved, not marginal, but invincible strategic dominance in the early 1980s. This apparent invincibility could be measured using a host of accepted strategic indicators such as:

Resources available,	Relative quality and reputation,
Scale in relation to rivals,	Distribution, Innovation,
Market position relative to rivals,	Proprietary technology,
Breadth of product line,	Superior high growth markets.

These strategic indicators plus IBM's decades of sustained superior financial performance surely indicated impregnability. Yet in 1992 it foundered and recorded one of the greatest corporate losses of all time and even in 1998 it still had not regained its previous dominance: the rules of the computer industry had changed and IBM's previous prowess proved puny against this new competitive agenda.

Four articles have been selected to illustrate the vital role of the strategist in signalling and then acting on industry transformations.

The first is *Becoming a Customer 'Owning' Corporation* by Sandra Vandermerwe. This article has at its core the belief that a major reason that companies suffer major strategic trauma caused by industry transformation is that they have focused on supplying products to customers rather than providing solutions to customers' lifetime needs. The author shows that outstandingly successful firms achieve their superiority by making the customer part of the strategic management process rather than as a consumer of end products, i.e. successful companies *own* their customers. The importance of having this open-ended pro-active view of redefining traditional product, industry and customer boundaries in an era of major transformation is well expressed by a quotation from AT&T's Head of Corporate Strategy which Vandermerwe uses:

> *People who see this (AT&T's new customer focused approach) as a win lose game between us and Baby Bells are missing the point." He sees the telecommunication pie growing bigger and bigger at the expense of other industries like transportation and sees a day when goods such as books are shipped around the country (direct from authors?) electronically and published in many places, rather than printed centrally, shipped and warehoused.*

When industries transform it is axiomatic that those firms which survive, or indeed prosper from, the transformation must also transform themselves. It is also axiomatic that the transformation of any firm can only occur through the transformation of the people who work in the firm. This type of transformational change is dealt with most comprehensively in *Strategic Change and Organizational Change at Hay Management Consultants* by Loizos Heracleous and Brian Langham. The authors first make the case that in order to achieve its ambitious goals Hay Management Consultants has no choice but to have major organizational change and second they assert that such change cannot be achieved without major cultural repercussions. They develop a cultural map of Hay Management Consultants and then provide four key points for managing the transition. The article has generic guidelines for managing the process and thus should be of interest to any readers who are concerned with implementing change programmes. Indeed an equally appropriate title for the article could be *'Managing Knowledge Workers in the Context of a Strategic Change Programme'.*

When genuine industry transformation occurs it is ruthless and indiscriminate and ultimately all players in the industry from the largest to the smallest will be affected. One of the world's best known and largest firms—Philips—clearly demonstrates this. The article by Nigel Freedman, *Operation Centurion: Managing Transformation at Philips* charts the programme of change that has taken place at Philips since the crisis of 1990 and the appointment, at that time, of Jan Timmer as President. Rebuilding the company had three major elements—Operational Improvement, Growth and Innovation and Operation Centurion was the structure that was used to achieve the changes necessary to achieve these goals. The article sets out the process of change that was used and also shows, perhaps more importantly, that key to change is the replacement of training by education and continuous learning. It is worth noting as well that the author does not believe that the transformation could have been achieved by using Philips staff alone. Key to the change process were teams comprising: outside facilitators (from business schools!) plus consultants plus internal Philips facilitators. Learning through action was a key feature of how these multi-perspective teams achieved their results.

The final article in this section emphasizes that today it is not just industries that transform but rather the whole environment in which all organizations face is increasing turbulent, unstable and unpredictable. How can firms, especially large ones, adapt to this turbulence? One approach is to use scenario planning and *Scenario Planning at British Airways* by Kathy Moyer charts how this company successfully developed scenarios for the future which helped guide the company's strategic development. The process is described in great detail and what is perhaps the hallmark of an effective strategic development is that, even at the height of a recession in the airline industry, British Airways continued to be profitable.

The Rise in Strategic and Industrial Importance of South East Asia

Although the Asia Pacific region is currently experiencing economic difficulties there would still be a strongly held view that the region will continue to be of great importance over the next decades. For example it has been forecast that between 1991 and 2011 the region's share of total world output is forecast to grow from 21 per cent to around 25 per cent and in some crucial advanced industries such as advanced structural ceramics it is forecast to become the world's largest producer. No book on gaining competitive advantage could be complete without including material which analyses how this region has developed and how it is likely to develop in the future. The distinctive nature of business in the region is considered at three levels in the three articles below.

Philippe Lassere's *Corporate Strategies for the Asia Pacific Region* is at the macro or regional level and it provides clear perspectives on key elements which have led to the region enjoying such sustained success. It is a most comprehensive article and contains a wealth of relevant information which will be of interest to planners from all sizes of firms. Lasserre seems to be concerned with the lack of substantial, or indeed any, presence that Western firms have in this 'engine for growth of the world economy'. Most persuasively he illustrates the multidimensional importance of the region in terms of its markets:

- as a resource base and
- as a source of learning.

It is perhaps the last of these issues that is most important from a strategic planning perspective in that many of the Western 'strategic rules for success' are not followed in this region and planners cannot afford to be ignorant of this alternative set of rules.

The second article is at the level of the firm. Closely related to the shift of industrial power towards South East Asia is the issue of why this shift has occurred. Although there are many reasons advanced there is one issue upon which strategic planners are likely to agree, namely that the ways in which business is conducted is somewhat different in Asia from the West. A corollary of this is that it is surely in the interests of all managers to ask the question: 'Is there anything to be learnt from this alternative approach?' At the heart of any approach to business lies the fundamental issue of who owns this company and in whose interests should it be run. *Whose Company is it? The Concept of the Corporation in Japan and the West* by Masaru Yoshimori addresses this issue. Yoshimori suggests that in terms of corporate governance companies can be divided into three types which are:

■ *monistic*, which is shareholder orientated and typical of many US companies,
■ *dualistic,* which is shareholder plus employees orientated and typical of many German and French companies and
■ *pluralistic,* which is orientated towards all stakeholders and typical of many Japanese companies.

The author shows the benefits and flaws of each system and concludes that there are new signs of convergence among the three systems and that, irrespective of the system followed, in the next century to survive more democratic and open systems must be developed.

The third article in this section—*Partnership with an Asian Family Business: What Every MNC Should Know,* by P. Narayan Pant and Vasant G. Rajadhyaksha—is very much a 'nuts and bolts' article which, as the title suggests, provides guidance for Western firms which opt to do business in Asia through partnership with a local family firm. The article provides an excellent set of questions to ask and answer before undertaking such a step.

Join up or split up?

In today's era of uncertainty it appears that large companies are often following two mutually exclusive strategies. One is the strategy of merger or forming strategic alliances in order to have scale benefits and greater control of markets while the other is to de-merge and have greater focus and strategic agility. These two strategies reflect a contemporary strategic paradox: namely in many industries, in order to be competitive firms must have a greater scale or critical mass than ever before and yet, simultaneously, because of the increasing rate of transformational change, firms must also be ever more strategically agile. This appears to be a contradiction as it is often argued that scale and agility are inversely correlated. Two articles illustrate this feature of contemporary strategic thinking.

The first is *Strategic Alliances in Fast-Moving Markets* by Victor Newman and Kazem Chaharbaghi which shows, with great clarity, how two companies—British Aerospace and General Motors —used a strategic alliance to respond to the challenges of scale and agility. They demonstrate how strategic alliances can range from the defensive—where the motive for the alliance is to protect existing markets—to the knowledge-led offensive kind. It is this latter type which they show is more likely to yield sustained competitive advantage.

Carol Kennedy's article *The ICI Demerger: Unlocking Shareholder Value* not only shows the strategic rationale and the actions taken in this momentous event but, perhaps even more importantly, she captures the thinking and uncertainty which led to the decision. This type of background to the de-merger decision is invaluable because in life it is often the case that when a successful major strategic decision is reviewed after a number years it is regarded, affectionately, as having been a sensible and logical choice. However any major strategic change such as this de-merger is always fraught with risk and fuelled by uncertainty: after all it tends to be an easier choice to maintain the status quo and to continue to accept disappointing but not disastrous results. ICI's management did have the courage to pursue what was probably regarded by many at that time as an heretical strategy and subsequent performance seems to have vindicated the choice.

PART II: WHAT HAS NOT CHANGED?

At this point it is important to reflect upon the contribution that strategic planning has made. Has the discipline failed?' Of course not. What appears to have happened, is not so much that the fundamentals of the discipline are flawed, but rather there has been an unquestioning application of what were believed to be strategic rules made certain by a previous era of greater certainty and clearer boundaries. As seen above this is now an era of competitive uncertainty and uncertain boundaries. So it appears that it is not so much that the rules no longer apply but for them to be robust their application and measurement must take place in the appropriate context. To illustrate, judgements about so many aspects of strategy are not made in absolute terms but in terms of position relative to rivals. For example the fundamental strategic issues listed below tend to be considered relative to rivals.

- Mission, goals and targets,
- Business definition,
  - Measures of strategic performance such as:
  - Relative Market Share,
  - Relative Product Quality and Service,

- Relative Unit Costs,
- Relative Capital Intensity,
- Relative Growth Rates etc.

In today's era of shifting industry boundaries it is not always clear that such measures yield true comparisons as it may not be the case that like is being compared with like. Thus, as already alluded to above, in the telecommunications business, when the mission, goals, targets and performance of a telecommunications company are being compared with those of a cable company which has telephone services as a minor aspect of its total business, the agendas and success criteria for each are likely to be very different. Thus it is likely that the telecommunications company will regard high returns from its telephone business as essential for its development and will have a strategy to provide this, whereas the cable company is likely to regard its returns from its telephone business as much less important than its returns from its television channels and will may well have a strategy which will promote its telephone services as 'a loss leader.'

Similar uncertainty applies about the use of the other measures listed above, not just in relation to rivals from non-related industries, but also in relation to industry rivals who may have different perspectives, e.g. national, regional global.

An additional difficulty which applies in the area of competitor analysis are the long-run relatively stable linkages between firms and their preferred suppliers and their preferred customers which have developed into federations or associations. The competitive insights likely to be gained from just an analysis of just the firm at the hub of these relationships seems increasingly inadequate.

However, when there is clarity about business definition, industry definition and competitor definition and how the strategic techniques or measures should be applied then the strategic fundamentals which have obtained for many years continue and are likely to continue to do so. This view is illustrated by four articles in the areas of:

- Developing missions,
- Benchmarking strategic performance,
- Managing mature businesses, and
- The benefits of adroit strategic planning.

Senior managers in all sorts of organizations expend enormous amounts of energy on developing mission statements. They must think they are important. They must think they add value. But do they? There would certainly be a view that, for some organizations anyway, mission statements are public relations blurbs whose function is to advertise the organisation as something better than it actually is. Yet from a strategic perspective it is difficult to think of any successful organization that does not have a mission. Although the mission of a successful organization may not be written it is still real and in many cases it will pulse through the company and give it its uniquely successful life. A problem with mission statements is their variability: it appears that those who develop mission statements may lack guidance on, first, what a mission statement actually is and, second, how to go about constructing one. *Creating a Sense of Mission* by Andrew Campbell and Sally Yeung remedies these problems. This article has two great attributes. First, it is based upon substantial empirical research and second, it sets out for those who wish to—planners or others—what needs to be done to create that vital success ingredient in all firms, namely a true sense of mission.

The second article is *Strategic Benchmarking at ICI Fibres* by Tony Clayton and Bob Luchs. Although benchmarking has been a favoured topic of business literature in the 1990s it has not featured quite so strongly at the strategic level. Clayton and Luchs neatly set out a comprehensive hierarchy of benchmarking, at the strategic, operating and process levels and show that irrespective of the degree of contemporary turbulence, when applied with rigour and circum-spection, fundamental rules of strategy still yield insights that enable dramatic performance improvements to be achieved.

The third article illustrates, from a different perspective, that some issues can never change. Thus one strategic reality that can never change is that there will always be mature businesses and mature industries. A corollary of this is that the management of such businesses will usually be seen as a problem area, especially when a corporate or portfolio perspective is applied. Thus it is not unusual for planners to express strategic problems related to the issue of portfolio man-agement of mature businesses in a manner similar to the following:

- *'When we look at our portfolio of businesses we see that, say, the bulk of our sales come from businesses that are mature.'*
- *'The industries that these businesses are in are in decline and will never yield the growth rates we need to achieve our ambitious targets.'*
- *'What we must do is reduce our dependence on those mature businesses and di-versify into those high growth businesses of the future.'*

Apart from the deleterious effects upon morale of those who are unlucky enough to be in such mature businesses this type of thinking often leads to the following dismal sequence of events:

- *Diversification* into the 'growth businesses of the future'.
- *Disappointing results* from the 'growth businesses of the future'.
- *Greater efforts* in the 'growth businesses of the future'.
- Even more *disappointing results*.
- *Disposal* of the 'growth businesses of the future' heralded by the strategy of *'back to basics'* which signals a return to the mature businesses.

For many planners the issue of maturity is all too real and the solutions to it are all too elusive and that is why *Parenting Strategies for the Mature Business* by Michael Goold is so important. It deals with a strategic topic which is very distant from the supposed glamour or high growth/high tech industries but which is really a much more relevant one for so many managers. In addition it shows that there appear to be generic strategies which, while not changing the characteristics of the business from being mature, do none the less, give that crucial guidance on how to manage them for competitive advantage.

In spite of what has been written above about change and its effect upon strategic planning one should not forget that the discipline is still key to the successful development of many organisations. One of the principal ways in which strategic planning retains its value is in *how* it is applied. This last section considers examples of best current practice.

In the article *Linking the Balanced Scorecard to Strategy* by Alan Butler, Steve R. Letza, and Bill Neale, the authors show that for true strategic insights into the performance of a company it is necessary to have a broader set of measures than just financial or marketing ones. This is expressing what most strategists would claim, namely *that it ought to be the strategy that drives the financials and not the financials that drives the strategy.* Thus, following the work of Johnson and Kaplan and others, in the company Rexham Customer Europe (RCE) they put strategy and vision at the centre of their process and claim that sustained superiority will be achieved through measuring and thus balancing three perspectives, namely:

- Shareholders' (or financial) perspective,
- Extraordinary growth perspective,
- Continuous improvement perspective.

These broad perspectives are refined into a detailed series of scorecards which are completed by managers and the result is an integrated strategic view of the firm which can be used for diagnostic purposes and for planning what the firm RCE (and so many other companies) really wants: extraordinary growth.

Finally, the article *The Return of Strategic Planning—Once More with Feeling* by Bernard Taylor provides a very useful review of the 'death and resurrection' of strategic planning. This is a most important article as it sets out quite objectively some of the problems that beset earlier efforts in the strategic planning area, why strategic planning is so essential today (because of massive industry transformation) and how to develop an effective process of strategic planning in any firm. The arguments are supported by short case studies based on well-known companies. Probably the most important aspects of the 'contemporary approach' to strategic planning is that it is essentially a learning process in which as many people as possible in the organization are involved.

PART I: WHAT HAS CHANGED?

1

Outsourcing IT: The Strategic Implications

Leslie Willcocks, Guy Fitzgerald and David Feeny

IT outsourcing is a growing phenomenon in the developed economies. However, it is not often managed as strategically as it might be. Drawing on evidence from 30 case histories in the United Kingdom, this article presents the basis for a strategic approach. It identifies six critical factors around which IT outsourcing decisions can be based, provides a framework for decision-making based on organizational experiences of different levels of success, and discusses the additional factors that need to be borne in mind as a reality check, to ensure that the IT outsourcing decision can be delivered upon. The paper argues for a more strategic approach to IT outsourcing and provides frameworks to enable decision-makers to think through the issues presented by an impending IT sourcing decision.

In this paper IT outsourcing means handing over the management of some or all of an organization's information technology (IT), systems (IS) and related services to a third party. The Yankee Group[1] estimated global revenues for all types of IT outsourcing as $33 billion in 1992, and projected a rise to $49.5 billion

Leslie Willcocks is Fellow in Information Management, Templeton College, and University Lecturer in Management Studies, University of Oxford. He is also Editor of the *Journal of Information Technology*.
Guy Fitzgerald is Cable and Wireless Professor of Business Information Systems, Birkbeck College, University of London. He is also an Editor of the *Information Systems Journal*.
David Feeny is Director of the Oxford Institute of Information Management, Templeton College, University of Oxford. Previously he was for many years a senior marketing manager at IBM.

for 1994. Recent research by Willcocks and Fitzgerald[2] found IT outsourcing spend at £800 million in the United Kingdom, with a forecast rise to £1.72 billion for 1998. 1993 comparators for France, Germany, and Italy were £600m, £200m, and £200m respectively. The figures indicate a general increase in IT outsourcing across developed economies in the 1990s. The article reviews recent research into IT outsourcing developments, in the form of 30 detailed case histories in the United Kingdom, and a 1994 survey of 162 European organizations.[3–5] Here we found some 80% of organizations surveyed had considered outsourcing, while 47% actually did outsource some or all of their IT activities. However, 70% of all organizations surveyed did not have a formal IT outsourcing policy in place, while only 43% of organizations that had outsourced IT had a formal IT outsourcing policy. In the main the survey found only a few organizations approaching IT outsourcing in a strategic manner, despite the fact that, where practised, IT outsourcing averaged some 24% of total IT expenditure.

We draw mainly on detailed analysis of the 30 case histories and the levels of success achieved with different IT sourcing decisions in various sets of circumstances. The cases are of medium and large European-based organizations in manufacturing and services in both private and public sectors. In each we conducted face-to-face interviews with individuals directly involved in the outsourcing decision for one to three hours. Interviewees included senior business executives, IT directors and vendor account managers as well as IT personnel responsible for gathering technical and financial information. Additionally we gathered relevant documentation such as the outsourcing request for proposal, outsourcing bids, internal bids, contracts, benchmarks, annual reports and organizational charts. We used the documentation to corroborate participants' statements and to analyze contract specifics. Additionally we have compared our findings and frameworks against other published research and case histories concerned with the outsourcing phenomenon.

The evidence suggests that a strategic approach toward IT sourcing decisions can pay long term dividends. We detail the major factors that need to be considered when determining how, if at all, the external IT and services market should be used. These are then utilized to develop a framework for assessing the business and technical imperatives that should govern IT sourcing decisions. We show how any strategic IT outsourcing decision needs to be checked against a final set of considerations that emerge strongly from the research as potential trip-wires to success.

The Need for Strategy

In our case studies we found organizations following one of three main paths into outsourcing. *Incremental outsourcing* involved starting small on an obvious discrete area, usually to achieve clear cost savings, and/or because of lack of internal expertise or inability to retain the IT staff required. A second, *'hard learning'*, approach was to drift or be pressured into some quite large-scale outsourcing with little experience of how it should be managed, and make many mistakes over several years and contracts. In a period that could stretch from four to eight years these organizations learnt how to draw up and manage contracts, but also identified the necessity for developing an outsourcing strategy which (to varying degrees in different organizations) fitted with what the business was requiring in terms of service from information systems. The third approach has seen a much greater emphasis on developing a *strategic* approach to outsourcing, both on how it fits with what the rest of the business is doing and on how IT outsourcing can be managed. In the latter case it was not always large-scale outsourcing that prompted moves toward being more strategic in approach. In some cases IT out-sourcing represented under 20% of the total costs of IT to the organization in any one year. However, in every case the organization tended to take a more strategic approach to its use of IT generally.

Amongst the thirty organizations we researched, five, in varying degrees, followed the 'hard learning' route. Clearly all outsourcing experiences will involve a degree of learning that will hopefully transfer back into future practice. But there are ways of cutting out much of the 'hard learning'. As one IT director commented on earlier experiences of out-sourcing in his organization:

> The key thing is for the business to decide what it wants, to have a strategy. You cannot drift into outsourcing. If you do everyone could suffer, and here everyone did. For example on one contract they (the vendor) lost a lot of money. They did not really know what we wanted. The contract was biased towards us on that occasion, because it was fixed price but it made for a bad relationship. Start with the strategy and once that is set up decide who you want to do it. But throughout you must be, as the customer, in control of your destiny. We learnt from that and have made sure we are now much more in control.

As a preliminary to making outsourcing decisions, it is useful to have an overview of what to keep in-house and what can be outsourced effectively. This is provided by Figure 1. The Figure is based on detailed findings from looking at successful and less successful IT outsourcing decisions and contracts. It shows only the major tendencies amongst those running contracts largely considered effective. In practice there may be variations from the pure model. Such variations are influenced by different risk assessments and circumstantial factors.

Several different terms used in Figure 1 need clarification. It is quite common for the following terms to be used interchangeably, but conceptual confusion can lead to mistakes in outsourcing decisions. Here Information Technology (IT) refers to the technical means available—equipment and attendant techniques, and is essentially activity based, supply oriented and technology and delivery-focused. Information systems (IS) are business applications, more or less IT-

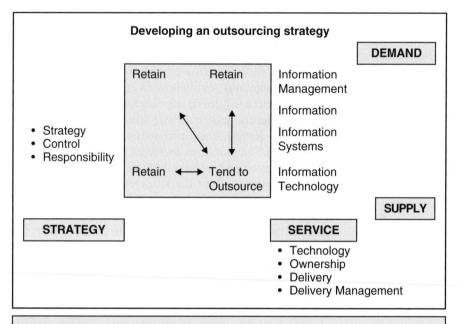

Figure 1. Making effective sourcing decisions.

based. The concern for information systems is a concern to be business-focused and demand oriented. Information systems are the business ends to which IT supplies the means. Information management is organization-based, relationships oriented and management focused. It deals with questions like 'how should we organize,' 'what policies should be in place,' 'who does what, where should IT be located'.[6]

The overall substance of Figure 1 is that it is unwise to outsource control of information management, IS and IT strategies. It is IT supply and service that can be outsourced, including operational management of that service, but strategy, responsibility and control should not be outsourced. The demand side of IS—that is the definition and management of business requirements—is best done in-house. The supply element of IS—running, maintenance and support of business applications—can be successfully outsourced, as many of our respondent organizations found. However, other organizations also chose to retain some or all of these in-house. Among reasons cited for this approach were: confidentiality of information, flexibility of running, to retain the advantages of existing strong links between in-house IT group and business users, user dissatisfaction with vendor cost/service levels.

An important issue here is the maturity of the organization about:

■ the relationship of IT to strategic business requirements; and
■ how this relates to the development of a strategic approach to outsourcing.

A further maturity factor that comes into play is the ability of the organization to develop a partnership-type relationship with the vendor company. Our own evidence is that the more an organization moves toward the top left corner of Figure 1, the more the risks of doing so need to be offset by developing longer-term partnering relationships with the vendor. As a general rule organizations with little experience of IT outsourcing would be advised to start out-sourcing on issues close to the bottom right hand corner of Figure 1 unless they have, or plan to put in place before outsourcing, most or all of the items in the checklist illustrated in Box 1. This checklist has been built up from detailed analysis of actual out-sourcing experiences discussed in our survey returns and case histories, and also from a review of the major available literature on the subject.

The major point of this section is that IT out-sourcing must be part of an overall strategic framework that takes into account business, IS and IT objectives and requirements. Outside such a strategic framework outsourcing is likely to remain an incremental, *ad hoc* response to circumstances driven by cost minimization criteria. This may well, and often does, produce tangible cost savings for each contract. However this approach runs a number of dangers. A piecemeal approach to contracts may not add up to total cost savings across all

---

We have an outsourcing strategy that fits with our business and Information Management, Information Systems and IT strategies. The strategy includes and goes beyond the period of any outsourcing contract we have or are planning.

Our outsourcing strategy includes plans for how to manage the IT supply and services market and how to choose, relate to, manage, and retain leverage with, vendors.

We are able to make decisions as to what IT services to outsource, and what to source in other ways. These decisions make sense on business and technical grounds.

We have in place a process and management capacity to select a suitable vendor.

There is a human resource plan in place to deal with the decision, transition and subsequent phases of outsourcing.

We have the management and specialist capacity to negotiate and draw up an outsourcing contract.

We have retained in-house sufficient management and technical capacity to manage the vendor, monitor contract performance and keep strategic business and technical options under review.

Box 1. Towards an IT Outsourcing Strategy.

contracts in the light of what else could have been done with IT. A further potential risk, particularly in an organization that does not identify IT use as strategic to the business, is to allow itself to get locked into seeing IT as a 'commodity' to be outsourced. With IT in the hands of a vendor, future opportunities for identifying IT as a source of strategic advantage and competitive differentiation for the organization can become cut off. A 'hollowing out' syndrome can occur, whereby the ability of the organization to compete through IT is increasingly adversely affected over time.

As we have argued elsewhere[7] taking a strategic approach to outsourcing means recasting the question 'to outsource or not?' into a more useful question with potentially more powerful answers. That question is: 'how do we use, if at all, the opportunity of what is available on the IT and services market to leverage business advantage?' The issue then becomes not outsourcing, but rightsourcing, with in-house options and a range of options for relating to and utilizing the IT services market always in play. The next section gives insights based on case histories researched by ourselves and others into the major critical factors that should be taken into consideration before making strategic sourcing decisions.

Making a Strategic Decision: Major Factors

There are high costs to getting outsourcing decisions wrong. The costs relate not just to additional management time and effort, unanticipated vendor bills, and the effect on the business during the course of an ineffective outsourcing contract. There may also be high switching costs going to another vendor or rebuilding the in-house technical capability. The costs of buying out of an unsatisfactory contract may also be high. Given the risk of such high potential costs, it is important to think through the issues in a structured manner. Here we first isolate the main contextual factors that direct IT sourcing decisions. Their interrelationships are then developed and explored through a framework that relates the market options to the business and technical imperatives facing an organization. From our analysis six contextual factors determine how (if at all) the external market should be used. These factors are:

The Potential Contribution of the IT Activity/Service to Business Positioning

An IT activity/service can be defined as a *Differentiator* or as a *Commodity*. Activities which are differentiators provide a potential basis for competitive advantage; executing them particularly well is important to the firm. In P&O European Ferries the central reservation system processes up to 12,000 customer reservations a day. The system is not only integral to most of the company's operations. It also gives it a distinct, and possibly sustainable, competitive advantage over other ferry companies operating on the same routes. In this case the system is run in-house.

An activity is a commodity if its execution does not distinguish the firm from a competitor in business offering and performance terms. This type of activity needs to be done competently, but no more. At BP Exploration and Civil Aviation Authority, for example, the computerized financial accounting systems have been outsourced to Arthur Andersen, the accountancy firm and IT consultancy. In BP Exploration's case the 1991 £55 million four year contract covers accounting services and transfer of 250 staff, as well as related computer systems.

In practice differentiators can quickly become commodities as competitors catch up or the basis of competition changes. Apart from this time element, the conditions that make a system a differentiator or commodity also vary from sector to sector. The following characteristics will push an information system application into being a differentiator:

■ High sensitivity to competitive exposure, e.g. information.
■ Strong need to retain intellectual property.
■ High business knowledge in the IT products/services.
■ Very competitive business environment.

The Relationship of the IT Activity/Service to Business Strategy

A distinction can be made between *Strategic* and *Useful* activities. 'Strategic' activities are integral to the firm's achievement of goals and critical to its existing and future business direction. Organizations need to maintain control of these. A strategic information system may, or may not, differentiate an organization from its competitors. The common thread is its criticality, the extent to which it underpins the organization's strategic direction. As one example Norwich Union Health Care are in the personal health care insurance business. In a start-up situation in 1990 it identified a strategic need for a computerized policy administration system. Though its development was initially outsourced, by 1992 the strategically important system had been placed under the control of an in-house IT department that had built up its expertise in the 1990–92 period. 'Useful' activities on the other hand can make incremental contributions to the 'bottom line' but do not affect the firm's competitive positioning. In fact 'useful' IT/IS can be 'mandatory' or 'discretionary'. For example, in many, perhaps most, industries payroll applications would be considered useful and mandatory but not strategic. In PC environments many software packages may well be seen as useful and 'nice to have', that is discretionary, but not mandatory, let alone strategic. PC maintenance of PCs will be seen as mandatory. Some firms decide to outsource such work. For example, as at 1993 and for some six years previously a major UK retailer had outsourced maintenance of over 3000 head office PCs.

The Degree of Uncertainty About Future Business Environment and Business Needs, and Hence Longer Term IT Needs

A high degree of business uncertainty seems to be a perennial characteristic of the external and internal environments of the vast majority of UK organizations in the 1990s. While there are variations in business volatility by sector and organization, all our case study respondents saw this as a critical determining factor when it came to outsourcing decisions. As one example Pilkington outsourced head office computing and IT development in 1992. The Head of Group IS comments:

> We are dealing with a terrific amount of change within the business and within head office itself over a two year period. We did not know what it was going to look like at the end, though we had some ideas on that. Luckily we (the senior IT staff) were very involved in the organization of that change from a business point of view. A long term contract would have been inappropriate here; there is too much change involved. In any case we wanted to retain a certain smount of negotiating independence on the back of that change (Bill Limond, Pilkington).

The problem lies in the way business uncertainty feeds into the ability to identify IS/IT requirements. Again, unlike in the Pilkington case, not all businesses keep IT staff highly involved or able to anticipate fluctuating business requirements. High uncertainty suggests that the 'buying in' of resources or partnership relationships with vendors are preferable unless the contract is very short-term.

Degree of Technology Maturity Associated With the Activity/Service in Question

Looking at technical factors, a particularly critical issue is that of technological maturity. The concept of technological maturity derives from research by Feeny, Earl and Edwards.[8] An organization is low on technology maturity when any of the following conditions apply:

- The technology is new and unstable in functions, specification, and performance.
- A well-established technology is being used in a radically new application.
- The organization has little in-house experience in implementing this technology in this application.

New technology/low maturity implies high uncertainty about future IT needs. Feeny *et al.* found that in situations of low maturity a 'user' focus was needed. Teamwork was important; business users needed to be highly involved in all aspects of planning, development, support and delivery, development; immediate goals were less clear than the overall aim of business effectiveness. However, as technological maturity increased and the technology became less problematic and immediate goals clearer a specialist focus could be adopted. Tasks could be increasingly delegated to IT specialists who could work to clear targets to produce an efficient result. Note here that even in situations of high technological maturity, activities concerned with Direction—that is determining IS and IT strategies—should remain a joint 'user focused' activity.

This research can be used to support the argument that outsourcing should be restricted to situations where IT is well understood and unproblematic to the organization, and where a specialist focus can be suitably applied by the vendor. In our detailed case studies, as a general rule, the prescription 'never out-source a problem' held up well. Where there were variations to this, in each case the successful organizations took a number of explicit actions to recduce the risks incurred. The rule emerged as particularly applicable in the systems development area.

Level of IT Integration

Some IT activities may have simple technical interfaces with the rest of the organization's systems, be easy to isolate and contract out. Additionally these systems may well have simple interfaces with business users, and the impact on business users if something went wrong could be isolated from large parts of normal business activity. In our cases this was found to apply to telecommunications networks at W.H. Smith for example, and to payroll and financial accounting applications in many organizations.

Other systems may be highly integrated, however. This means they will have complex and extensive interactions with a wide range of other systems. These systems may also interface in complex ways with many business users who will be impacted significantly by the levels of service experienced. Such systems tend to be more difficult to outsource successfully. We found organizations more reluctant to outsource such systems, in fact. For example while Citibank outsourced its London-based data centre in 1992, the bank has been more reluctant to outsource to a third party vendor its network and messaging infrastructure.

In-house IT Capability Relative to that Available on the External Market

A final factor relates to in-house technical capability. This factor is distinguishable from 'technological maturity' on two counts. Firstly, it is the in-house capability relative to that available on the IT service market that is important, not just the level of in-house technical capability itself. Secondly, the cost of utilizing in-house capability, including opportunity costs, as compared to the price of using equivalent capacity from the external market is also an important factor. High relative in-house capability will suggest keeping IT services in-house. However, one major UK retailer, for example, tends to redeploy in-house expertise on to developmental work and outsource what has been identified as 'low value' IT tasks, for example data processing. As at 1994, United Biscuits and ICI ran highly efficient data centres in-house, but constantly evaluated their costs against what is available from third party suppliers.

Making the Strategic Sourcing Decision

In this section we advance the decision-making process further by examining the trade-offs that organizations need to make on the critical variables in order to achieve effective decisions. The decisions arrived at then need to be tested against the 'Reality Check' outlined in the next section.

Our research helps us to identify what makes effective sourcing decisions in 30 case histories. Each case has been analysed primarily against the six critical variables identified above in terms of what type of sourcing decisions were made, and whether or not these were successful. The criteria for success, in number and type, varied from organization to organization. However, to generalize, where an external vendor was involved as a result of the sourcing decision, the criteria for success fell within the following range: targeted cost savings achieved or better than anticipated; service levels maintained or better; user management satisfaction; low levels of vendor–client dispute; vendor responsiveness and attention; general favourable comparisons between objectives and outcomes; and decision to renew the contract. Similar criteria, suitably adapted, were applied to where IT services were delivered by in-house IT staff.

In order to organize our results and discussion we have formulated a decision matrix, and this is shown in Figure 2. For mapping purposes we have conflated the 'differentiator-commodity' and 'strategic-useful' parameters into a 'Core' –'Non-Core' continuum. Additionally we have conflated the 'technology maturity' and 'in-house capability relative to that available on the market' into a High–Low continuum measuring 'Relevant Experience With Technology'.

When to Stay In-House

The most convincing case for staying in-house with IT is in the following set of circumstances:

- business positioning impact—HIGH
- link to business strategy—HIGH
- future business uncertainty—HIGH
- technology maturity—LOW
- level of IT integration—HIGH
- in-house versus market expertise—HIGH

The P&O European Ferries case and its central reservation system provides an example where these circumstances prevailed as at 1993/4. The IT/IS strategies here have been to continue to build up internal IT expertise and improve

Business uncertainty/ systems interconnectedness	'Core'	'Non-Core'	Experience with the relevant technology
High	In-House	Market-test: 'Best deal'	**High**
Low	Strategic Control: 'Discrete Commodities' only	↕ Outsource	**High**
High	In-house 'Buy-in'	Selective Outsource: 'Discrete systems'	**Low**
Low	Vendor as partner	Selective Outsource: 'Discrete systems'	**Low**

Figure 2. Framework for IT sourcing decisions.

IS-business user relationships within the company. The central reservation system represents, in the current competitive situation, a strategic differentiator that will not be outsourced. However within an overall 'core' system there may be parts that can be identified as discrete and not core (see Figure 2). In the P&O case, for example, the maintenance of ship-board systems was considered as a 'commodity' service and, as such, was contracted out to a third party supplier. The reasons were lower cost and to allow in-house staff to focus on systems development. In the event outsourcing resulted in a lower quality service and the business users demanded that the service be brought back inhouse.

Clearly an organization will have a portfolio of IT/IS applications, activities and services, and not all will fall into this 'must stay in-house' category. Even so companies like P&O European Ferries, having built up an in-house IT capability, may prefer in-house options even for non-core systems. Indeed the in-house option may well prove more cost-effective, as we found for example with mainframe data processing at United Biscuits and ICI. Alternatively even in situations of 'total' outsourcing, companies will find it necessary to retain certain vital functions in-house. These issues will receive more detailed discussion below.

The 'Best Case' Scenario

The surest case for outsourcing is where the following circumstances apply to the IT/IS in question:

■   business positioning impact—LOW

- link to business strategy—LOW
- future business uncertainty—LOW
- technology maturity—HIGH
- level of IT integration—LOW
- in-house versus market expertise—LOW

In fact our evidence suggests that outsourcing IT is most safely done on shorter term (1–5 year) contracts, for commodity type IT, in situations of high in-house experience of relevant technology, where discrete systems or activities can be identified, and in conditions of some business certainty leading to confidence about technological needs of the organization for at least the life of the contract. In such situations the cost effectiveness of the in-house operation can then be compared to what is available on the market by a market testing process, and a best deal sought (see top right of Figure 2).

An illustrative case here is the outsourcing (to DEC) of telecommunications networks at W.H. Smith, the UK retail and distribution chain. A discrete technology and service identified as non-core was out-sourced because a vendor could provide a similar or better service at lower cost. Future business uncertainty was adjudged low in this case as long as the contract was for three years, with an option to renew for a further two. Cost savings of between 20 and 30% per annum have been achieved on this contract. On similar criteria, Civil Aviation Authority outsourced their accounting systems to Arthur Andersen in the early 1990s on a contract to 1995. The difference was that, in the market testing phase, the vendor was chosen primarily for its greater expertise rather than on cost saving criteria as well.

Dealing with 'Mixed Case' Scenarios

Organizations that are successful in applying an 'incremental' approach to outsourcing invariably are found to have applied the criteria detailed above to their early contracts. However, when looking across the portfolio of IT/IS applications, activities and services that an organization has, it is unlikely that circumstances for many of the items will be so clear cut in their pointers for decision-making as those outlined in our first two scenarios.

In practice we have found most organizations taking a selective approach to outsourcing. North West Thames Regional Health Authority has been a successful practitioner of selective outsourcing. Here mainframes and data centres were outsourced together with IT staff, to Sema Group in April 1991. The staff had high experience with the relevant technology, a fairly short term (5 year) contract was signed to minimize risk but also because the systems had limited usefulness beyond 1995, and the outsourced assets, including staff, were considered 'non-core'. Outsourcing also offered prospective cost savings. Essentially NW Thames were not outsourcing a problem here, and this is a typical pattern amongst the more successful contracts we have studied.

Certain other items were outsourced separately on *ad hoc* contracts. One of these was applications development. Here, though in-house technology maturity was low, it was felt that no great specialist skills or NHS knowledge was required by the vendor because the policy was to move to packages already available rather than commission new development work (see bottom right, Figure 2). The development of a Wide Area Network for the RHA, however, was seen as a strategic project involving highly interconnected systems and potentially touching many users within the Health Authority. It was retained in-house, the aim being to build up in-house skills on this technology. A 'Buy-In' (or 'insourcing') strategy was pursued here. To balance the outsourcing, further elements identified as 'core' were retained in-house. These included IT/IS planning, liaison, training and consultancy and ability to manage the outsourcing contracts. Where these were inadequately resourced a strategy of 'insourcing' IT capability, basically recruiting experienced staff, was adopted.

Pilkington, the UK-based glass manufacturer, provide an illustration of selective outsourcing within Pilkington as a whole (manufacturing systems were left largely under in-house IT staff) but almost total outsourcing at Pilkington Head Office. The situation in 1991/2 was one of considerable business and organizational change, devolution of the business, and the head office being slimmed down. Head Office IT was outsourced to EDS. The items outsourced consisted firstly of the ageing data centre mainframes and most of the IT staff, including the IT manager, who became the vendor's account manager. This was seen as a positive move, guaranteeing continuity and minimizing the risk. Pilkington knew who they were dealing with and also had guarantees that transferred staff would stay working on this contract. The circumstances are represented accurately by the top right hand box of Figure 2.

More unusually, as part of the deal, Pilkington also outsourced applications development of new office and network systems. Pilkington were low on skills here. We have found that generally the more effective arrangement in these circumstances for development work is to use a 'Buy-In' approach. This is certainly the case in Quest International, for example, where in several 1990s contracts vendors were seen as team members who help to build up in-house development capability. Pilkington looked to the vendor to provide additional skill/expertise through training transferred staff, and bringing new staff on to the contract (Figure 2, bottom right). This outsourcing approach has proved successful because of action taken to minimize its risks. Pilkington knew the vendor staff and account manager—the relationship side was fairly secure and guaranteed some flexibility. Secondly there was a short term contract. Thirdly, Pilkington made sure it would own the assets being developed. Fourthly, Pilkington retained in-house capability to manage the contract. More broadly, Pilkington identified as 'core', and retained, their ability to manage strategy, contracts and business knowledge, together with a pool of technical skill needed to control the overall architecture of the company.

The 'Total Outsourcing' Decision

When talking about effective decisions, in several ways the phrase 'total outsourcing' must be a misnomer. Generally speaking in effective 'total' outsourcing contracts 'strategic differentiators' would not be outsourced; 'strategic commodities' might well be. Of course there can be mistakes in definition, but generally speaking companies will recognize most of IT/IS as 'non-core' before they decide on the 'total outsourcing' route. However, case study evidence from Huber[9] and Lacity and Hirschheim[10] support our own findings that where all IT/IS is deemed 'non-core' and outsourced, there always have to be certain IT/IS capabilities left in-house.

This was recognized at NV Philips, the electronics manufacturer. From the mid-1980s the company consolidated and rationalized its IT capability. Business exigencies required shedding of labour and non-core activities. As a prelude to total outsourcing Philips pulled out of its in-house IT department some 100 business systems analysts and put them back into the businesses that made up the company. This meant that each business had its own IT capability on the demand side. Philips then outsourced all its software and systems development, including 180 related staff through forming a separate partly owned company in a joint venture with a Dutch software house. Philips also outsourced all its communications and processing capability, including some 140 staff, through setting up another partly-owned company that could sell its services on the open market. Following Figure 1, Philips have outsourced IT supply but have retained in-house capability to define business demand. Also there is a central management capability to define strategy, identify and coordinate IT/IS needs across the Group, provide internal consultancy and manage contracts. The risks of total outsourcing are also ameliorated by the 'vendors' being partly owned and highly dependent on business from Philips. Also there are strong pre-existing mutual relationships and business knowledge held by client and vendors .

This section has given only a few examples by way of illustration of the principles we have found guiding effective sourcing decisions. However, a general point can be made here. Many organizations deviate from the principles behind the 'best case' scenario for outsourcing described above. In many such cases in our research base the outsourcing subsequently proved successful. In each case the managers involved could describe policies, tactics and practices they had consciously adopted to minimize the risks of outsourcing in less favourable circumstances.

Developing the Decision: A Reality Check

The strategic IT outsourcing decision needs to be checked against a number of other factors. Our evidence suggests that the following questions are highly pertinent:

Is There an Economic Rationale?

Our survey found a primary widespread concern to link IT outsourcing to cost savings, or at least cost control. Some organizations, however, utilize outsourcing for other purposes; even so it is important that the decision makes economic if not economical sense. Thus Whitbread wanted to refocus management attention against a background of declining and volatile mainframe processing demand:

> Over five years it breaks even. The savings are about efficiencies in development support, support of application systems, and greater productivity in, for example, function points delivered. It takes a long time for them to come through and be measured but it wasn't a cost thing, apart from avoiding a lot of redundancy costs (Fraser Winterbottom, Whitbread).

However, declaring the objective and delivering upon it can be in two different worlds as several cases discussed in this study will attest. Before outsourcing it is therefore very useful to examine carefully the implications of proposed actions and any proposals by potential vendors. In particular four major issues that need to be explored are:

- Are projected in-house costs static, or can we take action to reduce them ourselves?
- Will the vendor motivation to increase profit by reducing its costs affect service quality?
- How 'fixed' is the price? Will there be expensive add-ons? How does and will price compare to what else is available on the market?
- Even if we do not expect to make cost savings, are we still likely to pay too much for what we get from IT outsourcing?

How Does the Decision Fit with the Rate of Technological Change?

An important supply side issue is uncertainty/volatility in the technologies available. Technologies for business have changed, and will continue to change dramatically, not least as a function of competitiveness in the IT industry. The degree of volatility in this supply side of the business environment and how future IT could support the business, feed into what sorts of IT/IS outsourcing decisions can be made:

> We have reservations about long-term contracts. You are seeing terrific changes in information technology and IS. For instance if you are going through downsizing, what you start out with will not be necessarily appropriate at the end of ten years. One thing you can be sure of at the end of ten years is that the technology will have changed completely—as will what you need to have in an outsourcing contract (IS Director).

If going down an outsourcing route, the dilemmas and decisions relate to type of contract and type of relationship with the supplier. Are these flexible enough to permit the organization taking business advantage of unanticipated technical developments without prohibitive costs from the vendor? A further important question relates to the vendor's technical capability—can the vendor actually supply/support future technical developments? And even if the answers to these questions are affirmative, the vendor will have its own interests and these may differ from the client's. Something that makes technical sense to your organization may not make technical sense for the outsourcing vendor.

Are There Issues Around Ownership when Transferring People and Assets?

Respondents to the survey placed a major emphasis on the risk of irreversibility of contract. This raises questions about the wisdom of transferring people and ownership of assets to a vendor. The following salutary experience suggests it might be sensible to prepare for divorce even while negotiating the 'marriage' contract:

> After a costly battle to end the contract, the client company is rebuilding its internal group minus several good people who found other jobs during the chaos. Rebuilding that staff is turning out to be far harder than expected. You can't put Humpty Dumpty together again as easily as they'd thought (Industry Consultant, quoted in Houghton[11]).

Organizations might feel the need to take action to minimize the likelihood of such costly outcomes. Turning to assets like hardware and software, many organizations have found it advantageous to sell off equipment to the vendor in order to get it off the balance sheet and also gain a cash influx. This will gain present financial advantage, but could be at the expense of future technical security or flexibilities. However, another reason for transferring asset ownership can be to get rid of old equipment—ageing mainframes for example—and prepare the ground for their replacement. The reality check questions here are:

- What advantages do we gain from transferring all/any people and/or assets to the vendor?
- Are there critical skills and assets we should NOT transfer?
- What are the identifiable risks in making the specific transfers we have planned?
- Can we protect ourselves against the risks of transferring people and/or assets?

Is a Suitable Vendor Available?

It is not enough to make an intellectually appealing decision; is there a vendor that can actually deliver on identified requirements? Generally speaking, we have found that vendors are better at selling their services than client organizations are at buying them. Despite the richness of what is available generally on the market, vendors are also in high competition against one another over clients and contracts. It falls ultimately on the client to identify the strengths of possible vendors against the client's own identified requirements. However, what each client needs from a vendor will probably be very specific to that client and its circumstances. In the outsourcing cases we have reviewed this has invariably been the case. Thus Whitbread chose FI Group because as a vendor its core competencies were in the areas required—support and enhancement. The competencies of other bidders seemed to be focused mainly around data centres or development. National Grid needed a vendor with proven experience in the specific hardware and software outsourced that could match the company's geographic requirements and was a large vendor in the market to stay. When BP Exploration chose SAIC it was partly because of its large size, its outsourcing experience, but also because they had a base of scientific and geologist staff. For an oil exploration company this meant that the vendor could be a partner that could add some value.

Do We Have the Management Capability to Deliver on the Decision?

An organization whose strategic decision-making has pointed to outsourcing should ensure that it possesses enough management capability to:

- select a suitable vendor;
- negotiate a contract;
- draw up a contract;
- manage the contract and relationships with the vendor;
- manage relationships with and needs of business users; and
- identify and look after existing and future IT/IS needs of the organization.

While this may sound obvious, it is all too clear from our case studies that organizations inexperienced in outsourcing frequently underestimate both the degree to which these capabilities are required and the number of staff that might be needed to fulfil these responsibilities. Like every solution, outsourcing brings its own set of problems. For one thing the character of management needs to change. It may well be that the managers involved will need to be replaced or reinforced. Those able to run an in-house IT department may not have the skills required to fulfil the above responsibilities, at least by themselves. On the first three areas mentioned above, we found several inexperienced organizations taking more expert advice from outside, but also, where applicable, from other companies within the same Group. On the fourth point, this will need specific skills and may require a new appointee; it is quite common to underestimate the large time requirement for this role, especially in the first eighteen months of a new contract, even where it is running fairly smoothly. On the last two points it is clear from our case study work that whatever the degree of outsourcing, in addition to the above capabilities these two issues must be covered by retaining in-house the following:

- Ability to track/assess/interpret changing IT capability and relate this to the needs of the firm.
- Ability to work with business management to define the IT requirements successfully over time.
- Ability to identify the appropriate ways to use the external market to help specify and manage 'rightsourcing' .

These relate to retaining strategy and control capability within the client organization.

Will Significant Human Resource Issues Arise?

This final check list item does not appear that significant in our survey findings. However, when we turned to examining case histories in detail, all respondents remarked on the need for sensitivity on human resource issues. In particular several respondents from organizations more experienced in outsourcing remarked on how easy it was to get wrong and gave us case histories from their own organizations to illustrate the point. Two of the largest outsourcing contracts signed in the UK during 1994 were at British Aerospace and the Inland Revenue. Both experienced strikes from IT staff during the build-up to awarding contracts. They were not alone in experiencing staff problems in this respect in that year in the UK, and strikes are only the more visible versions of potential problems on the human resource front. Clearly the objective should be to manage sourcing decisions and their communication in such a way that staff do not feel the need to take strike action. The problem may rest as much with how a sourcing decision is implemented as with the actual content of the decision. Therefore an important reality check on an outsourcing decision is to assess whether or not the content and method of implementation will secure in-house and vendor staff motivation across the contract. As one example, in the North West Thames Regional Health Authority case the first inclination was to go for a total outsourcing approach. But staff enthusiasm was low for both this option and that of a management buyout. Eventually the decision was to go for a selective outsourcing route, ensuring that the vendor selected was the one offering the best deal to the staff to be transferred.

Conclusions

We have identified the general conditions for effective IT outsourcing decisions—high 'technology maturity'; vendor offers better deal compared with in-house; IT identified as 'non-core', that is IT is not a strategic differentiator;

discrete systems; in situations of reasonable business certainty across the life of a contract. However even where all these favourable conditions apply there still needs to be in-house management action during the contract on a number of fronts which we have identified. Additionally we have found examples of organizations outsourcing IT where not all or even only some of these favourable conditions apply. But success seems dependent on taking careful action to minimize the additional risks to which the conduct of the contract then becomes exposed. The following formula may be suggested for IT outsourcing:

- Market Logic **not** Management Despair
- Rationalization **not** Rationing
- Commodities **not** Differentiators
- Targeted **not** Total

The suggestion here is that if you are outsourcing IT out of despair with in-house IT, seeking to cut costs, are outsourcing differentiators and are going down the total outsourcing route, then the organization will probably end up in serious trouble. Sourcing decisions should follow a market logic. From a management perspective the issue is not whether or not to outsource IT, but whether or not, and if so how, to use the market for IT and associated services for organizational advantage. In some situations 'insourcing' approaches may well be more appropriate. A sourcing decision should be based on in-house rationalization first and outsourcing should focus essentially on commodities. Furthermore a targeted rather than a total outsourcing route reduces risk. It may be that targeted outsourcing eventually, or quite quickly, becomes total outsourcing; however the point is that the targeting stage should be part of the way in which a decision is arrived at.

References

1. Yankee Group. Quoted in L. Loh and N. Venkatraman, Diffusion of Information Technology outsourcing: influence sources and the Kodal Effect, *Information Systems Research* **3** (4), 334–358 (1992).
2. L. Willcocks and G. Fitzgerald, *A Business Guide To Outsourcing I.T. A Study of European Best Practice in the Selection, Management and Use of External IT Services*, Business Intelligence, London (1994).
3. G. Fitzgerald and L. Willcocks, *Information Technology Outsourcing Practice: A UK Survey*, Business Intelligence, London (1994).
4. L.Willcocks and G. Fitzgerald, Market as opportunity? Case studies in outsourcing Information Technology and services, *Journal of Strategic Information Systems* **2** (3), 223–242 (1993).
5. G. Fitzgerald and L. Willcocks, Outsourcing Information Technology: Contracts and client/vendor relationship, RDP 94/10, Templeton College, Oxford (1994).
6. M. Earl, *Management Strategies for Information Technology.* Prentice-Hall, London (1989).

7. D. Feeny, L. Willcocks, T. Rands and G. Fitzgerald, Strategies for IT management, In S. Rock (ed.), *Director's Guide to Outsourcing IT*, Institute of Directors/IBM, London (1993).

8. D. Feeny, M. Earl and B. Edwards, *Organizational Arrangements for IS Roles of Users and IS Specialists,* Oxford Institute of Information Management RDP 94/6, Templeton College, Oxford (1994).

9. R. Huber, How Continental Bank outsourced its crown jewels, *Harvard Business Review*, January/February, 121–129 (1993).

10. M. Lacity and R. Hirschheim, The Information Systems outsourcing bandwagon, *Sloan Management Review* **35** (1), 73–86 (1993).

11. J. Houghton, Outsourcing Information Technology services, *CIRCIT Policy Research Paper No. 17*, CIRCIT, Melbourne (1991).

2

Innovation in Banking: New Structures and Systems

Robert E. Morgan, Eileen Cronin and Mark Severn

Despite a number of recent strategic manoeuvres, the retail banking sector is still suffering from symptoms of intra-type competition and competitive intensity. Bank strategists are constantly seeking to develop a unique service mix and new product lines in response to changing market demands, but have recently recognized that there are more fundamental issues which need to be addressed within the sector. The old models of service delivery are cost-laden and outdated and new models for success are needed in order to alleviate the pressure on margins witnessed in recent years.

This article examines the evolution of banks' delivery programmes and organizational forms in the retail sector and describes the reasons underlying these changes over time. The authors take account of the problems and challenges that face these contemporary structures and explain the rationale underlying the current requirements for further change. The *servuction system* is used as the basis for explaining the mediating effects of changes in a bank's governance structures (all internal and operational issues that affect the structural configuration of the bank) and their impact upon the delivery of services to customers. In order to illustrate these issues, some governance structure responses from Barclays Bank plc, are described, and the experiences and lessons from this example suggest that it is more than fine-tuning of existing governance structures which is required. A new organizational mindset is necessary in banking which completely reappraises governance structures and retail service delivery programmes so as to balance the desire for operations efficiency with marketing effectiveness.

Robert E. Morgan is Lecturer in Marketing and Strategy at Cardiff Business School.
Eileen Cronin is Regional Planning Manager at Barclays Bank plc.
Mark Severn is Risk Director at Barclays Bank plc.

More than a decade ago, *Long Range Planning* published an article by Morison and Frazer (1982) entitled, 'Shaping the future of retail banking'.[1] In this article, the authors attempted to identify some of the factors which would most likely impact on the development of retail banking as a distinct business domain. Whilst not intending to forecast the future of banking and its activities, they identified some significant factors which have become apparent during the 1990s. For example, they observed that branch network expansion would become one of the main ways for banks to compete, but anticipated that such a pattern would be unlikely to be sustained. It is the authors' intention to provide some insight into this issue in view of the changes which have taken place.

Within the financial services industry, there are many types of delivery system used to link customers and service providers. Some examples are the full-service branch, the limited service branch, and the speciality branch. There are obvious additions to these, most of which use electronic hardware and information technology in some manner—remote systems such as automated teller machines (ATMs), electronic funds transfer at point of sale (EFTPOS), intelligent terminals and tele/home-banking.[2] Historically, the principal delivery system that most UK clearing banks have adopted has been the full-service branch type. These are typical high street branches acting as retail outlets for a bank's full range of services which are targeted at a wide variety of customer segments. There are many strategic groups in the UK financial services industry that do not require a retail outlet network. For example, the merchant banks do not need them, finance houses usually demand only small networks and building societies require them in only parts of their service provision. Undoubtedly, the largest networks of all are held by the clearing banks, and their branches constitute the main channel of distribution for their retail banking services.

Historically, the formation of these large branch networks in the UK was the result of a few key factors. In the last century the national clearing banks became firmly established and branch networks slowly expanded throughout the country. The 1960s witnessed a number of mergers which produced a dominant group of clearing banks, each with its own oversized branch network.[3] An added ingredient to this branch expansion was the upgrading of various sub-branches, which was thought to be necessary because of the enormous proliferation in financial services provision during the 1980s. There are a number of strategic benefits that can accrue from operating large networks such as these, but one of the most significant concerns that has occupied boardroom discussion recently, is the excessive cost incurred by operating such delivery systems. This is such a critical area of strategic concern that it has led a prominent international consultant to conclude that there is no other part of retail bank decision-making which impacts upon profitability as much as branch policy and location.[4] Therefore, the traditional concept of branch banking has come under increased scrutiny due to competition, deregulation, and, most importantly, increased operating expenses. Indeed, one recent pessimistic view has suggested that a combination of ATMs, mutual funds, home banking, and loans-by-phone, will soon have a deleterious impact on approximately 200,000 branches in North America and Europe. A consequence of these high operating costs has been that banks have been exploring new and alternative delivery systems to service customer needs. Some popular alternatives have been listed above and even though these options do exist and have been in place for some time, it is largely considered that branch networks are likely to remain and continue as an important distribution channel,[5] despite the high costs associated with their operation.

Environmental Challenges

The acquisition of new customers, the provision of financial services, and the retention of existing business has never been more competitive. Legislation, such as the Financial Services Act and The Building Societies Act, coupled with deregulation, has broken down some of the traditional boundaries between financial institutions. This previous delineation was reflected in customers having fairly rigid views of where and from whom they should obtain financial services: for example, current accounts from banks, mortgages from building societies, and insurance services from brokers or insurance companies.

As the barriers to competition were removed, the distinction between traditional providers of financial services became less clear cut. The introduction by the building societies of the current account, previously the prerogative of the banks, and the payment of interest forced the banks to rethink their strategy and in 1989 all the major UK banks re-introduced their current accounts with interest-paying options.

Credit Cards were until fairly recently dominated by the clearing banks, but now Barclaycard Visa and Mastercard Access have been issued by building societies and other operators such as Save and Prosper and Adam and Co. The smaller issuers are endeavouring to attain market share by aggressive pricing, although they admit that their market will be small. New entrants such as Ford and General Motors, whilst offering apparently lower rates, also tie in the customer with offers of incentives. The main card issuers recently responded with cash discounts on condition that customers transfer their balances from one card house to another.

Consumer lending was traditionally the domain of the banks and finance houses, with the latter using hire purchase as the major lending vehicle. Point-of-sale credit and in-house credit cards have eroded the market share of traditional lenders with major store chains such as Marks and Spencer offering personal loan facilities, in addition to their in-house store cards. The major car manufacturers have also entered the market with 'lease-like' facilities offered to the personal market—examples of these are the Ford Options scheme and General Motors options 1-2-3.

Mortgages were almost the exclusive province of building societies until the banks entered the market in the early 1980s. Banks now have a sizeable market share and are committed to retaining and indeed increasing this involvement as part of their strategy to capture and retain personal customers.

The introduction of direct selling (e.g. motor and home/contents insurance sold direct by Direct Line), introduced a new concept of selling financial services to the public. Many large insurance companies have followed suit, attracted by the cost cutting benefits of removing the 'brokerage' layer to whom commission was paid.

As a result of the environmental challenges, the 1980s witnessed a sharp decline in the number of traditional bank branches because institutions became disillusioned with pursuing strategies of branch development for a number of reasons. Deregulation, greater market sophistication and segmentation, and a volatile economic climate all combined to act as a catalyst in encouraging strategic decision-makers to question their branch network presence in the UK. Figure 1 illustrates the scale of this branch reduction.

These factors combined with other effects to provide a disruptive influence on branches. For example banks have faced their principal competition from building societies who have captured market share in the 'traditional' banking segments. These building societies generated a greater customer-base from smaller, and therefore less costly, branch networks. The Halifax Building Society (which is the largest of its type) has only 750 branch outlets and 20,000 employees which yields a costs/income ratio of 43.5%. This compares very

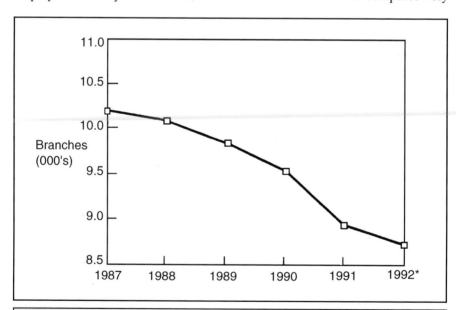

Figure 1. Reduction in the UK branch outlets of the *Big Four* banks (Barclays, National Westminster, Midland, and Lloyds). * Morgan Stanley Research estimated for 1992. *Source*: CLSB.

favourably when set against the large clearing banks who have recently reported ratios of 63.9% (Barclays), 63% (Lloyds), 65.9% (National Westminster) and 72.9% (Midland). The burgeoning electronic banking age has meant that there is less of a requirement for cheque transactions nowadays, leading to greater use of electronic payment procedures which do not require branches for processing. Recent developments in technology based delivery systems mean that home banking will become the service of the future. Most clearing banks and some building societies now have, or are piloting a home banking service. First Direct, the Midland Bank subsidiary, was the first UK bank to offer a complete banking service via the telephone, although Nationwide and Abbey National have had telephone services for some time. The final factor is the recent reduction in the UK's base interest rate which has put greater pressure on overall branch profitability and margins. Gapper[6] has suggested that bankers require a minimum of 8% base rate to make traditional branch banking a feasible form of delivery system.

These factors provide adequate testimony to the problems that retail banks are currently facing. This has no doubt increased the need for improved retail performance and effectiveness in branch banking at the field level.

Servuction in Banking

At present, most of the UK banks are examining ways of improving their returns from the expensive servicing of their branch networks. As it is becoming increasingly difficult to generate profits via interest-related activities[7] banks are seeking greater earnings on fee and commission-based services to improve margins and to maintain their competitive profiles. In order to operationalize these tactics, banking staff in the field have had to increase their marketing awareness in the realization that they are involved in *service encounters* with customers,[8] that is to say, that due to the largely intangible nature of banking services, the one-to-one interaction between the service provider (bank employee) and the customer is critical in terms of marketing opportunities. Not only is the relationship between provider and customer of vital importance in quality perceptions and customer satisfaction, but appreciation should be given to the *context* of the whole interaction. In fact, this has been recognized as a *research priority* by the Marketing Science Institute which researches the design and delivery of services that advance the state-of-the-art in marketing practice. Figure 2 outlines the key elements within the production, delivery, and consumption of services, otherwise known as the *servuction system.*[9] At its most basic, servuction is a descriptive model which extrapolates the elements that determine the effectiveness of any service relationship. In applying the model as a template to different service settings, it can be used as a diagnostic tool to audit the process of service provision. Implicit within the servuction system is the notion that every element is dependent upon, and should be supportive of, all other elements within the model.

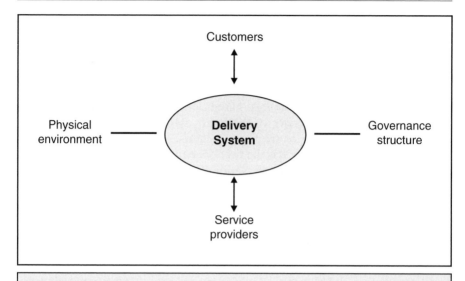

Figure 2. The servuction system.

Characteristically, the production of services is not as straightforward as it is for manufactured goods in that the customer has partial responsibility for the production process itself; the customer is an inherent part of the servuction system because the production, delivery and consumption of services takes place simultaneously. The five factors which impinge upon the effectiveness of servuction are customers, service providers, physical environment, governance structure, and the selected delivery system. First, customers are obviously linked to the process because, without them, no service is required and servuction as a process model would become redundant. Given the very nature of service production and consumption, customers are not passive recipients without a 'voice' in their encounters with service providers, but are directly engaged as important resources in the service exchange process with both providers and receivers taking on mutual responsibilities. For instance in banks, customers are active in operating ATMs, paying funds into accounts and speaking to personnel at enquiry desks. Second, the service provider defines the front-line contact point. In the case of banking services, this can be the telesales staff, the branch tellers, or even ATMs. Most often, the front-line service provider is one of the most important resources for the service firm. As customer-contact personnel, they are in the privileged position of being able to interpret the wishes and demands of customers and either respond immediately or take corrective action. This is obviously less likely when the service provided is a physical resource or item of technological hardware. Third, the physical environment contains tangible cues and atmospherics with which the client can evaluate the visible part of service provision, such as branch layout, bank uniform, branch interior design, product brochures, and such like. Fourth, the governance structure which the service firm selects involves the laying down of policies and procedures which determine the way in which employees are able to offer services. Thus, it involves all internal administrative and operational issues that affect the structural design of the service firm. Finally, the delivery system is central to service equilibrium, because it is the vehicle which allows the transaction of exchanges between customers and service providers to take place, and it is the distribution point for servicing customer demands.

In applying the servuction model to UK retail banking, it becomes apparent that changes are taking place in every facet of the system. However, particularly noteworthy are the governance structure elements which involve innovative adaptations to organizational structures, patterns, and procedures. The large UK clearing banks tended to operate a uniform approach to customer transactions with no substantial competitive differentiation visible in the marketplace. Nowadays the situation is markedly different and, in a recent study conducted by Stephenson and Kiely,[10] UK banks were investigated and analysed on the basis of their physical organizational changes which are being implemented following the recognition of a number of environmental challenges. Figure 3 gives a summary profile of some of these responses and details the banks' current tactics which represent the management agenda in each respective institution.

The selection of the most appropriate governance structure is a two-way concern involving both the service provider and the receiver. For instance, the service firm would wish to minimize the cost of the service encounter and increase efficiency, whilst the customer seeks ongoing satisfaction and exchange experiences from the encounter.[11] These two may reflect incompatible demands, but provided they can be reconciled in the governance structure, the likelihood of effective service delivery is much improved. Notwithstanding its simplicity, this logic is providing something of a dilemma for banks, and has resulted in a variety of responses.

Governance Structure Responses

The principal costs in branch-based systems are staff and premises which in 1992 accounted for £12.6 billion out of a total of £16.6 billion of operating costs in the large UK clearing banks. Recent years have witnessed attempts to cut such costs in the form of new governance structures, delivery systems, dis-investments, and cost-rationalization efforts. As a consequence, banks are faced with a wide number of strategic alternatives from which to choose. Although these options are extremely varied, Channon[12] has provided a useful five-point framework from which to observe the strategic choices facing bankers at the corporate level. First, increased *specialist branches* are tantamount to high-calibre specialist branches where a superior level of expertise and client support can be offered to key customer groups. Second, *limited service branches* are traditional, large-

National Westminster

- Strategic studies of branch locations

- Cautiously experimenting with new types of outlets e.g. retailing environments selling only mortgages and investment services

- Aware of significant cultural and organizational change required within the bank and customer base for this to succeed

Midland

- 350 branches in best retail locations identified as 'key sites'

- Major investment in 'key sites' to make them more customer-oriented

- Dramatic changes in branch layout with removal of traditional enquiry counters to ensure all enquiries are dealt with by trained staff

- All interfaces with staff more customer-oriented

Barclays

- Attempting to move from a 'processing culture' to a 'sales culture'

- Significant changes in branch structure with regrouping of branches into four or five banks around a central bank

- New groupings designed to give customer access to a greater level of expertise

- Reduction in employee base as part of a long-term overhaul of retail branch networks

Figure 3. Developing a sales orientation. *Source*: Adapted from Bill Stephenson and Julia Kiely.[10]

scale, full-service branches that have been slimmed down so that they are able to act as satellite or support branches with machine and teller activities. The slimming down effect has given these outlets the name 'thin branches'. Third, *automated branch experimentation* is a growing concept in bank delivery arrangements and one which is sure to remain in some form or other. Typically, these branches offer a limited number of services, most often for the targeted retail customer segment. Fourth, *electronic/machine banking* banks; all fall within this grouping in that they use electronic banking at some point in the service delivery. The ATM is the classic illustration which, with home banking, electronic terminal banking, and such-like provides a comprehensive portfolio of delivery arrangements via electronic systems to corporate and retail customers. Finally, *branch closures* involve the massive reduction of branch numbers which has been witnessed throughout the world in recent years.

It should be noted that the above are not mutually exclusive. Many banks operate a combination of these measures when implementing their delivery strategies. A number of UK banks are currently pursuing a *mixture* of such tactics which are aggregated in the form of a 'hub and spoke' branch system. The hub contains the support and administrative personnel necessary to deliver services to the branches (spokes).

Experience with this system in the US has shown that it lowers operating expenses and thereby improves branch profitability. Nevertheless, even though these strategies are well-intentioned and intuitively appealing to the strategic decision-maker, most rationalization efforts fall '...woefully short of addressing the fundamental structural problems facing the industry...banks are still over-branched'.[13] In fact, some evidence suggests that there is 30 to 40% excess capacity in current branch networks. Despite competitive cost-cutting, the experience of leading banks suggests that branches are still the cornerstone of retail banking strategy. The concept of the traditional full service branch is not dead, but rather experiencing a process of evolution.

Organizational Responses

Barclays Bank plc provides an excellent case example of the tactical responses being implemented to achieve more cost-effective and improved delivery arrangements. Barclays is a leading multinational financial institution which maintains operations in over 70 countries. Its market capitalization amounts to £5290 million and it has total assets worth £140.1 billion. Recent figures indicate that net operating income has been £1174 million with pre-tax profit at £51 million. Notwithstanding the size of the institution, Barclays has recently been suffering, along with all the other banks, from an unsatisfactory financial performance.

Barclays, like others of its ilk, had full service branches in most towns and cities across the UK. Branch managers and their staff provided a diverse portfolio of services to a demanding customer base. There was little or no specialization and as part of their day-to-day operating duties, it was expected that branch managers would know a great deal about each service line and facility available to their customers. Inevitably, problems of *role ambiguity* occurred where it became increasingly difficult, if not impossible for individuals to be able to offer guidance and advice on, and sell such a wide proliferation of banking services. Furthermore, this had a deleterious effect on perceived service quality from customers in that they tended to expect full service knowledge from all contact staff.

In order to tackle this vital strategic problem, Barclays designated certain branches as business centres which provide services to corporate clients, whilst allowing the retail branches to concentrate on providing personal and small business customers with enhanced service levels. From these changes it became apparent that the most important requirement of any restructuring programme was a marketing infrastructure which could provide:

- clarity in understanding specific client needs, which would be of paramount importance in service development planning and decision-making;
- a realignment of all systems and procedures to meet customer requirements;
- a re-orientation of all customer contact staff to understanding, serving and satisfying customer demands; and
- developing a delivery mechanism which would ensure both consistency in the service *offer* and high quality customer service/satisfaction.

In order to create this marketing infrastructure, a number of internal changes were required. First, a customer service programme was developed to establish the areas of Barclays' strengths and weaknesses. External consultants were commissioned to undertake three research exercises on a national basis aimed at providing Barclays with market intelligence on the performance of the branch network. The programme included branch visits, mystery shopping, branch telephone calls, and a customer satisfaction postal survey. In order to give some indication of the scale of the survey, the sample amounted to 1.2 million personal customers, which awarded a response rate of 22%. By and large, the results were very favourable with a significant majority of customers satisfied with key areas of common banking problems such as counter service, complaint handling, professionalism and courtesy, ATM network and telephone responses. Second, branches were grouped on the basis of customer profile, central market concentration, homogeneity of customer base and community working, and shopping patterns. Third, various departments were centralized to facilitate control in decision making.

Overall, the new configuration of branching from a regionally based structure to a more market-specific approach required changes to systems and procedures as well as additional investment in many areas. Efforts have been made to divide workloads more effectively between teams of management and staff within branches, as well as some branches within a group concentrating on targeted market segments and service lines. The principal advantage which this system provides is that specialization in branches reduces the wide range of product knowledge formerly required of individuals, allowing them to gain greater expertise in areas.

Clustering at Barclays

As part of an effort to group branches and change the overall governance structure, Barclays have followed a strategy of clustering. Figure 4 illustrates the clustering under a group parent. This type of approach reduces the size of the

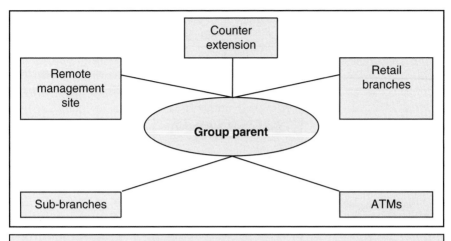

Figure 4. Clustering around group parent 'hub'.

overall network and provides more comprehensive control points. The group parent with higher grade managers ultimately makes more decisions at branch level, thereby speeding up decision time and making it possible to reduce the size of the controlling regional office.

The group parent branch (hub) holds centralized data for many retail branches, ATMs, sub-branches and counter extensions. The retail branches then report directly to the group parent branch for all decisions outside their control. This obviously takes a great deal of pressure off regional offices, who prior to clustering, would have received all queries and lending referrals directly from the retail branches. From the hub, extend sub-branches where customers can discuss general banking problems. They are strategically positioned and may be open less frequently than the normal branch network, sometimes only 2 or 3 days per week. The counter extensions are simply used for depositing or withdrawing funds and again are only open at certain times of the week. The ATMs are located at critical sites where their usage is warranted. Some group parents also have a remote management site, where senior level management are available for consultation.

Figure 5 illustrates the specialization of corporate and personal sector managers. Prior to clustering these functions were amalgamated, with product knowledge demanded of individuals being considerable. The diagram now shows the products which are offered within the corporate and personal sector manager's portfolios, and also highlights the operations manager's responsibilities, which have altered as a result of these changes.

The pattern of historical evidence suggests that bank costs are dependent upon three characteristics: margins, loan quality, and non-interest expense. By and large, a bank's true margin values and loan quality are mainly outside its direct control, being subject to external influences. On the other hand non-

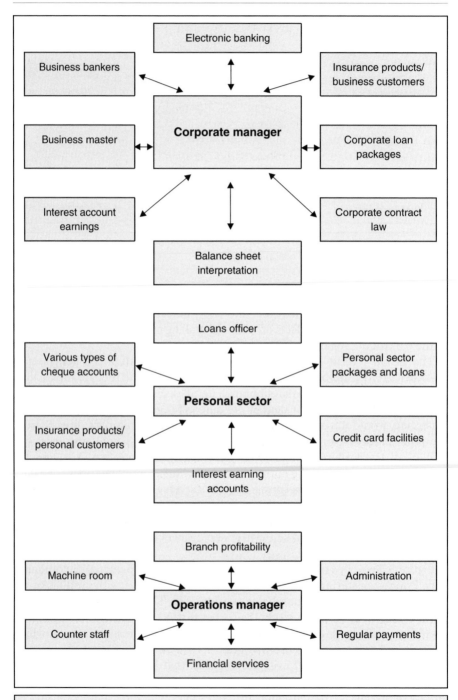

Figure 5. Sector specialization in the corporate, personal and operations functions.

interest expense, with its largest ingredient being human resources, can be managed and controlled. For instance, an analysis of 16 retail-oriented regional banks conducted by Marine Midland Bank showed that a clear correlation exists between returns on assets and non-interest expense. This study found that 60% of non-interest expenses are human resource related, whilst 20% are occupancy costs. Consequently, the outstanding players in banking are the institutions with the lowest staff numbers at the branch level. Doubtless as roles change, re-training and redeployment of human resources will be required. Given the potential internal hostility to these changes, open lines of communication have been encouraged with managers and other staff being kept informed of changes and decisions in order to increase awareness and reduce uncertainty.

These changes are being *phased in* over a period of years and aim to achieve the following:

- reduction in employee base to an appropriate lean level (via voluntary redundancy);
- introduction of new information technology;
- retraining and redeployment efforts;
- extensive internal communication with all staff;
- increased sales efforts for improved marketing performance; and
- emphasis on excellence in customer service.

Structural Implications

Given the turbulence facing not only the banking sector, it is not surprising that organizational strategies are being regularly monitored for potential problems. Strategic change will have an impact on the structure, the administrative and processing practices, and the overall governance of banks. The problem for organizational design consultants and strategic managers is how best to cope with the increasing diversity and align elements such as technology, environment and firm size, the strategic concerns of product mix and market expansion, priorities of market share, growth and profitability, and a wide range of performance goals with structural issues of decentralization, organizational form, dependencies and cross-fertilization, reward systems, control, and the like.

It has become fashionable to attempt to identify future trends and the implications for organizational structuring. Nevertheless, it is apparent that organizations approach these issues in varying ways and that their strategic priorities differ markedly (Figure 3). Rather than continuing the search for state-of-the-art models or frameworks of best practice, it is far better for them to strip back their activities and pursue transformations of structure from within. This reflects the views of a number of distinguished authors. In the late 1980s Professors Bob Eccles and Dwight Crane from Harvard Business School, examined management practices in 17 US investment banks.[14] Their observations have proven invaluable to understanding service firm structure. One key characteristic of the firms examined relates to the extent to which individuals throughout the firm (especially at the grass-roots level) could effect and bring about changes in organizational design. In a similar vein, Tom Peters[15] has argued that service firms are fluid networks engaged in constant redesign activities, so that organizational design is more organic and bottom-up, than structured and top-down. Given the rapid change in the business environment the traditional view of organizational structure representing a response to strategic conditions is no longer adequate. Rowe *et al.* have argued that

> ... a structure is not simply a rigid artifact that reflects the manner in which strategies are carried out. Rather, organizations are constantly changing and adapting to external exigencies and to internal political coalitions and technology requirements.[16]

A transformational approach is necessary which will ensure that new structures are customized to the needs of the organization and this should be the outcome of an organic process of change from within the firm.

Conclusions

Banking institutions are undergoing a series of challenges which do not so much constitute fine-tuning of their current arrangements and activities as involve a completely new approach in all areas of their operations. A product of this climate of change and turbulence should be an improvement in customer service, more cost-effective delivery systems, reduction in slack within processing systems and overall advanced marketing effectiveness.

Doubtless, retail banking institutions will continue to witness fierce competition and greater intensity for capturing market share. There will, however, have to be winners and losers. The winners will be those organizations that are best able to recognize changes in market preference and respond by offering services which readily meet the demands of customers. Service innovation, though, is just one determinant of organizational effectiveness; banking institutions will have to maintain the realization that a host of other factors impinge on successful competitive advantage. For instance, markets will continue to fragment, requiring more sophisticated segmentation and targeting efforts. Organizational image and service line positioning will thus be paramount issues in capturing market-share, as will service mix (breadth and depth) and controlling loan quality with improved risk management. All of these variables have strategic relevance and importance in decision-making, but one factor which must never be overlooked is the need for internal operations to respond to, and conform with, the demands of effective service delivery. Thus, once the current wave of governance structure changes across the industry is in place, regular assessment and appraisal will be essential to recognize the need for further and subsequent change.

References

1. Ian Morison and Patrick Frazer, Shaping the future of retail banking, *Long Range Planning* **15** (4), 105–115 (1982).
2. Derek Channon, *Bank Strategic Management and Marketing,* John Wiley and Sons, Chichester (1986).
3. Barry Howcroft, increased marketing orientation: UK bank branch networks, *International Journal of Bank Marketing* **9** (4), 3–9 (1991).
4. Peter Carroll, Rationalising branch location, *Journal of Retail Banking* **14** (2) Summer, 5–9 (1992).
5. Christine Ennew, Mike Wright and Trevor Watkins, Personal financial services marketing strategy determination, *International Journal of Bank Marketing* **7** (6), 3–8 (1989).
6. John Gapper, Banks launch root and branch reform, *Financial Times*, January 18, p. 11 (1993).
7. In fact, most UK banks have suffered a decline in their domestic net interest margins over recent years. For example, Barclays Bank plc, have suffered a domestic net margin fall from 7.8% in 1980, to 3.9% in 1990.
8. Robert Morgan and Sanjay Chadha, Relationship marketing at the service encounter: the case of life insurance, *Service Industries Journal* **13** (1), 112–125 (1993).
9. Eric Langeard, John Bateson and Pierre Eglier, Marketing of services: new insights from consumers and managers, Report No. 81–104, Marketing Science Institute, Cambridge, MA.
10. William Stephenson and Julia Kiely, Success in selling—the current challenges in banking, *International Journal of Bank Marketing* **9** (2), 30–38 (1991).
11. Gareth Jones, Governing customer-service organisation exchange, *Journal of Business Research* **20** 23–29 (1990).
12. Channon, *op. cit.*
13. Quotation taken from p.7 of Jeffrey Maddox, Securitisation is killing branch banking, *Journal of Retail Banking* **12** (2), 7–15 (1990).
14. R. G. Eccles and D. D. Crance, *Doing Deals: Investment Banks at Work*, Harvard Business School Press, Reveling, Mass (1988).
15. Tom Peters, *Liberation Management: Necessary Disorganisations for the Nanosecond Nineties,* Macmillan, London (1992).
16. A. J. Rowe, R. O. Mason, K. E. Dickel, R. B. Mann and R. J. Mockler *Strategic Management: A Methodological Approach*, p. 509, Addison-Wesley, Mass. (1994).

The views and opinions expressed in this manuscript are the authors' own (except where acknowledged citations are given) and not necessarily those of Barclays Bank plc.

The authors would like to acknowledge Mr David Webb (BMI-Insight, South Africa), Mr Gareth George (Regional Director of Barclays Bank plc) and anonymous *LRP* reviewers for helpful comments and guidance in revising earlier drafts of this manuscript.

3

Becoming a Customer "Owning" Corporation

Sandra Vandermerwe

> You know you "own" the customer when . . . You are their first choice. They look to you to solve their problems. They share confidential information with you. They talk to you about their plans. They accept your advice and ideas. You are involved early on in their decisions. They discuss options (as opposed to just price and discounts) with you. They give you feedback (good or bad) before you ask. They recommend others to you (and you to others). They trust you to take decisions on their behalf. They want you to succeed.

What we have learnt over the past few decades is that the most important capability a corporation needs in order to sustain competitiveness is knowing how to "own" customers in its selected markets—both existing, emerging and imagined.[1]

Some people object to the word "own" when they first encounter it. Amongst other things, they say, "you can't/shouldn't try to own anyone". But the notion of "owning" is actually a very effective way of driving a customer based transformation because it gets people to think differently about how to take their corporations into, and compete for, a future in which capturing the long term value of the customer is the primary concern.

It focuses thinking, energy and efforts from all parts of the corporation, thus opening up wider debates around issues which are tangible and relevant. People are able to compare the transactional business model, which primarily drives for

Sandra Vandermerwe is Professor of Marketing, Imperial Management School, University of London, UK.

market share through products or services, with the new business logic, which genuinely begins with customers. With customer "owning" as the dominant logic an important void is filled—not only do people talk about being customer driven, they begin to use terms and tools to make it happen, enabling the interests, language and ideas from people from different parts of the company, distribution channel, globe and industry to converge around common goals.

Importantly too, the notion of "owning" customers gets people to acknowledge that the corporation has to be good at quite different things than in the past, if they are to get customers to do and want to do business with them over a lifetime. And that requires thinking holistically about providing value for customers, which firms acknowledge can't be done alone. This becomes a platform for corporations and their partners to become the "gateway" to the total results needed by customers, rather than simply continuing to fight for increased market share based on the specification and price of their products and services.

Demystifying Marketing

In this process of transforming to "own" customers some myths and misconceptions must be consciously eradicated by change leaders. For example marketing—or management's interpretation of it—has been a serious barrier to "owning" customers. Marketing was often seen as solely responsible for the relationship between corporations and customers. But it never has, nor ever will be, remotely possible to have one single link responsible for the relationship between a firm and its customers. Paradoxically, many corporations built themselves in such a way that marketing was kept separate from day-to-day operations with customers. This proved fatal, since while marketing and sales were making the promises, the people customers saw most—and indeed often only saw—were those in operations.

Aggravating all of this was the passion and push for getting as much volume sold as possible. This led marketing to use several creative ways to broadcast corporate and brand virtues, rather than promote genuine dialogue between the customer and the corporation, and to monitor the firm's short term results, rather than long term results obtained by customers.

Aiming at End Users

Customers were often considered to be the ones next in the distribution line, and that was inevitably regarded as the end of the line and responsibility. Not surprisingly therefore many firms lost "ownership" of their market. Making the point was David Whitwam, CEO of Whirlpool, the North American appliance manufacturer, in a *Harvard Business Review* article:[2]

> "Until you stop thinking about the retailer as the customer and start thinking about them as part of the process, you're going to be deliver-

ing the wrong kinds of products. Sears Roebuck is a great example. We developed products to sit on their floors in competition with other products that were sitting on their floors. If they said "I want this washing machine with three whistles and two bells, and we want it to be pink", we gave it to them. Little did we know that the customer (end users) didn't want machines with whistles. Today we don't treat each other as customer/supplier. We see ourselves as partners trying to solve a common need."

New corporations who want to "own" customers go into the market to find out about end users, even though they may be far removed on the traditional distribution chain. This was one of the first moves Peter Lewis made when he arrived as the new CEO at Jiffy, the UK packaging company (of Jiffy bag repute). Since the corporation had always relied exclusively on distributors for information and feedback, Lewis's first question upon arrival was: how did end users feel about their packaging? Did they know what to use and when? Were the products available? Were they getting the value out of the products being made by Jiffy? Who were "they" anyhow?

Being on the Move with Customers Also on the Move

Another myth was that marketing could find out what customers wanted. We now know that customers don't always know, neither can they always articulate what they want. Also, customers too are undergoing major change. "Owning" customers is more like being "on the move with others also on the move" than having a strict formula to meet fixed and repetitive needs. Also, customer "owning" corporations go beyond traditional theories of segmentation. They follow and grow with customers, individualizing their offerings to suit their unique and changing needs.[3]

There were also serious limitations to what existing data could tell a corporation about its customers—let alone non-customers. Much of the information was history by the time corporations got it, and by definition it seldom revealed the new opportunities in emerging and imagined markets. Dissatisfaction with customer satisfaction data—no matter how robust—grew, because it didn't tell a corporation whether customers intended to continue to do business with them, a major concern in customer "ownership" . For example in the USA automobile statistics showed that between 65% and 85% of customers who switched automobile brands had said they were very satisfied.[4]

But probably the main culprit was an obsession with market share which drove firms conceptually, structurally and financially in a product rather than customer direction. Deep down it was believed that if market share was OK corporations were OK. But what is market share? Share of what? Rank Xerox were looking at copiers when they defined their huge market share in the 1980s. But while they were telling customers to "make one and photocopy the rest" the real competition, Hewlett Packard (HP), was saying "make as many as you want with our printers". And when all this was happening Canon came along and redefined the game away from products (copiers or printers) to what they then called "distributed information".

Finance Baffles Brains

Throughout the 1980s and into the early 1990s, IBM's financial results looked excellent; revenues almost trebled from $23 to $63 billion between 1979 and 1989. Profits were growing: it remained the market share leader in each of its computer businesses, with the highest market value and strong ratios. Until net income fell in 1989, when management responded by an attack on costs. 1990 was a very good year—profits were up 60%, and revenues 63%. An extension of the mainframe range, "the most important new product introduction in 25 years", led to predictions of even larger revenue growth.[5]

Despite massive restructuring efforts and cuts in operating expenses, in 1991 IBM reported its first ever real loss. Then in 1992 followed the biggest loss in US history. What went wrong? Amongst other things IBM thought it was leading in the leading markets: in fact, if it was leading it was doing so in the shrinking markets. Its relationship was with products, not customers—it was afraid to switch from one product to another for fear of cannibalization. Like others, IBM scrutinized and crunched out the numbers. Management continued to cut costs through major restructuring—whereas what IBM needed was much more radical.

Eliminating the Bias

If still being run by the analytic bias of the industrial era, management takes a narrow view of reality. Historic (hard) facts overrule intuitive or creative feelings about market position or potential. Conventional accounting and financial measures are used to assess the corporation's performance but this is a snapshot showing only what is brewing on the surface, and what has been accomplished in the past. Conventional ratios are compared to those of others within the industry whereas competition is much more likely to come from without.

"Owning" customers requires a different set of economics. Accounting systems have to be created to support the people within the organizations who have to change their behaviour and do different things.[6] The real financial questions and decisions on investment and performance revolve around building a portfolio of capabilities which offer, and will offer, customers—existing, emerging and imagined—value. A new set of questions are asked:

- What return can we get from customers over their lifetime, if we do it better than anyone else?
- What will this take?

- What will this cost?
- What will we lose if we don't do it?
- And what will that cost?

Defining New "Market Spaces"

Giving people the terms and tools that are new, relevant and workable is a critical part of what makes a transformation aimed at customer 'ownership' do-able and successful. Switching from old notions of product market shares to 'market spaces' is top of the list.

It involves changing the fundamental assumptions underlying value, namely:

- Value is not what goes into products or services, it's what customers get out of them.
- Customers get this value out over a period of time, rather than at a point in time.
- Value happens in the customer's space rather than in our space—in our space we only accumulate costs.

But as the following examples demonstrate, conventional wisdom based on more, bigger, better and cheaper products/services ran counter to this:

- Matsushita found that a large proportion of its Japanese customers were getting inferior listening performance from their increasingly superior video and TV products. Why? They were buying machines that were too big for the size of their rooms; they were not maintaining them well enough; and incompatibility between curtaining, carpet fabrics and acoustic technology adversely affected the sound quality.
- Despite buying good lubricants, Northumbrian Water was spending lots of money on downtime delays, shortened life of machines and time wasted because its engineers were having difficulty lubricating the pumps which were needed to move water supply and sewage. (70% of all machine failures in the UK are due to poor lubrication!) Here were some of the reasons engineers gave: machine suppliers put oil into the pumps, which could not always be mixed with other lubricants in stock; tins were difficult to open with consequent mess and wastage; difficulty was experienced getting oil out of cans into pumps, and dirt in cans led to contamination.
- Ciba (Ciba Geigy's) farmer customers in parts of the US were buying the best chemicals that could be made for weed and pest elimination. But while pesticides got rid of the bugs farmers were not necessarily getting a lifelong safe crop. Other plants were being affected by the pesticides which killed off the following season's production.

Ironically defining products, instead of value, inhibited product innovation. Had for instance the telephone utilities of yester-year thought in terms of "mobile communication", "office liberation", "mobility" or "independence" instead of phones, they may not have allowed other corporations like the Finnish company Nokia to get in on the emerging "alternative global office" through cellular phone technology. Had they become masters at connecting people, instead of just lines and cables, they may have asked the correct questions earlier and built the right capabilities sooner for the information and communication networking revolution.

Of the global appliance industry, David Whitwam of Whirlpool went on in the *Harvard Business Review* article to say that so much focus was on the machines that there has been little radical improvement in appliances in the last 30 years. He now talks about the new approach where individual customers undergo activities which lead to "total fabric care", the accumulation of which is the new "market space" opportunity:[7]

> "Going beyond traditional product definitions we are now studying consumer behaviour from the time people take off their dirty clothes at night until they've been cleaned and ironed and hung in the closet. What are we looking for? The worst part of the process is not the washing or drying. The hard part is when you take your clothes out of the dryer and you have to do something with them—iron, fold, hang them up. Whoever comes up with a product to make this part of the process easier, simpler or quicker is going to create an incredible market.[11]

Articulating the "Market Space"

New "market spaces" expresses in deliberate language what customers do to get the results they want rather than just what the products can do. Expressing new "market spaces" rather than product market shares requires a holistic approach to customers.

Value is defined through the verbs like "providing total fabric care" or "delivering global logistic management" rather than through the nouns or things, i.e. washing machines or courier services.[8]

Framing verbs to express and rescope what customers—existing, emerging and imagined—should/could do to get the results they want, enables corporations to articulate the new "market space" opportunity and thus focus energy and efforts. This set of activities is framed around a descriptor which, as the focal point for creating added value, is probably the most important breakthrough for any company in the process of transforming. Rank Xerox used "global document management" ("if you see your documents differently you'll see your business differently", Paul Allaire CEO said to customers) and it became the powerful lever in identifying the "market space" they wanted to dominate as opposed to previous eras in which the boxes (mainly copiers) were the mainstay of the business.[9]

Once done, the object is then (and only then) to decide:

- What added value is needed to "own" customers within these market spaces?
- Who does what? (What do we do? What do partners do? How do we structure/organize for this?)
- How to build the capabilities to achieve 100% of the market potential inside these "market spaces" (as opposed to a market share of product categories).[10]

Broadening the Core Business to Encapsulate Customer Value

To achieve capabilities to "own" 100% market potential in new "market spaces" requires a shift from old notions of core business to wider, richer definitions encompassing the entire customer experience so that customers get the results (the verbs) they want. For instance Federal Express talks about total "global logistic management". Its market share 10 years ago was 68% of the easy-to copy overnight delivery service product. It has half that now, but its capability and activity portfolio is much larger and relevant for long-term customer "ownership" and thus profitability.

An important part of the success of the Northumbrian Water (now part of the French Group Lyonnaise des Eaux) transformation in the mid 1990s was through having shifted the notion of their core business. Some years prior they had received a letter from Ford Motor Company—a standard letter sent to all the water companies—asking them whether they would be interested in managing Ford's total water activities in the UK. A carefully worded "thanks but no thanks" letter was drafted by them to Ford. Said Ian Macmillan, Service Director at the water utility then:

> "Water management wasn't our core business. We were good at getting large quantities of water to factories and collecting and treating the sewage and waste to very high standards. So we said "no" to the opportunity to work with one of the biggest companies in the world!"

From a very insular mindset and narrow core capability focus, Northumbrian Water began to build capabilities for managing the customer's total set of needs around water and utilities. As Macmillan put it:

> "We realised we needed to get "behind the factory gate" if we were going to deliver real value add to customers. Industrial customers are very reliant on water for the quality of their products—the taste of everything you eat and drink is affected by water as is the consistency of that taste from day to day or country to country. The drugs you use could contain as much as 90% water. The quality of the microchips in PCs depends on water. It takes 30,000 litres of water to build the average car and 8 pints to make 1 pint of beer. But some of our largest water-using industrial clients were taking their water (conforming to 99.8% industry standards) and putting it into tanks marked "raw ingredient". Only then did the real value adding opportunity begin."

Seeing a "Market Space" First

Seeing a "market space" first, articulating it and then building the capability for it takes courage, energy and vision. A good example is Citibank. John Reed positioned Citibank as the global bank in the 1980s. Before, being global had meant being in several countries. But, typically, mobile local customers had had to scramble to manage and co-ordinate their financial affairs cross-border. Reed was determined to change this for, as he saw it, there were emerging global financial market spaces in which upper income mobile customers would demand integrated and consistent services wherever, whenever, whatever.

Only now is Citibank beginning to enjoy the fruits of its efforts to build the customer business independently of geographic considerations for an emerging customer in a new "market space". Reed believes this has put Citibank way out front (though competitors thought they were crazy at the time).[11]

Becoming the "Gateway" to Customer Solutions

Once new "market spaces" have been identified and articulated the new corporation needs to determine how to become a "gateway" to the solutions customers need if they are to get the results they want. "Gateways" provide sets of solutions, across product and industry, rather than solutions around single products and services. They do the following which makes them different:

- Proactively they anticipate and push for new opportunities for customers on three levels—existing, emerging and imagined "market spaces"—as opposed to reactively solving problems only related to their products and/or services.
- Through them the various solutions are channelled and flow—they add their value to produce a total result for customers.
- They connect and integrate the various solutions, not just inside their own corporations, but between themselves, other companies and industries, in order to produce this total customer experience.
- They become therefore the dominant powerful "centre" for the customer value creation and delivery system, not just the dominating member of a linear supply and distribution chain.
- They align with others strategically, in order to provide the total customer experience to ensure "ownership" rather than just join forces to save costs or gain distribution.

New corporations become "gateways" because they extend their thinking, market activities and capabilities beyond making and selling more products and services to "seeing" new "market spaces" and concentrating on building capabilities to provide and continue to provide the value add potential within these "market spaces". This they do by putting value in and taking non-value out over the total life of a customer's activity. What they can't do themselves, they get done through partners operating in one system.

Rolf Huppi, who masterfully led the global transformation at Zurich Insurance—a challenge which began in the early 1990s and continues to break ground in countries all over the globe—is an example:

> "The Zurich" he describes as an integrator and contributor to people's lives—at work and at home. "We continually ask ourselves: how can we be a part of customers' daily lives—what we call "total care". Making relationships with customers more meaningful and helping them with the unforeseen is our key task today. When there is a problem we want to be there (first) to help. If something goes wrong in the home we want to take the first steps. If a pipe bursts we want to (or get someone to) clean it up—generally help the customers to protect and manage their assets whether or not it involves a claim. In fact the claim is secondary."

Total care, as Huppi explained it, is not just related to the insured assets because customers have needs outside of that narrow focus. Any problem, emergency or accident at home or in a foreign country is handled, and help or advice needed by customers in protecting or managing their assets is provided—either executed by Zurich themselves or found by them and delivered by others.

Actualizing the obvious tie-up between packaging and transportation, Peter Lewis from Jiffy Packaging, looked at getting packages to their destination on time as well as in one piece, as part of the move to make his corporation customer "owning" by providing ongoing added value. Costs had been unconsciously incurred by customers because they were using old product logic. Said one executive:

> "Bulk packaging costs money to store. As well, since packaging was such a minute part of overall expenses, buyers didn't take it seriously and often made bad application decisions. But so often if package decisions were poor or a shipment badly packed, millions in damage—reputation, time and hard cash—occurred. "

With TNT, the international courier operator, Jiffy re-assessed the role of packaging and transportation in delivering total customer value. In the motor industry for instance 45% of the body panels manufactured in the UK arrive at their destination damaged. So they worked in that industry first, finding that the real opportunity for value adding began right at the outset with the design of the new auto model and the various components that go to make up the vehicle through production on to delivery and then maintenance and repair.

Moving Through the Stages to "Gateways"

Let's look at the progression of thinking from products through solutions to "gateways". Table 1 tracks the journey, using Rank Xerox to demonstrate.

In transforming to become the leader in the global document management space, Rank Xerox must connect the various solutions that go to make one

Table 1. Moving through the stages to "gateways": Rank Xerox

Stage 1 1960s	Stage 2 1970s	Stage 3 mid-1980s	Stage 4 mid-1990s+
Value = features Offering = products or services.	Benefits Products augmented by services	Solutions Products and services	"Gateways" "Products" of the products and services
Object = market share (boxes)	Market share "products"	Markets share products	Share of potential market activity in "market spaces" becomes the integrator of improved life and business performance through documents
Market power = sell (boxes)	Help customers make better documents and make documents better	Software and services help specific user groups to use documents better and differently	

on-going experience for customers by creating, distributing and communicating documents around the world through its own and others' products and services.

Looking at the table you will see that none of the stages excludes the others. That is:

■ Features of the basic product or service have to be there, constantly improved through ongoing learning (Stage 1).

■ Benefits for specific groups of customers are necessary depending on specific user needs (Stage 2).

■ Solutions should be customized to solve specific user group's problems (Stage 3).

■ And all of the solutions need somehow to be linked into one integrated "gateway" result (Stage 4).

"Gateways" work with partners to achieve one integrated ongoing customer result consisting of all of the stages. Rank Xerox and AT&T USA have developed a distribution and print on demand system. Features include security, file storage and status checking (giving permission for access to buyers). Benefits range from reduced warehouse and shipping costs, allowing smaller investors to avoid huge investments in private infrastructures. Solutions are customized for specific sender and receiver user groups—from students to software houses. Into the global offering go the various solutions to form a "gateway"—software, distribution, shipping, storage, printing, binding etc.—that ultimately produces a result for people both sending and receiving documents in the form individual customers require, when and where needed.

Working to offer a total result, they redefine boundaries across product and industry lines according to customer needs and jointly compete for customer "ownership" in existing, emerging and imagined "market spaces". As AT&T's head of corporate strategy USA said:

> "People who see this (AT&T's new customer focused approach) as a win–lose game between us and Baby Bells are missing the point".

He sees the telecommunication pie growing bigger and bigger at the expense of other industries like transportation and sees a day when goods such as books are shipped around the country (direct from authors?) electronically and published in many places, rather than printed centrally, shipped and warehoused.[12]

Becoming the "Gateway"

Becoming a "gateway" for customers entails doing the following:

- *Understand your role in relation to others in getting the value to end users.* For a company like Rank Xerox this means articulating the role of "document management"—in, say, a bank, tax authority, insurance company or aircraft manufacturer—first in the protection and transferring of ideas, information, intellectual property and know-how in order for them to help firms compete more effectively. Take a simple example. One life insurance company found that part of the delay in getting the OK to people wanting life cover was due to hold-ups on the part of so-called third parties like doctors, accountants, other insurance companies or brokers. A large part of this was obviated by reducing the complexity of their documents.

- *Be prepared to influence and collaborate so that other products or services used by customers are interconnectable and inter-operable.* As we saw from the Matsushita, Northumbrian and Geigy examples, a lack of compatibility between products and customer usage makes getting value out to customers impossible. The superior Matsushita video equipment couldn't produce superior sound because of the textiles used by carpet and curtain manufacturers; the engineers couldn't mix the lubricants or get them easily from tins to the pumps so they ended up frustrated and delayed; the farmers had problems getting safe lifelong crop performance and ongoing productivity, due to mixes working for some aspects of the crop but killing off others. Louis Gerstner who took the reins of IBM in 1993, as the first non-IBM chief executive is trying to achieve common standards in the computer industry: the industry still doesn't work to make things easier for customers, he admits. His personal experience is testament to this—he once commented that he has eight computers in his office and everyone turns on and boots up differently. From this realization came his vision for the new IBM (he first said IBM didn't need a vision and then retracted his words[13]) in the new global electronic networking "market space": enabling people—both corporate and domestic customers—to connect and co-ordinate, taking action in real time, simultaneously.

The new corporation increasingly sees itself as one of a total package of events that go to make the overall customer experience. And they proactively push for the whole result rather than their own small bit. Knowing that their pesticide chemicals are only one of many that go to make a totally integrated solution for farmers in the USA, Ciba Geigy for instance now provide a "tank mixing" system. Items from different manufacturers can now be mixed and made to work together optimally.

■ *Be prepared to sell less of what you were good at making and moving in the past, and more of what makes customers good at what they do.* As increasingly "owning" customers depends on the results they get, corporations find themselves investing in new services rather than just the basic product or service. In their efforts to become a "gateway" through superior water and water treatment management, Northumbrian is working with key corporate customers to increase their market performance through better, more cost-effective and environmental products and processes, rather than just trying to get them to buy and use more water. In some cases this may mean helping to reduce corporate water bills.

■ *Know, understand, and—when applicable—recommend, sell and maintain competitive products and services.* For the automotive after-market SKF, the world wide manufacturer who made headlines when they made their then revolutionary jump from making and moving bearings (the noun) to selling "trouble free operations" (the verb), provides kits—which include up to 15% of bearings SKF purchases from competitors. Additionally, the kits contain several products from other manufacturers, e.g. seals and gaskets put together specifically for each of SKF's 8000-odd distributors in Europe, depending on the dealers and end user markets for whom they cater.

■ *Do things for and with customers—before rather than after the fact.* Remote diagnostics versus repair is probably the preventative example cited most often. But in a world dedicated to achieving real customer "ownership", the notion of working with customers in the long term to get ongoing results, thus preventing rather than curing, can go a lot deeper. For example what if:

- Pharmaceutical firms were judged, not on how many pills doctors prescribed, or how many pills people swallowed, but on how many "well" customers they had (as Chinese doctors are) and on the caring for and getting patients through the various stages of their lives?

- Or life insurance companies were judged on whether people lived longer/better rather than how quickly claims were met? (Aegon in the Netherlands pays a premium to people at a certain age if they are healthy).

- Or insurers prevented accidents instead of selling more policies to cover accidents? Zurich Insurance go into retail stores and factories and ask: what causes the millions of small incidents that could lead to small accidents that could lead to the bigger ones and ultimately to the disasters? How can we help customers prevent them?

- Or lawyers were rewarded not for winning a case but for how few clients had to go into litigation?
- Or auto dealers made money not on how often or well mechanics fixed cars, but on how seldom it was needed?

Accelerating "Time to Acceptance"

Accelerating "time to acceptance" of a new way for corporations to work in the marketplace is integral to becoming a customer "owning" corporation. In an ideal world everyone would be thinking and feeling the same way at the same time, and corporations could just get on and do whatever needed doing. Top management would definitely all be tuned in and turned on at the start, so that the new dominating logic could move swiftly through the ranks and drive behaviour in a neat orderly way. And every country would be on the same wavelength, responding in concert.

This doesn't work in real life however, where individuals, units, countries and companies understand and buy into and implement change at differing speeds. Resistance or support is not linked to seniority. Some of the strongest resistance is to be found in the highest places, while people who motivate and drive the corporation forward can be found everywhere within the organization.

That change no longer moves hierarchically either "top-down" (or "bottom-up" for that matter), has therefore been an important lesson in the past decade. (In May 1994, at the height of the IBM crisis, the Wall Street Journal reported that some 20% of its top 1400 managers still hadn't accepted the fundamental need for change.[14]) "Pockets of resistance" need to be found and managed by change leaders. Similarly, "pockets of support" need to be consciously identified and ideas converted into specific initiatives in order to make the right things happen at the right time.

People influence others by their behaviour, and they thereby bring about the transformation. Rather than expecting everyone to react or move at the same time or pace, corporations who want to "own" customers must work with a few key players and build a strong coalition with them to grow understanding, commitment and sponsorship.[15]

The same principles apply externally as do internally. Commitment early on from the correct customers will accelerate "time to acceptance" of new ideas and enable an organization to ultimately get to the bulk of their market. Therefore, not only must new corporations persuade and educate their own people to think, talk and behave differently, they must be prepared to influence partners and customers.

Choosing Corporate Partners with Whom to Leap

Picking customers early on is critical to success. It entails finding and getting to the "innovator" and "opinion leader" individuals or organizations early on and/or to the "pockets" or persons within corporations who are influencers, leaders or sponsors for a new way of working, remembering that often the biggest corporation (in revenue terms) won't be the first to accept or be the best bet in the long term.

The best choice for choosing corporate customer partners initially are those which will:

- act as a reference source, both in product and experience terms;
- give you an entree to the correct people and thus an early start;
- allow you to make a tangible difference to their business results;
- invest time and money in making both the offering and the relationship work;
- respect transparency and value sharing;
- believe enough in the benefits to push new ideas within their firm.

Success as a Motivator

That change happens at different speeds in different parts of the organization is significantly different from the old days when a new book of rules was produced and sent down the organization to be obeyed. Today we recognize that once a transformation starts, diffusion will take place through the innovators who are situated everywhere, and influence 360 degrees around themselves. Old notions of "bottom-up" or "top-down" are replaced by finding the correct people and working through them, in order to make things happen, spreading the learning and their successes, thereby building new role models. Said one executive of a large (mature) global corporation: "We've learnt, you can't tell people they are wrong and expect them to change what they are doing—you have to do it, prove it and sell it."

How fast, and how well, institutionalization of new customer ways progress largely depends upon opinion leaders taking on projects which form the "pockets" of energy which pull other "pockets" along. Projects—call them what you may—thus become an important lever in the transformation process. They mobilize the innovators and opinion leaders and act as a role model for the early and late acceptor groups of employees. Through them, new principles become new practice—visible, tangible and transferable.

Building "Model" Concepts

Since not everything can be done by everyone or financed all at once, firms have to build "model concepts" relating to ways of doing things that lead to customer "ownership". "Model concepts" are literally new ways of working with and for customers, which are made to work and then "modelled" so that others can learn from and copy.

The notion of a "model concept" (rather than the old pilot test) is preferable for corporations transforming to "own" customers for these reasons:

- A pilot test is about trying something and dropping it if it fails. Whereas the "model concept" is about actively putting resources behind a new initiative to make sure it works, learning and then making the necessary adjustments.
- The pilot assumes that there is enough time to test things out. The "model concept" is based on the principle of "doing and learning", to accelerate time to market acceptance.
- The pilot test is usually kept isolated for fear of failure. Whereas building a "model concept" involves getting the correct high impact people and customers involved, and making the process transparent.
- The pilot is made to be representative of the average. In a "model concept" people are chosen because they are different, out front willing and able to take risks before anything has been proven to everyone's satisfaction and make it work. Their successes incite and influence others.
- Pilot tests have a definite beginning and end. A "model concept" continues. Once begun they are developed, and the learning spills over into other projects in the transforming organization.
- Pilots exclude the customer—the corporation "gets it right" and then goes to market. Part of the objective of a "model concept" is to build relationships and share the learning, which includes experimentation—with chosen customers. The situation must therefore be win/win for both parties. If a learning consortium of sorts can be formed so much the better, where all parties invest and have something to gain.
- And finally, unlike pilot tests, "model concepts" become a reference source for other customers. Once successful, they can be used as a live laboratory, testing ground or show-case.

To "fix Europe" and integrate 500 scattered branches offering customers a total financing experience in the newly emerging global financial management "market space", the then head of Citibank's Consumer Services, Victor Menezes chose four countries—those he felt could adapt most readily and speedily. The other countries he continued to manage in the usual way. The country branches had always been highly decentralized, each doing its own thing, each with its own business proposition and, ironically, those with the larger networks and revenues were the most conservative of all.

One of the four countries chosen was Greece. Tom Sisson, who had been selected to head Citibank Consumer Banks in Greece, picked a small group and set about making some visible things happen fast. The model branch had been developed by Sisson in Chile, one of several projects initiated in New York with a view to getting "Citibanking" implemented world-wide. Immediately Sisson sent his people over from Greece to Chile to see it in action.

The "model branch" was not a premises or architectural issue, but rather a part of the new way Citibank was to do business with customers, navigating them through their entire and ongoing banking experience. In retrospect, Sisson believed that the "model branch" served several specific purposes in driving the "Citibanking" implementation.

■ It provided an ideal vehicle for getting customers to "see" the new company way and to try new services.

■ It was a valuable place for people to experiment, observe, learn and adapt *in situ*.

■ It acted as a role model for other branches and countries.

■ It made the global "Citibanking" vision tangible and thus gave it solidarity and cohesiveness.

■ It helped build consistency in the transformation process from branch to branch, country to country.

Initially small groups were put together by Sisson who intended to (and did) convert all 19 Citibank branches in Greece into Model Branches over time. He insisted that every experience throughout the bank system be shared. When one person or branch had a failure or success, the learning from this experience was made known to the others. "Strategy Review Sessions"—where lead countries came together regularly—were deliberately set up by Menezes to transfer know-how and successes on the model branch and other projects from one country to another.

"The Pan-European rollout from country to country in order to get cross country customer 'ownership' was deliberate and conscious", recalled one executive "even though we didn't have a pre-set plan and had to learn as we went along". Branch managers from the countries joined in these meetings. This sped up the rollout and built networks and friendships. One branch manager elaborated:

"It was so interesting. We really got to know each other, so when we picked up the phone for a request for one of our customers who might have been travelling, the person at the other end knew who we were, and, more importantly, wanted to help . This helped us think about being global and offering each other's customers the services and service levels they wanted."

Changing the Economic Rules

Because customer "owning" initiatives cannot pay off in the normal way or over the usual time horizons, how to get them funded is sometimes the biggest challenge:

■ How much time, energy and money will be invested to get the learning and know-how?

- How much of the exercise is expected to be profit generating, and how much will go to make a worthwhile learning experience?
- How can the learning gained be used in a tangible way?
- How can this be expressed in the economics?
- What can be saved if working practices which cost money but add no real value to customer value are eliminated? (e.g. bidding, contract renewal)?
- Who does what, who pays for what, who gets what afterwards?
- How should the best people on both sides be resourced to make it work?

One way to finance initial customer commitment is to make projects part of "customer R & D", a financial budget category that is still very rare. But since most corporations have product R & D budgets it is often a way to get support and realistic return time frames agreed upon.

Many of the projects can be made self-financing, since the transforming organization will not only be creating but also be extracting know-how and value. Also some expenses will disappear as those activities no longer relevant to customer "owning" activities become redundant. And some projects may be deliberately chosen to fund the longer-term, more costly ones.

Nonetheless, quantifying gains is still important in answering questions like:

- What new product opportunities will come from this which can be used for other customers?
- What information and know-how can we extract that will improve our overall ability to "own" customers?
- What is thus the potential worth of the information, know-how, learning, confidence and credibility we will gain?

Operating on Twin Tracks

To become a customer "owning" corporation, key people need to take the risks associated with making "model concepts" work and making these role models for others. Rooting changes into a customer focused culture involves explicitly stating (and rewarding) new desired behaviours, and how and why they differ from the old, and also articulating the connection between new behaviours and customer successes as demonstrated by "innovators" in new projects, otherwise people quickly revert back.

It's about people experimenting with and about customers, testing and implementing new ideas, based on a commonly shared interpretation of the priorities and opportunities in existing markets as well as those emerging or imagined.

A new set of tools and terminology aimed at lifelong relationships with customers provides a framework in which people can begin to do different things as well as do things differently. And, importantly, build confidence in taking personal initiative, instead of experiencing the constant insecurity born of, and perpetuated by, the industrial era.

Living with Ambiguity

People can and want to take new initiatives at differing speeds. But often they don't know how. Many may have long wanted to do much of what is now being advocated, but never dared, in the controlled environments in which they had to work. The best ideas therefore must be seeded, encouraged to grow and be shared through projects over time, which not only builds critical capabilities but, by doing so together with customers, obtains tangible results through doing, learning and adapting.

Ambiguity is a normal part of any customer driven transformation. The unexpected will invariably happen. Not surprisingly, this frightens and confuses many people. New corporate leaders are having to say:

> "We can give you clear direction but we don't know exactly how we are going to get there."

> "There is no manual, no book of rules, no magic strategy document from the top."

> "We can provide and help you discover new frameworks, ideas and tools, but you must translate them into daily behaviour."

> "We can provide the resources, support and infrastructure, but you have to do the doing."

Working on the Fast and Slow(er) Track Simultaneously

In his book, *Managing with Dual Strategies*, Derek Abell, a former colleague of mine at IMD in Switzerland, discussed the fact that management as a human endeavour differs from others—because at times we invest and at times we consume—running a business and changing it simultaneously are not sequential but parallel pursuits.[16]

For this we need to be able to work on different tracks and balance long and short term goals as we go. New corporations develop capabilities therefore to work in the present and the future simultaneously. They keep within the "sphere" of their stated vision to maintain the focus and direction of the transformation, but always with one eye stretching to horizons beyond what they can presently "see" or prove exists.

Such corporations know they need to operate on twin tracks at different speeds, making sure that the one doesn't interfere with the corporation's ability to achieve the other. Both aspects have to be balanced:

> "You can't predict or plan"—"You must keep coming back to the basic strategy."

> "Move faster than ever before"—"Go only as quickly as people can tolerate."

"Move quicker or people will revert back to old behaviour"—"There are limits to the amount of change people can tolerate."

"Do what's possible and can be done naturally well in a reasonable time frame" —"Do what's impossible, if it needs doing, no matter how long it takes."

"Keep the bonfires burning"—"There is too much change happening."

They also know how to manage the contradictions. Working on two fronts simultaneously, change leaders are able to alter the pace depending on with what and with whom they are dealing. With 36,000-odd people involved in the Zurich Insurance transformation, Rolf Huppi conscientiously managed different tracks within the different countries and parts of the business. The fast—which he defined as the "do-able"—focused on more operational aspects, and he pushed to get these done quickly. On the slower track, he knew initiatives would take longer. But they had to be done to fulfill his vision of creating a customer "owning" corporation.

Some corporations see more than two tracks, and explicitly state this to their people. By splitting initiatives out into the different categories, they are better able to manage the various paces moving simultaneously toward the goal. Citibank for instance divides projects into three categories: one, the visible high priorities which should and could be done immediately; two, those involving "stretch goals"; which need more time and systematic change efforts; and three, those requiring what Citibank calls super-stretch-capabilities and goals taking a longer period to accomplish.

At some moment, the fast and slow(er) track(s) must converge. While change leaders cannot manage each piece or project in the quest to become customer "owning", they must manage the dynamics between the pieces and projects to accomplish this. Only they can pull them together, building bridges between the fast and the slow(er) tracks knowing which levers to pull, with whom, when and where.

Funding the Future

Initiatives which lead to transformations aimed at customer "ownership" don't show quick bottom line results. Yet firms continue to use economic minds and methods which are based on the short term. They focus on a point in time rather than demonstrating the value of and for customers over time. They continue to ask: what will it cost now and what will be our return now?

In truth most corporations continue to judge in the short term, because they are judged in the short term. With pressure to show results quickly, get the ratios right and watch the share price on a minute for minute basis, without some alternate or supplementary way to express what they are doing with customers, why, over what period, to what end, corporations will continue to be caught in this short term "capital pathology" trap aiming to please short term investors.

Old and New Financial Questions

New corporations increasingly work not just with old but also with the new economic questions shown on the right hand side of Table 2.[17]

They know, however, that the old economic figures can only go so far looking at customers as costs rather than investments. They put energy into funding a sustainable future through fast and slow(er) track initiatives carefully balanced, making customers their major investment.

Like any other investment, investing in customers means accepting that a lot of the time and energy and money spent initially will take a period to pay off. And people have to be rewarded accordingly. It is said that salespeople working at the Lexus dealerships in the USA only get part commission when the deal is struck. The rest comes when the customer returns for their next car. At Citibank's corporate banking division, where the entire vitality of the business

Table 2. Old and new financial questions.

Old Questions not just	New Questions but also
How do we increase market share?	What will it take to commit the customers we want for a lifetime?
What is the value of our customer(s) as a percentage of sales?	What is the lifetime worth of our customer(s)?
Can we cut unit costs/hold margins to maintain profitability?	How can we better serve customers to get a deeper share of their spending?
Are our products /services/countries/ units/ companies/branches profitable?	Are our customers profitable?
What are our cost of sales and services?	What's the cost of losing a customer?
How do we get costs down?	What costs can we eliminate because they add no value to our customers?
What is the cost of the activities we do?	What is the opportunity cost of the activities we do?
What are the unit costs of our products and services to us?	What is the total integrated cost of our products and services to our customer?
How do we allocate costs to products/services/units/companies/ countries/branches?	How do we: ● Share resources? ● Allocate value for contribution for customer profitability?
What will it cost to increase customer value?	How do we increase value for customers and simultaneously decrease costs?

hinges around expanding relationships and frontiers with customers, account managers spend a good chunk of their time being with prospective customers, assessing new trends, giving them proposals and ideas before any deal is signed. Ed Holmes, managing director of Citibank N.A., says this is a very frustrating period because very little happens. He calls it "the two year tunnel":

> "To get through this tunnel you have to reward people for doing the right things, even though they don't get the business immediately. Customers may initially say: we like your ideas and your people, we see what you can do, but at the moment we don't have business for you. You can actually feel the moment when that changes, when you start getting to the end of the tunnel and you are going to have a different life with the customer. But you need to learn to live with the period in between if you want get onto a higher plateau with customers. You need to take the enthusiasm and creativity people have generated and make it worth something—to them and to the organization."

Conclusions

Becoming a customer "owning" corporation entails using an alternative logic and a new set of terms and tools. It is only in this way that corporations can be moved from where they are to where they must go if they are to profit from existing, emerging and imagined market opportunities.

To break the existing paradigm needs both the opening and changing of minds and the converging of ideas and actions on twin tracks—the slow and fast(er)—around organizing principles which are both customer relevant and powerful for the times. Getting a common language helps set and gain common ground—everyone acknowledges that the correct moves are those which attain the customer "ownership" goal. "Owning" customers means being the first choice for individuals who want you as a lifelong partner because you represent a long term value to them in the same way that they do to you—and individual customers need offerings to suit their unique and changing needs over time.

Whereas market share was the main objective in previous times, we now understand the limitations. To get results for customers means understanding what they do in "market spaces" and adding value to these activities rather than just producing new products. This means extending core business notions and aligning with others to become the "gate-way" to lifelong customer solutions.

This article tries to show why old minds, methods and models have inhibited customer "ownership", and provides a new set of tools and terms by which corporations can genuinely focus on customers and take advantage of opportunities to add value. In sum the major points are these:

■ Articulate new "market spaces" around what customers do to get the results they want and determine which capabilities will be needed to own 100% of the market potential within these "market spaces."

- With others, across unit, branch, company, country, industry, become the "gateway" to customer solutions, by providing ongoing results for customers, regarding them as lifelong investments.
- Make delivering value add to the customer—existing, emerging and imagined—so that he or she gets/will get the total experience in the "market space(s), the prime motive for strategic partners and alliances, because that is how the customer will get results, not just through improved versions of your products and services".
- Focus financial questions on investment and performance around how to get the value to customers and quantify the costs and risks of not doing so. Compare this to the long-term value of customers.
- Support this with rewards, accounting systems and projects on new ways of working with customers and make them into "model concepts" from which others can learn and apply.
- Learn to operate on twin tracks—the fast and the slow(er), understanding the contradictions and ambiguities associated with having to transform a corporation from one which has been competitive because it knew how to make and move products/services to one which now has the capabilities to "own" customers and thereby compete in, and for, the future.

Acknowledgements

Unless otherwise stated, information and quotes come from interviews conducted by the author in a research project on customer driven transformations spanning the last decade. The author gratefully acknowledges the research support for this work provided by the International Institute for Management Development, (IMD) Lausanne.

References

1. As far as I know the word "ownership" has not been used in this way before. For market "ownership" see W. A. Sherden, *Market Ownership,* AMACOM American Management Association, New York (1994). For more on customer "ownership" in this context see S. Vandermerwe, *The Eleventh Commandment: Transforming To "Own" Customers,* Wiley, London (1996).
2. From D. Whitwam, The right way to go global: an interview with David Whitwam, *Harvard Business Review,* March–April (1994).
3. On so called markets of one see: D. Pepper and M. Rogers, *The One-to-One Future: Building Relationships One Customer at a Time,* Doubleday, New York (1993). For an interesting discussion of the evolution of segmentation and markets of one, see P. Kotler, From mass marketing to mass customization, *Planning Review,* (September 1989). For more on individualization see S. Vandermerwe, *The Eleventh Commandment: Transforming to "Own" Customers,* John Wiley, London (1996).

4. Figures from paper by F. Reichheld, *The Satisfaction Trap,* Bain & Company, USA (January 1993).

5. IBM material other than from personal interviews see: P. Carroll, *Big Blues: The Unmaking of IBM,* Weidenfeld, London (1993); T. Clarke and J. Jaben, IBM's destiny: marketing challenge hinges on meeting customer demands, *Business Marketing* (May 1993); M. Dunn, IBM chief warns big changes needed, *Newsbytes* (21 April 1995); C. Ferguson and C. Morris, *The Computer Wars: The Fall of IBM and the Future of Global Technology,* Random House/Times Books, New York (1993); S. Greyer and N. Langford, IBM: When the numbers failed to compute, Harvard Business School Case Study (1993); R. Heller, *The Fate of IBM,* Little Brown & Co., New York (1993); W. Ketelhohn and B. Robbins, From big blue to Baby Blues, IMD Case Study (1994); D. Lichtenthal and W. Copulsky, How Big Blue Became black and blue, *Industrial Marketing Management,* **22** (1993); G. Lloyd and M. Phillips, Inside IBM: strategic management in a federation of businesses, *Long Range Planning,* **27**, 1994; D. Quinn Mills and G. B. Friesen, *Broken Promises: An Unconventional View of What Went Wrong at IBM,* Harvard Business School Press, Boston (1996); W. D. Yoffie and D. Pearson, Transformation of IBM, Harvard Business School Case Study (1991);W. D. Yoffie and J. Cohn, Transformation of IBM—Supplement, Harvard Business School Case Study (1993) .

6. P. Drucker, *The Leader of the Future,* Drucker Foundation Future Series, New York, p.37 (1996).

7. D. Whitwam, *op. cit.*

8. S. Vandermerwe, *From Tin Soldiers to Russian Dolls: Creating Added Value Through Services,* Butterworth-Heinemann, Oxford (1993); S. Vandermerwe, Jumping into the customer's activity cycle, *Columbia Journal of World Business,* Summer (1993).

9. Material other than interviews on Rank Xerox from: In-house publication *The Document Seminar,* Revision 3 (May 1994), J. Brown, Seeing differently: improving the ability of organizations to anticipate and respond to the constantly changing needs of customers and market—the Xerox experience, Marketing Science Institute Conference (1993); S. Charkravarty, Back in focus, *Forbes* (June 1994); R. Howard, The CEO as organizational architect—an interview with Xerox's Paul Allaire, *Harvard Business Review* September (1992); H. Motroni, Xerox company study—a turnaround: putting the customer first, *The Journal of Business and Industrial Marketing,* Fall (1992); E. Ramcharandas, Xerox creates a continuous learning environment for business transformation, *Planning Review,* April (1994); R. Walker, Rank Xerox-management revolution, *Long Range Planning,* **25** (1992).

10. For interesting reading related to this idea, see B. Henderson, The origins of strategy, *Harvard Business Review,* November (1989).

11. J. Reed and Citibank quote from Citicorp faces the world: an Interview with John Reed, *Harvard Business Review,* November (1990), and Citicorp: John Reed's second act, Fortune, April (1996). See also S. Hansell, Citibank's global goal: the McDonald's of consumer banking, *International Herald Tribune* (15 July 1996).

12. A. Kupfer, AT&T, Ready to run, nowhere to hide, *Fortune* (29 April 1996).

13. See Gerstner's new vision for IBM, *Fortune* (November 1995), and address given by him to *Comdex Computer Show,* Las Vegas (November 1995); D. Kirkpatrick, Gerstner's Visions For The 1990's, *Fortune* (15 February 1995).

14. L. Hays, Blue period, *The Wall Street Journal* (16 May 1994).

15. For original work on diffusion theory see E. Rogers, *Diffusion of Innovations,* The Free Press, New York (1982). For more on the diffusion theme in transformation see S. Vandermerwe, The process of market-driven transformation, *Long Range Planning,* April (1995), and S. Vandermerwe, *The Eleventh Commandment: Transforming To "Own" Customers,* Wiley, New York (1996). For coalitions diffusion and transformation, J. Kotter, Leading change: why transformation efforts fail, Harvard Business Review, March–April (1995).

16. D. Abell, *Managing With Dual Strategies: Mastering the Present, Pre-empting the Future,* The Free Press, New York (1993).

17. For general reading on new economic questions in table see J. Anderson and J. Narus, Capturing the value of supplementary services, *Harvard Business Review,* January (1995); D. M. Brown and S. Laverick, Measuring corporate performance, *Long Range Planning* **27** (4), (1994), R. Cooper and R. S. Kaplan, Profit priorities from activity-based costing, *Harvard Business Review,* May–June (1991); A. De Meyer, Creating product value, putting manufacturing on the strategic agenda, *Financial Times* (1993); F. Gouillart and J. Kelly, *Transforming the Organization,* McGraw Hill, New York (1995); R. S. Kaplan and D. Norton, Balanced scorecard: measures that drive performance, *Harvard Business Review,* January (1992); J. Quinn, *The Intelligent Enterprise,* The Free Press, New York (1992); F. Reichheld, *The Loyalty Effect: The Hidden Force Behind Growth, Profits, and Lasting Value,* Harvard Business School Press, Boston (1996), especially Chapter 8, The Right Measures; J. Ribera and M. Rosenmuller, The value of a satisfied customer, Technical Note, IESE, International Graduate School of Management, University of Navarra, Barcelona-Madrid (April 1995); A. Slywotzky and B. Shapiro, Leveraging to beat the odds: the new marketing mind-set, *Harvard Business Review,* September (1993); T. G. Vavra, *Aftermarketing—How to Keep Customers For Life Through Relationship Marketing,* Business One Irwin, Homewood, Illinois (1992); T. Wallance, *Customer-driven Strategy and Winning Through Operations Excellence,* Oliver Wright, London (1992).

4

Strategic Change and Organizational Culture at Hay Management Consultants

Loizos Heracleous and Brian Langham

In summer 1994 Hay Management Consultants responded to market and stakeholder demands by embarking on a strategic change programme which aims at transforming the way the organization operates over a 5-year period. Experience from leading and researching the change process suggests, among other things, that diagnosing and considering the implications of organizational culture at the initial stages of a change programme, as well as conducting subsequent periodic cultural audits, is extremely helpful to its effective management. Moreover, the case highlights important issues relating to the management of knowledge workers in the context of strategic change. Within a simplified framework of strategic decision-making we discuss the importance and role of organizational culture in strategic change programmes, as well as other change management issues and lessons arising from this case. In so doing we illustrate the use of a potent diagnostic tool—the 'cultural web'—which has assisted the executive to plan and manage the change process and is currently used for monitoring the change.

Loizos Heracleous is a doctoral researcher at the Judge Institute of Management Studies, University of Cambridge, UK.
Brian Langham is Executive Director—Change Management at Hay Management Consultants, London, UK.

The aims of this article are two-fold: *1.* to highlight and illustrate the importance of organizational culture in strategic change processes; *2.* to discuss some change management issues and some lessons arising from leading strategic change at Hay Management Consultants, a major international human resources consulting firm.

The data used in the discussion of the case and the construction of Hay's 'cultural web' was collected as part of an ongoing longitudinal qualitative case study of Hay's strategic change process.

The philosophical commitments of the research programme lie within the interpretive approach, which holds that in contrast to natural events, social action is characterized by a subjectively meaningful character which researchers should try and grasp. Social reality is seen as consisting not of 'objective' hard facts, but of structures of signification, domination and legitimation which are affirmed, sustained or challenged by social action.[1] The methodological paradigms followed, in accordance with the interpretative approach, are an integration of semiotic ethnography and action research.[2]

The research strategy employed is that of a longitudinal case study utilizing theoretical and methodological triangulation in order to increase the internal validity of the findings.[3] Five main methods are utilized: in-depth interviews of employees at various levels and in various roles; cultural audit sessions with 6–8 participants;[4] participant and non-participant observation; document analysis using current and past documents; and organization-wide descriptive surveys.

Strategic Change at Hay Management Consultants

Hay's operations in the UK have been the most successful, sustained over several years, in relation to other countries in which it has been operating. During the last few years, however, there has been a growing awareness among the senior group that things needed to change, escalating to significant levels during summer 1994. There were several signals which could not be ignored. Environmental projections by independent research organizations showed that the human resources consulting market was expected to grow at an annual rate of around 12%. Internal data showed that the field in which Hay has traditionally been a leader (job evaluation) was decreasing in terms of overall returns, and others such as organization change, human resources planning and development consulting were growing rapidly. Periodic client satisfaction surveys have indicated certain areas where improvements could be made.

The need for transformational change was based on the fact that because Hay had been operating at near full capacity, and with a relatively reliable projected market growth of around 12%, the strategic options it had were to either remain at its existing size, with the implication that it would gradually lose market share to competitors with more spare capacity or who intended to grow, or set and pursue growth targets which would at least meet or exceed market growth. The second option was chosen, and Hay set growth targets of about 15% per annum (compound) which will lead to growth amounting to twice its size in 5 years.

In addition to substantial growth, Hay's strategic redirection includes:

■ A more focused client relationship management process where consultants will focus more effectively on clients within specified size brackets, as opposed to 'owning' a portfolio of clients with varying sizes, needs and demands developed in an *ad hoc* manner. ˌ

■ An increased breadth and depth of consultants' expertise, within an approach to expertise development and selling which moves away from simply providing tools and methodologies to providing integrated solutions to client needs. This necessitates consultant skills which enable an accurate understanding of the nature of complex client issues and the subsequent application of packages of tools and methodologies as the solution, as opposed to providing a single tool or methodology.

■ The integration of consulting methodologies in their provision to clients as a package, which is based on such broadening and deepening of consultants' expertise.

Strategic Change and Organizational Culture

Studies of strategy development over time and in context[5] have demonstrated the close links between strategy development and organizational culture. Normative rationalistic approaches to strategic management were found to be inadequate in explaining actual processes of strategic development in organizations. Observed patterns in strategy formation, such as incrementalism, whether intended or unintended,[6] were shown to be rooted not solely or essentially in rational and objective planning procedures, but in the cultural, social and political characteristics of the organizations concerned. While strategic planners themselves report that they follow the steps of normative models of strategic management,[7] this process takes place within a context of taken-for-granted and tacit beliefs and assumptions about the organization and its environment—the organizational paradigm.[8] This set of core values and beliefs about the organization and its environment develops over time out of the learning experiences of the organization as it copes with its problems of external adaptation and internal integration.[9]

The organizational paradigm, as a set of taken-for-granted beliefs and assumptions, is enshrined within a cultural web of artefacts which are both the behavioural manifestations as well as the legitimations of these beliefs and assumptions.

The cultural web (Figure 1) is a construct which encompasses elements from both ideational views of culture which emphasize shared cognitions (being the paradigm in the cultural web), and adaptationist views of culture which em-

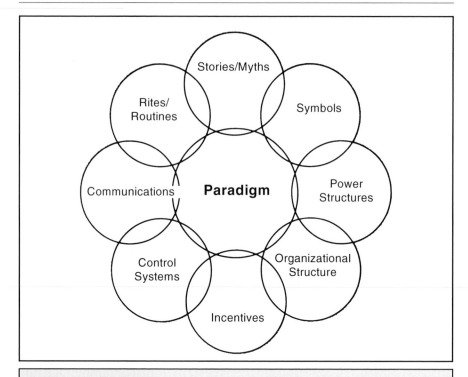

Figure 1. A cultural web.

phasize behaviour (manifested in terms of the artefacts around the paradigm),[10] drawing attention to the close link between the two. As such, the cultural web is consistent with seeing culture either as a root metaphor for conceptualizing organization within an interpretive frame of reference (something an organization *is*), or as a variable within a functionalist frame of reference (something an organization *has*).[11] These orientations are not inherent in the cultural web as a construct, but can be manifested in the specific use it is put by researchers or managers.

Incrementalism in strategy development has been viewed as an essentially logical and rational process in response to an uncertain environment, where managers are said to proceed cautiously and experimentally in order to try and reduce this uncertainty.[12] It has been argued however, based on the findings of longitudinal qualitative studies of strategic change, that it can be accounted for not as much by such logical processes, but by the filtering influences of the organizational paradigm on managerial interpretations and actions.[13]

The main implications of this approach for transformational change are that it is seen as exceedingly difficult to achieve because of the substantial influence of cultural beliefs and assumptions on individuals' interpretations and actions, their taken-for-granted nature which effectively precludes them from open debate[14] (unless they are surfaced using constructs such as the cultural web), their close link with the power centres of the organization and the internal consistency, self-legitimacy and self-sustenance of the cultural web.[15] In this view transformational change is possible, but it has to be pursued in an evolutionary manner, by committed leaders who are intellectually and politically able to make it happen.

Having briefly explored the theoretical origins and implications of the cultural web, we now proceed to discuss its value as a potent empirical tool for gaining a deeper understanding of various dimensions of the internal situation of an organization. Figure 2 is a simplified framework of how strategic decision makers might approach their task, and will be used to structure our discussion of the strategic change programme at Hay Management Consultants. It should be emphasized that it is not a model of how strategic decision-making is carried out in practice. Strategic decisions are influenced by social, cultural and political factors,[16] in this sense they are not fully rational, but there are strong arguments that they should try to be,[17] by following procedures which are likely to minimize such factors. Figure 2 portrays an example of such a process, which needs to be repeated continually because *1.* as time goes by, both market and internal conditions change so the premises for forthcoming and previous decisions need to be reconsidered leading to feedback loops in the process; *2.* as regards planning for organization change, it is implausible to plan for every issue in a single session. The product of the necessarily intuitive, synthetic and creative act of strategic thinking by direction-givers[18] needs to be given initial form by more down-to-earth, operational considerations.

Figure 2. A simplified framework for strategic decision making. The management cycle.

The functions of the cultural web in this process, which will be discussed further below, are:

- *Situation analysis.* The cultural web helps to portray and clarify several internal characteristics of the organization.
- *Policy and strategy making.* The cultural web surfaces the beliefs and assumptions which have guided—and are still subconsciously guiding—the interpretations, decisions and actions of the policy and strategy-making bodies.
- *Implications.* A valid cultural web can help to show clearly which beliefs, assumptions and artefacts need to change in accordance with the new strategic direction and which ones should be maintained and strengthened. The cultural web can also help change agents predict likely areas of resistance to change by assessing the nature and salience of existing cultural beliefs and assumptions, and the extent of interconnections between these and cultural artefacts.
- *Change management.* The cultural web portrays a substantial range of the elements which should actively be managed for a strategic change to be successful, e.g. communication, changes in control systems, incentives and organizational structure.
- *Monitoring and evaluation.* Constructing a cultural web periodically (say every 6–9 months) and examining any alterations in the presence and relative strength of its elements can help the organization track its progress in changing internally to reach its strategic goals.

Where Are We Now and Where Do We Want To Go?

Organizations should continually be scanning their environments and detecting relevant opportunities and threats, as well as assessing themselves internally for their strengths and weaknesses. This should be done in a climate of open, critical inquiry, as the dangers of 'groupthink'[19] are real and pervasive.

Since summer 1994 one of the authors was collecting data on the organizational culture and employees' views and concerns about the change, and working closely with the organization change steering group. A cultural web of Hay Management Consultants was constructed using qualitative triangulated data (Figure 3). The inner circle of the web (the organizational paradigm) portrays the cultural beliefs and assumptions of the organization, which are supported by and interconnected with the cultural artefacts on the outer circles.

Over the three decades during which Hay has been operating in the UK it has developed a rich professional organizational culture. This was characterized by the following perceptions, which have been shared by members of the organization to varying (but relatively high) degrees:

- Hay's core business was perceived by many, both consultants and clients, as being job evaluation (which had been its core business for decades in the past, but not any more in terms of sales). This was mainly manifested in consultants' daily communication amongst themselves using terms related to this methodology, as is the case in several organizations where a shared vocabulary helps to constitute an identity for organizational members.[20]

■ Clients are considered as all important in Hay, often taking priority over internal systems and commitments. Consultants' explanations of their actions or inactions, as one of the authors has observed, mainly rest on the premise of acting in the best interest of the client. Moreover, Hay's client orientation is reflected in its carrying out periodic client satisfaction surveys, the substantial power base of individuals with significant client portfolios and relationships, and its flexible structure allowing it to respond swiftly to clients,

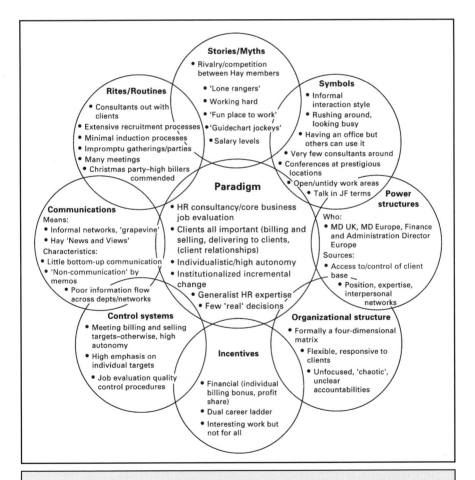

Figure 3. Cultural web of Hay Management Consultants—constructed summer 1994.

being a four-dimensional matrix (regions, practices, sectors and client project teams).

- Hay has been characterized by individualism and high autonomy of its consultants since its inception. This is exemplified by its mythological figures of 'lone rangers', currently senior people who have exhibited highly individualistic behaviours in dealing with clients and 'guidechart jockey', who would 'ride' in an organization with their job evaluation guidecharts to be used as a tool to solve client problems. In the section on managing knowledge workers the interconnections of Hay's individualistic climate with several cultural artefacts are sketched out.

- Hay has been carrying out reorganizations on an annual basis, referred to as 'autumn manoeuvres' by its members. The autumn manoeuvres have been institutionalized as part of its culture, which has created problems for the present strategic change, as will be discussed below.

- Consultants have tended to consult on a variety of human resource fields, which led to an internal perception of generalist expertise.

- Lastly, mainly due to the high autonomy and individualism of consultants, the perception developed that there are few 'real' decisions taken by the executive.

What Implications Does This Have for Our Values, Beliefs, Structures and Processes?

One important issue which is often ignored is that there cannot be a transformational (as opposed to incremental) change without major cultural repercussions. Taking Hay as an example, it has been determined that if the strategic change is to succeed, significant changes should take place in the cultural beliefs and assumptions of the organization. In particular, it was decided by the change steering group that all beliefs and assumptions portrayed in the inner circle of the cultural web had to change except the belief that clients are all important:

- *Human resources consultancy*. Core business job evaluation. Job evaluation had provided Hay with most of its revenues for decades. The perception that job evaluation is Hay's core business still exists both in Hay's market as well as internally, although this specific activity accounts for less than 25% of Hay's consulting revenues, and less than 60% of reward as a whole. If perceptions that 'Hay is Pay' are to be broken, Hay needed to broaden its consultants' understanding of the integrated human resource offering, and to position job evaluation as one of its main areas of expertise.

- *Client focus* is clearly of strategic importance to any organization as a driver and the *raison d'etre* of organizational synergies, capabilities and competencies which can produce a sustainable competitive advantage. Hay's client-oriented vision for the future provides a common thread between Hay's past and the desired future state. This common thread legitimizes the vision and helps to ensure employees' commitment to it:[21] to "be the consultancy of choice for helping our clients realize their strategy through people".

■ *Individualistic/high autonomy.* Consulting on the job evaluation area had frequently been done by individual consultants, the lone rangers of Hay's mythology. They had high autonomy and were rarely in the office, something which is still the case. If the organization is to grow significantly and offer its many services to a demanding market, this individualistic climate has to change to one of teamwork and more co-ordinated resource allocation and consultant development, which had previously been based almost exclusively to the operation of an internal market.

■ *Institutionalized incremental change.* Hay have made sure that their early almost monopolistic power in the job evaluation area did not lead to a complacent approach to their development. Hay has institutionalized internal change on an annual basis, the autumn manoeuvres of the organizational vocabulary. This, however, has had an 'anaesthetizing' effect on the organization with regard to change and led to a difficulty to convince employees that the current change is not an autumn manoeuvre but a transformational one. This belief has to change to one that Hay can achieve transformational change.

■ *Generalist expertise.* The individualism of Hay and the perceived high emphasis on financial performance for consultants' appraisal has led to their tendency to consult on a variety of areas within the human resource field. If, however Hay wishes to offer deep integrated expertise to the market on varying fields through teamwork of its consultants, then this has to change. The aim is to have experts on particular areas (with a broader understanding of other areas) as members of teams which as a whole can offer leading edge advice on a variety of fields.

■ *Few real decisions.* This belief emerged from the employee's perceptions that although decisions are taken, nothing ever changes (referring to Hay's beliefs and assumptions). The autumn manoeuvres have been incremental changes, not having challenged any cultural values. The individualism and high autonomy of consultants has also meant that certain changes in systems have been 'implemented' but not followed by them, again reinforcing the belief that there are no real decisions. This also has to change, with decisive leadership and decisions directly supported by control systems.

Figure 4 portrays the cultural web aimed for, with the desired changes in italics.

How Should We Manage the Transition?

There are different ways to manage change, depending on the extent of potential change, the time and information available and the power distribution in the organization.[22] Some important issues are:

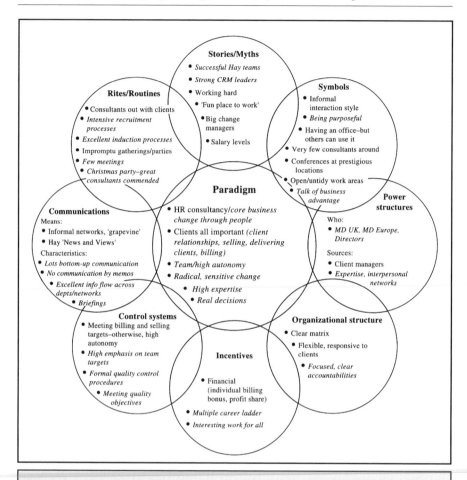

Stories/Myths
- *Successful Hay teams*
- *Strong CRM leaders*
- Working hard
- 'Fun place to work'
- *Big change managers*
- *Salary levels*

Rites/Routines
- Consultants out with clients
- *Intensive recruitment processes*
- *Excellent induction processes*
- Impromptu gatherings/parties
- *Few meetings*
- *Christmas party–great consultants commended*

Symbols
- Informal interaction style
- *Being purposeful*
- Having an office–but others can use it
- Very few consultants around
- Conferences at prestigious locations
- Open/untidy work areas
- *Talk of business advantage*

Communications
Means:
- Informal networks, 'grapevine'
- Hay 'News and Views'
Characteristics:
- *Lots bottom-up communication*
- *No communication by memos*
- *Excellent info flow across depts/networks*
- *Briefings*

Paradigm
- HR consultancy/*core business change through people*
- Clients all important *(client relationships, selling, delivering clients, billing)*
- *Team/high autonomy*
- *Radical, sensitive change*
- *High expertise*
- *Real decisions*

Power structures
Who:
- *MD UK, MD Europe, Directors*
Sources:
- Client managers
- *Expertise, interpersonal networks*

Control systems
- Meeting billing and selling targets–otherwise, high autonomy
- *High emphasis on team targets*
- *Formal quality control procedures*
- *Meeting quality objectives*

Incentives
- Financial (individual billing bonus, profit share)
- *Multiple career ladder*
- *Interesting work for all*

Organizational structure
- Clear matrix
- Flexible, responsive to clients
- *Focused, clear accountabilities*

Figure 4. The cultural web aimed for.

- There should be visible, active and credible leadership of the change process. Leaders' actions are highly symbolic,[23] and leaders should show by their own actions what is going to be valued in the organization. At Hay management has consciously taken some visible steps towards demonstrating its commitment to carrying the change through, such as frequent and clear communication, organization-wide meetings and utilizing one of the authors to conduct personal and group interviews and surveys to gauge employees' attitudes over a significant time period. A lot of attention, moreover, is paid to encouraging senior consultants to role model the new behaviours that Hay wishes to institutionalize.
- Participation: it was shown long ago[24] that involving the people who will be affected by changes in their planning decreases resistance to change because

it builds ownership of the process through participation. At Hay there have been several internal projects under way which came up with detailed suggestions for operational changes in processes and systems. Attention is being paid to integrating the various smaller scale initiatives that are taking place towards reaching the strategic aims.

■ Communication: there is an insatiable need for information at times of change. It is important to communicate a clear rationale for the change and identify the end state with outcomes which are important for the stakeholders, as well as to build their confidence that the organization can reach this end state with the right efforts.[25] It is important to use personal means of communication as often as possible and seek employees' views and concerns. The rationale for change has been clearly articulated in Hay, and it is now clear to most employees why it has to undergo a transformational change although it does not face any crisis. What is also now apparent is the importance of communication not only in informing, motivating and co-ordinating, but also in managing employee expectations. If changes are expected to occur over a long period and are likely to involve high ambiguity at some points, then this should be clearly communicated in advance in order to avoid potential loss of momentum, disappointment and cynicism in certain groups of employees. Lastly, it is important that if communication is going to be more effective in motivating employees, it should address their actual concerns which can be elicited through meetings, group sessions and interviews. In Hay employees have in the early stages expressed their thoughts and concerns about the change which were addressed in subsequent communication and by project groups and initiatives.

■ Proper investment should be made for the development of any new skills which will be required by the changed organization, especially if the change involves new technology and new roles. At Hay one of the most important new roles is that of the regional 'team managers' who will have greater responsibility for work allocation, consultant development, coaching etc. The skills needed to fulfil these roles were identified and training programmes planned.

How Will We Know How We Are Doing?

Any change needs to be actively managed throughout its duration and monitored through both 'soft' and 'hard' data. Ideally there should be periodic feedback from individuals elicited in a non-threatening but in-depth way. Assessing changes in the elements of the cultural web (as well as in their relative strength) is one important internal indication of the progress of the organization in reaching its strategic goals. One of the authors is undertaking the task of tracking such changes and eliciting employee feedback in Hay.

Current data has indicated certain shifts in the cultural web, but not adequate to justify construction of a new web. The cultural web identified in summer 1994 had evolved over three decades and, as confirmed by data, has not been altered significantly (although 'unfreezing' of certain elements was observed). The extent of the cultural change aimed for makes this a long-term effort, with a realistic timescale of around 5 years to achieve cultural transformation.

Managing Knowledge Workers in the Context of Strategic Change Programmes

In general, the prescriptions of the change management literature do not distinguish between different work contexts, skills and tasks of employees, but give generalized prescriptions with the implication that they apply across the board. While certain prescriptive guidelines such as those above were shown to apply to Hay's case, certain issues specifically related to consulting staff arose. While the generalizability of these issues to other knowledge-intensive organizations (their population validity) is unclear, as would be the case in any case study research design, some initial directions are suggested for further research into the specific issues facing the management of knowledge workers in the context of strategic change. Such research is urgently needed given the dearth of published studies on this issue.

The central challenges which arose with regard to the management of knowledge workers at Hay relate to teamwork, specifically *1.* how to encourage a teamwork orientation away from a highly individualistic style which has characterized Hay's operations for over three decades and *2.* how to manage the ambiguity and complexity involved in consultants' simultaneously belonging to several and shifting teams, without encroaching on consultants' autonomy which was shown to be positively correlated with their commitment to Hay.[26]

Encouraging a Teamwork Orientation

As can be seen from Hay's cultural web (Figure 3), individualism is a highly entrenched feature of Hay's culture. It is directly or indirectly interlinked with all other cultural artefacts, e.g. the lone rangers and guidechart jockeys of Hay's mythology (stories and myths), the informal interaction style and control of their own time–space movements (symbols), an important base of power being the client base that they individually 'owned' (power structures), the loosely coupled organizational structure which enabled and encouraged individualism, the individual financial incentives, the individual billing and sales targets (control systems), the high reliance on each individual's informal communication networks for obtaining task-related information (communications), the short induction processes after which it was up to individuals to develop their internal networks through which they could get involved into projects, as well as manage their own expertise development and the praising of individual 'billing stars' at Christmas parties (rites and routines).

After the important step of bringing these systemic processes to conscious awareness, through the construction and interpretation of a valid cultural web, the approach taken at Hay was *1.* clear communication by the Managing Director on the necessity of and rationale for teamwork to all members of the organization; *2.* encouragement of senior consultants to role model the desired behaviours; *3.* in the longer term, reviewing the incentive and control systems with a view to reducing their individualistic bias toward team-oriented rewards and incentives; *4.* gradual re-allocation of clients based on their sales size in order to achieve greater client focus but also to reduce the importance of long-term 'owning' of clients as a power base; *5.* generally ceasing practices which have inadvertently symbolized the desirability of individualistic behaviour, and replacing them with practices which symbolize the desirability of teamwork-oriented behaviour, e.g. not praising individual billing achievers at Christmas parties or other occasions, but praising teams which carried out successful client projects as a whole.

Managing the Ambiguity and Complexity Deriving from Membership to Shifting Teams

Hay is a matrix organization, and teams have to be formed and re-formed according to project demands and other contingencies. Every single consultant can simultaneously belong to a regional team, an industry sector team, a consulting practice team as well as one or more internal project or client project teams.

Simultaneous membership to teams of varying stability creates problems of ambiguity and complexity, especially with regard to the effective management of such processes as personal development, induction, feedback and work allocation, about which consultants require clarity. The problem of ambiguity, moreover, was exacerbated at Hay because of an individualistic cultural context which has placed responsibility on the individual for such things as managing their expertise development, quality-controlling their work and gaining access to projects via the internal market. In addition, during the initial phases of the change process a significant number of internal projects addressing various aspects of the change were initiated which has increased individuals' team membership and responsibilities.

Management of the issue of ambiguity and complexity arising from membership to multiple and shifting teams involves a dilemma—how to achieve effective and efficient co-ordination of internal processes, while at the same time avoiding the creation of a stifling climate and allowing operational autonomy to the consultants in achieving their tasks and providing opportunities for personal growth and development factors which were identified as key motivators of knowledge workers.[27]

We will discuss Hay's approach to this dilemma by using the expertise development process as an example. We have chosen this process both because of the obvious importance of expertise development for providing a sustainable competitive advantage to knowledge-intensive firms as well as the existence of initial interview and survey data which have indicated consultants' concerns with various aspects of this process.

A working group, overseen by a steering group was formed and charged with addressing the expertise development process. The expertise development process was linked to Hay's strategic aim of growth by viewing the ultimate purpose of the expertise area as helping to grow the business by enabling consultants to develop client solutions which may not be easily replicable and therefore represent high added value for the client and good margins for Hay. An expertise framework was developed which interlinks business drivers sparking client issues, client issues themselves, provision of solutions via the use of tools and methodologies, and core capabilities, these being methodologies which are research based and difficult to replicate. New roles of 'client issues managers', 'methodology keepers' and 'core capability keepers' were created and the responsibilities of each clearly defined. Five key processes related to expertise development were identified: scan for and determine expertise requirements; develop and update Hay's approaches and services/client solutions; enable and equip people to sell and deliver new approaches and services; quality assure delivery; maintain skills data base. For each of these processes, specific sub-processes were identified. Lastly, a force-field analysis of forces for and against successful implementation of these changes was conducted.[28] After this initial analysis appointments to the new roles were announced, and the expertise group communicated its intention to define key clusters of client issues, priority tool and methodology developments and training needs relating to these issues during the next quarter.

The above approach, being highly analytical, contrasts sharply with the previous individualistic cultural context where consultants were tacitly 'expected' to define their own direction for the development of their expertise by deciding which training sessions they wished to attend. The main point is, however, that while the resulting expertise development process will be structured, this is not likely to reduce substantially consultants' autonomy but rather condition it in a manner that many of them would accept. Concerns with the expertise development process were stated at in-depth interviews and exploratory surveys, mainly centring around negative evaluations of the unstructured nature of this process. Many consultants have clearly stated or implied that they would welcome guidance regarding this issue (but not being forced to develop their expertise in a direction they are not interested in).

This points to the importance and desirability of carrying out further research to clarify exactly in what sense and in what processes knowledge workers would welcome structured processes without perceiving encroachments to their autonomy, as was the case in Hay. Initial guidance in the interpretation of such findings and in conducting further research can be provided by findings regarding the motivation of knowledge workers. For example, what we see here is knowledge workers welcoming structured processes relating to their personal growth, which has been identified as their primary motivator, while simultaneously not perceiving any threat by this structured process on their operational autonomy, identified as their second motivator.[29]

Conclusion

In this article we have:

- Highlighted and illustrated the close interrelationship between strategic change and organizational culture.
- Presented a simplified framework for strategic decision-making and discussed some important issues of change management arising at each stage.
- Introduced and explained the use of a useful diagnostic tool—the cultural web.
- Discussed some implications arising from the case for managing knowledge workers in the context of strategic change.

Apart from the 'conventional' lessons on change management which were confirmed in Hay's case, there are some additional lessons which stand out:

- Importance of conducting a cultural audit and of considering the cultural implications of the desired strategic direction of the organization. Related to this is the importance of an external viewpoint from a trained process consultant who has not been enculturated by long-term membership to the organization and who can bring required process consulting skills to the situation, such as conducting group sessions aiming to surface the tacit beliefs and assumptions comprising the organizational paradigm.
- Importance of using communication not only to inform and co-ordinate, but to manage employee expectations in order to later avoid potential feelings that the momentum of change is waning, something which can feed the cynics and slow down the change.
- Importance of recognizing that knowledge workers are likely to have different concerns and needs than other types of workers and should therefore be managed differently, especially in the context of strategic changes which present a period of high risk and increased uncertainty to the organization.

References

1. G. Burrell and G. Morgan, *Sociological Paradigms and Organisational Analysis,* Gower, Hants (1979); A. Giddens, *The Constitution of Society,* Polity, Cambridge (1984).
2. See C. Geertz, *The Interpretation of Cultures,* Basic Books, New York (1973) for an explanation of the semiotic approach to ethnography; E. Schein, *The Clinical Perspective*

in Fieldwork, Qualitative Research Methods Series, Sage, CA (1987) for a discussion of the characteristics of action research.

3. For a discussion of the merits of triangulation see T. Jick, Mixing qualitative and quantitative methods: triangulation in action, *Administrative Science Quarterly* **24**, 602–611 (1979).

4. Using a culture-deciphering process described by E. Schein, *Organizational Culture and Leadership,* 2nd edn, Josey-Bass, San Francisco, CA (1992).

5. G. Johnson, *Strategic Change and the Management Process,* Blackwell, Oxford (1987); A. M. Pettigrew, *The Awakening Giant: Continuity and Change in ICI,* Blackwell, Oxford (1985).

6. H. Mintzberg, Opening up the definition of strategy, In J. B. Quinn, H. Mintzberg and R. M. James (eds), *The Strategy Process: Concepts, Contexts and Cases,* pp. 13–20, Prentice-Hall, Englewood Cliffs, NJ (1988).

7. P. M. Ginter, A. C. Rucks and W. J. Duncan, Planners' perceptions of the strategic management process, *Journal of Management Studies* **22** (6), 581–596 (1985).

8. G. Johnson, *Strategic Change and the Management Process*, Blackwell, Oxford (1987); G. Johnson, Managing strategic change—strategy, culture and action, *Long Range Planning* **25** (1), 28–36 (1992).

9. See E. Schein (1992) *op. cit.*

10. Y. Allaire and M. E. Firsirotu, Theories of organizational culture, *Organization Studies* **5** (3), 193–226 (1984).

11. L. Smircich, Concepts of culture and organizational analysis, *Administrative Science Quarterly* **28**, 339–358 (1983).

12. J. B. Quinn, Logical incrementalism, *Sloan Management Review* **1** (20), 7–21 (1978).

13. G. Johnson (1987) op. cit.; G. Johnson, Managing strategic change: the role of symbolic action, *British Journal of Management* **1**, 183–200 (1990); G. Johnson, Rethinking incrementalism, *Strategic Management Journal* **9**, 75–91 (1988).

14. See E. Schein (1992) *op. cit.*

15. Where the differences among organizational subcultures are substantial, then the organizational paradigm can be limited to any beliefs and assumptions that are relatively commonly shared. Alternatively, it may be useful to produce different cultural webs.

16. G. Johnson (1987) *op. cit.*; A. M. Pettigrew (1985) *op. cit.*

17. J. Hendry, Rational planning in a non-rational world Part l: Strategy formation and the policy context, *Journal of General Management* **20** (4), 54–64 (1995); J. Hendry, Rational planning in a non-rational world Part II: Competing strategy programmes, *Journal of General Management* **21** (2), (1995).

18. H. Mintzberg, The fall and rise of strategic planning, *Harvard Business Review,* January–February, 107–114 (1994).

19. I. L. Janis, Sources of error in strategic decision making. In J. H. Pennings (ed.), *Organizational Strategy and Change,* pp. 157–197, Josey-Bass, San Francisco, CA (1985).

20. See e.g. R. Evered, The language of organizations: the case of the Navy. In L. R. Pondy et al. (eds), *Organizational Symbolism,* pp. 125–143, JAI Press, Greenwich, CT (1983).

21. L. R. Pondy, The role of metaphors and myths in organization and in the facilitation of change. In L. R. Pondy et al. (eds), *Organizational Symbolism,* pp. 157–166, JAI Press, Greenwich, CT (1983).

22. J. P. Kotter and L. A. Schlesinger, Choosing strategies for change. *Harvard Business Review*, March–April (1979).

23. G. Johnson (1990) *op. cit.*

24. K. Lewin, Frontiers in group dynamics 1, *Human Relations* **1** (1), 5–41 (1947); L. Coch and R. French, Overcoming resistance to change, *Human Relations* **2** (4), 512–532 (1948).

25. A. A. Armenakis, S. G. Harris and K. W. Mossholder, Creating readiness for organizational change. *Human Relations* **46** (6), 681–703 (1993).

26. Unpublished comparative research by A. Decker for an MBA degree at Henley Management College (1993).

27. M. Tampoe, Motivating knowledge workers—the challenge for the 1990's, *Long Range Planning* **26** (3), 49–55 (1993): The general ranking of these motivators is personal growth, operational autonomy, task achievement and money.

28. See K. Lewin (1947) *op. cit.*

29. See M. Tampoe (1993) *op. cit.*

5

Operation Centurion: Managing Transformation at Philips

Nigel Freedman

In 1990 Philips Electronics, one of the world's largest companies went through a crisis as its share price plunged. 'Operation Centurion' was launched as a broad turnaround programme designed to revitalize the company. Probably the most up-to-date thinking in the field of management has been applied to tackle the size and complexity of this challenge, and progress is now evident. This paper describes the design of the change process, the key experiences so far and the implications for leadership and management development.

The Crisis of 1990

For nearly 100 years Philips had been one of the world's largest electronics companies, with a high reputation for innovation through inventions in lighting, the rotary shaver, the audio cassette and the compact disc (see Figures 1 and 2). In early 1990 the situation became desperate as financial institutions lost confidence and the share price dropped to an all-time low. Disillusionment due to poor and inconsistent performance quickly led to the appointment of Jan Timmer as the new President in mid-year. It was already clear, after years of declining profits in the face of murderous competition, that responses were

Nigel Freedman is Deputy Director of Philips Company Training, Eindhoven, The Netherlands.

- Headquarters: Eindhoven, The Netherlands
- Established in 1891 as lamp factory
- Six product sectors: Lighting—Consumer electronics—Other consumer products—Components & semiconductors—Professional products & systems—Miscellaneous
- Shares listed on 16 stock exchanges in 9 countries
- Strong technology basis:
  R&D: 6–7% of sales
  —research labs in 5 countries
  —65,000 patents
  10,000 inventions
- 254 production sites in more than 40 countries
- National sales organizations in more than 80 countries
- Sales and service outlets in 150 countries
- Multinational workforce of 265,000 employees
- Turnover 1995: NLG 64.5 billion

Figure 1. The Philips Company

1994	World	Europe
Lighting	1	1
Consumer electronics	3	2
PolyGram	1	1
Shavers	1	1
Coffeemakers	3	3
Colour tubes	1	1
Semiconductors	10	3
Medical imaging equipment	3	1
Analytical X-ray	1	1
Dictation equipment	1	1
Congress systems	1	1

Figure 2. Ranking Philips' market position.

needed that went to the very roots of the company's way of operating. The challenge of revitalising a company of over 250,000 employees and worldwide sales of more than $25 billion had begun.

The Change Process

Jan Timmer decided to embark on an ambitious programme known as 'Operation Centurion', the architecture of which was strongly influenced by Professor

Phases	Activities
I Restructuring (performance gap)	1. Sealing the leaks 2. Efficiency drives (personnel, stocks, fixed assets, debtors/creditors, purchasing)
II Revitalization (opportunity gap)	3. Daily sales go on; customer and quality campaigns 4. Strategic direction and growth 5. Workforce revitalization

Figure 3. The Centurion design model.

C. K. Prahalad from the University of Michigan, who became the leading advisor supporting the operation. The key feature of the approach was to avoid the frequently seen 'slash and burn' technique of pure down-sizing, by taking a longer-term view of what it takes to 'create a winning company'. Learning has been a critical theme from the start.

The Centurion design provides a phased sequence which balances the attention given to improving operational performance and the attention given to innovation and growth (see Figure 3). While all five of the items in Figure 3 have been dealt with to some degree from the start, the priorities for attention have shifted.

In the first instance a small number of severely loss-making activities were sold or terminated. Then a start was made with the long-term process of creating a winning company.

In practice, work on Phase II, e.g. via task forces on a new strategic direction or on fundamentally new ways of organizing work and involving people, needs to be established early on in the change process.

It was considered very important that as many people as possible had the overall model in mind, because to anticipate the hoped-for 'light at the end of the tunnel' is crucial for its motivational effect at all levels. 'Restructuring' is hardly a motivating theme if sustained for long, but the pain can be justified if more exciting innovation possibilities are seen to be ahead.

The key features of Operation Centurion follow.

Cascade

The Centurion 'cascade' communication process involves three main elements:

1. Top-down 'Centurion sessions'.

2. Bottom-up town meetings.
3. 'Customer Day' satellite and group discussions.

Centurion sessions consist of meetings lasting approximately 3 days, with 30–70 participants who represent three or four hierarchical levels and, except at corporate level, usually within one business. An external consultant provides process facilitation and specific cognitive inputs are given as required, with the manager responsible for the business as 'owner' or chairman.

Initially, the agenda on the first day (see Figure 4) confronts participants with the state of the business, benchmarked against the best in class, followed by group work on formulation of the key issues facing the business. In businesses where a major turnaround is necessary, this is the point at which the whole group is quite intentionally confronted with harsh reality and is pulled into the so-called 'Valley of Death'. This establishment of a sense of urgency is a critical *emotional* part of the change cycle, in order to prepare for the personal commitment to 'stretch targets' in the following steps.

Day 2 is used to present modern concepts and illustrations on 'building a winning organization', including strategic intent, core competences and approaches to major transformation in other large companies. This builds the knowledge and the faith needed for the following phase, in which participants work in groups on the formulation of and commitment to stretch targets that will take the business to new levels of performance. The third day is devoted to project formulation, action planning and making firm commitments.

This process is cascaded downwards in similar sessions with large groups to lower levels, where specific targets are put up for 'buy-in' discussions and translation to the next operating levels:

Day 1	Day 2	Day 3
A crisis scenario Magnitude of the task	*Examples of change in other firms*	*Priorities, commitments, projects and action planning*
Coming to terms with reality	Fighting back	Identifying and accepting goals for performance improvement
—performance, choices and managerial orientation	—a methodology for revitalization	—role of top management in revitalization
Source: C. K. Prahalad		

Figure 4. The structure of Centurion I.

■ The whole cascade process was started with the top 120 managers including the Board of Management (labelled the 'Centurion I' group), and continued for each Product Division normally to 'Centurion III or IV' level, and for most national organizations or regions.

■ Most groups have continued to hold follow-up sessions at intervals of 4–6 months to review the implementation of the change projects, and to plan the next stages. Some 30,000 people have been involved in Centurion sessions, and over 600 change projects have been launched.

■ The Centurion I group has established *22 corporate task forces* to tackle major issues such as customer orientation, control of inventory and receivables, purchasing, accounting systems, R & D effectiveness, management skills, values and behaviours and strategic direction.

'Town meetings' have involved large groups of up to 400 people, from the operator level upwards and including senior management, in facilitated meetings lasting several hours. Questions are usually submitted in advance and lead to discussions on how to improve the business. All questions are answered immediately if possible, or within 2 weeks. Hundreds of such meetings have now been held in all parts of the world, and have led to a considerable improvement in the communications and to a large number of practical suggestions for change.

External consultants have helped us substantially with the cascade process on a world-wide scale, bringing the advantages of objectivity and the ability to confront; also external information, examples and best practices, plus meetings facilitation and advisory capabilities.

Customer Day has become an annual event, where 200,000 employees across the world spend a day in working groups by department, searching for better ways to satisfy customers and involving two-way communication with the President via a satellite link.

Urgency

Critical to the whole process is instilling among senior management a shared sense of urgency for major change, e.g. by well-prepared competitive benchmarking comparisons, presented in a manner that quickly shakes managers out of any complacency.

An important factor here has been the application of much more stringent criteria for profitability, cash flow and investment: also the label 'strategic' for a business activity has been re-defined, since it was often a cover for continuing losses supposedly in support of some other part of the firm.

Stretch

A key theme in the Centurion process design is the notion of 'strategic intent',[1] a concept that has been at the heart of achieving the commitment or 'buy-in' to reaching new levels of performance among large groups of employees at all levels. Prahalad and Hamel's idea of 'the impossible, achievable target' has been made operational by using outside examples of how 'stretch' can lead to creativity and supreme performance when properly managed.

Emotion, Consensus and Commitment

A basic assumption underlying the Centurion model is that people will not be committed to new challenging goals unless they feel an emotional identification with them. This they will have only if they have either personally been involved in setting these goals, or they are provided with sufficiently appealing incentives to adopt them. Centurion meetings give an opportunity for the free expression of personal feelings and no 'sacred cows' are permitted. Often a great deal of emotion is shown in putting away the past and adopting new stretch targets in a mutually supportive atmosphere. The 'Valley of Death' phenomenon mentioned above is recognised as a key factor in developing an emotional commitment to change.

The first decision in the Centurion I meeting in October 1990, to cut the headcount by some 45,000 people, was reached by 120 people collectively and not by a top-down instruction from the Board. In a highly emotional process managers found that they could do collectively what was previously impossible individually.

Projects, Action Learning and Building Competences

Centurion meetings provide an excellent platform for collective learning and action learning. The solid output from each session is a set of stretch targets and projects that are selected to achieve new levels of performance. The intention is to change the way we manage, by forcing people to find new ways of doing things.

Similarly the 22 corporate task forces provide a vehicle for involving hundreds of people in searching for new approaches. Most of them have undertaken extensive external benchmarking to establish targets for best practice.

Projects have proved to be a very effective way of learning and of building new capabilities.

Changing Behaviour and Style

A great deal of emphasis has been placed on the 'soft' aspects of management as pre-conditions for reaching 'hard' results. The goal is to establish a new mindset.

The *Centurion spirit* is about raising ambition, about change, challenging established beliefs and norms, and listening to others. Trust, openness and honesty are key requirements for the Centurion approach.

Corporate task forces were set up to advise on *values and behaviours*, and on *corporate governance*. One result was a set of five simple statements comprising *The Philips Way:*

- Delight *customers*.
- Value *people* as our greatest resource.
- Deliver *quality* and excellence in all actions.
- Achieve a premium return on *equity*
- Encourage *entrepreneurial behaviour* at all levels.

These five values are becoming the 'Credo' to which reference is made in a wide range of situations, at all levels.

Centurion Progress

Since the middle of 1990 the Centurion process has led to an improvement in almost all operating ratios, despite the recession and the particularly unfavourable market conditions for companies in the consumer electronics business (see Figure 5).

The figures for 1995 showed improvements in sales and profits, however analysts reacted negatively to the third-quarter results which hinted that asset management was not improving as fast as had been expected. This has led to increased attention to the 'unfinished business', i.e. to more and continuous efficiency improvement. The competitors are not standing still and complacency should not be allowed to creep in.

What We Have Learned About Change

Five years of Operation Centurion have given Philips management a number of insights into change processes that may well be of value to other organizations,

	End 1990	End 1995
Sales (NLG)	55.8	64.5
Net debt: group equity*	56:44	34:66
RONA† (excl. Restructuring)	8.5%	18.1%
Income from operations (% sales)	4.2%	6.3%
Net inventories (% sales)	20.7%	18.8%
Receivables (months)	1.9	1.5
Personnel (comparable)	304,600	265,000
Share price (guilders)	20.30	58.00
*Gearing or leverage †Return on net assets NLG 1.0 = US$0.6		

Figure 5. The turnaround: the financial results.

particularly large complex firms. The most significant feature has been that we had to begin in a time of crisis, whereas firms such as General Electric have had the foresight to start a radical change process early.

The following points stand out.

The design of the change process. The 'Centurion key themes' are sequence, cascade, urgency, stretch, emotion, consensus & commitment, projects & action learning and changing behaviour & style. The change process has been less effective where one or more of these has been given less attention.

Several units in the company were already active with major change programmes of the 'traditional' reorganization or restructuring type. Other units which have faithfully followed the Centurion design appear to be performing better than those which took the conventional approach. Without the combination of the 'Centurion key themes', we believe that lasting change is unlikely to be achieved. Our conclusion is that commitment to the change process is critical, and now we recognize that it should have been made mandatory for all units of the company.

It was necessary to attend quickly to operational performance improvement at the outset, while starting the discussion early about giving attention later to growth opportunities. A widespread clear understanding of the sequence of priorities for change can be valuable in providing a logic for the pain of downsizing. The terms 'performance gap' and 'opportunity gap' have been used at many levels to show where the process was heading. The idea of a 'light at the end of the tunnel' is very important for motivation.

Creating and sustaining a sense of *urgency,* by using carefully presented facts or scenarios, has been a difficult but critical factor in focusing management's attention on the need for fundamental change. Relentlessly benchmarking the best-in-class has helped a great deal.

Emotion is a critical component of the change process and needs to be used wisely. An 'emotional cycle' was a key design feature of the earlier Centurion sessions. The sequence—confrontation with harsh reality; a feeling of despair; hope arising from examples of other companies' successful transformation approaches; the challenge of formulating stretch goals and action projects—has helped participants to adopt the mindset for implementation with personal commitment.

Resistance to change can be greatly reduced by 'peer pressure' in large groups. Less familiar perhaps is 'peer support', whereby difficult decisions become easier when all the team face them together. The initial headcount reduction by 45,000 people proved to be surprisingly less impossible than most people thought, because all colleagues were faced with the same challenge and the same pain. The exchange of experience was also very helpful in managing this process.

The place of total quality management (TQM) in the overall transformation operation was a source of considerable discussion among senior managers, faculty and consultants. TQM offers approaches that lead to continuous *oper-*

ational improvement, e.g. via the re-engineering of business processes, but managing *strategic direction* requires different strategic management skills and practices. The Centurion model includes these vital elements.

Speed is essential. Despite the rapid response which Philips management made to the crisis in 1990, with hindsight some have said that they would have preferred to have moved much faster. The lesson here is ...*change at least twice as fast as you can. And start long before it is possible!*

Communication. A cascade process involving large multilevel meetings, re-peated every few months, can provide a status-free forum for achieving real change. For top-down sessions you need a minimum time, of 2–3 days, for the dynamics to work effectively. Consensus takes time: compliance can be decep-tive: achieving genuine commitment requires considerable effort.

The units which held Centurion sessions at top level but did not cascade the process to lower levels usually found that the implementation of stretch goals did not work well. The critical 'buy-in' process was missing. There is a (subtle) major difference between a traditional hierarchical deployment of targets, and a translation by lower levels of proposed stretch goals into accepted and owned commitments.

The softer issues, involving values and behaviours, need persistent revisiting and commitment from the very top. There is a danger in simply broadcasting a new code of values which may not be acted on by senior management.

Learning. One of the major positive 'soft' changes that we have seen is the *increased readiness to learn.* The exchange of best practice across divisions, benchmarking against competitors and comparing with firms in other industries, a willingness to listen to more junior and younger people and a marked increase in the demand for management and technical training programmes, are signs of a healthier respect for learning. The earlier arrogance is departing.

The cascade process has been coordinated by the Corporate Management Training & Development function, and for 2 years all normal management training programmes were suspended. Instead, Centurion became a new way of combining management meetings with education. Many corporate-level task forces recommended new or revised training programmes, which gave the impetus for re-thinking and expanding internal management training.

Two key areas which are now receiving much greater priority are:

- *action learning* through work on live issues or projects;
- *collective learning* in 'business' or 'family' teams.

There are numerous examples of situations where a large number of people know what should be done, yet nothing happens. Actions leading to real change happen when a critical mass of critical people are dissatisfied with the current situation and they are aware of each other's readiness to act.

A number of trends were recognised, which together influenced the emerging policy for management training (see Figure 6).

Effective management education requires a shift:

From	To
Knowledge	Capability
Individual	Team performance
Depth only	Breadth
Functional	Cross-functional
Results	Process-orientation
Stability	Flexibility
Individual	Collective learning
Teaching	Action learning
Sporadic	Regular, planned
High-fliers focus	Main contributors

Figure 6. Trends in management learning.

The importance of projects. Culture change cannot take place without changing business practices: knowledge and attitudes are not enough. More than 600 Centurion projects were in progress by 1992, with the primary aim of reaching their stretch targets. A secondary aim has been to use projects as vehicles for changing the way people manage. Cooperation across boundaries, teamwork in task forces, greater delegation and priority setting, have all been affected positively.

The problem caused by the huge load of extra projects has sometimes been overwork and stress. Managers have had to learn the hard way to re-set priorities, to adapt their own agencies, to delegate, to re-think the way work is done ...and to stop doing certain things.

Assessing the progress of change. Measuring the progress of change is a complex matter. A comprehensive yet easily understandable model is a valuable guide in steering the change process. The model in Figure 7 has been developed and applied to design a survey that was carried out after 2 years of the Centurion Operation, to find out how people at different levels perceived the change process. The results helped considerably in planning and directing the subsequent phases. Reading from right to left, it is clear that the 'hard' *outputs* can only emerge when the necessary *competencies* have been developed or acquired: these require changed *behaviours*, which in turn will only come when people have gained an appropriate *mindset* or attitude.

The four-step change model has been helpful in understanding and explaining the natural sequence of building sustainable capabilities. The management of change is a long-term process. It begins with an appropriate collective mindset.

The five company values which describe *The Philips Way* have also been a useful reference for assessing the company's progress regarding both the 'hard'

Creating a shared mindset	Changing behaviour	Building competences and capabilities	Improved business performance
A sense of urgency	An empowering leadership	Marketing capabilities	Profitability and operating costs
External focus	Customer driven	Technical capabilities	Market share
Collective ambition	Mutual sharing of information	Manufacturing capabilities	Geographic coverage
Commitment and motivation	Cross-functional cooperation	Strategic positioning and portfolio management	Share price
Open and action oriented	Learning behaviours	Organization capabilities	
		External linkages capabilities (JVs, supplier and customer management)	
Source: N. J. Freedman			

Figure 7. Assessing the progress of change.

issues and the 'soft' issues. Each item is regularly assessed either qualitatively or quantitatively, e.g. through customer surveys, a detailed company-wide employee motivation survey, the achievement of quality awards or by increasing profitability.

Leadership. A change process of this size clearly demonstrates that a variety of leadership styles are necessary to ensure that all aspects in the change model are covered appropriately. Both the 'performance gap' and the 'opportunity gap' have to be managed in parallel and with the right emphasis at the same time. The skills needed for the improvement of efficiency and asset management are different from those needed for growing new businesses.

'Hierarchical' leadership behaviours are not to be totally buried and forgotten and replaced by 'adhocracy and entrepreneurship'. A much more subtle interplay of skills is needed, among members of a management team and often in the same individual. Transformational leadership requires that competences in several styles of management must be brought into play as the change process develops.

An insightful model of managerial leadership skills is provided by the 'competing values framework', shown in Figure 8, which was developed by K. Cameron

A model of organizational paradox and effectiveness

Flexibility
Individuality

Culture type:
CLAN

Managing teams

Managing interpersonal
relationships

Managing the development
of others

Culture type:
ADHOCRACY

Managing innovation

Managing the future

Managing continuous
improvement

Internal
maintenance

External
environmental
positioning

Culture type:
HIERARCHY

Managing coordination

Managing the control system

Managing acculturation

Culture type:
MARKET

Managing
competitiveness

Energizing employees

Managing Customer
service

Control
Stability

Source: R. Quinn and K. Cameron

Figure 8. The competing values framework.

and R. Quinn at the University of Michigan.[2, 3] This model describes 'hierarchy' skills, 'market' skills, 'clan' skills and 'adhocracy' skills, and gives a simple, realistic but comprehensive framework for assessing and developing leadership capabilities. It fits well with managers' intuitive and practical observations. Substantial research has shown that the most effective leaders have at least average competencies in all four quadrants, i.e. a balanced leadership profile. By using this model it is possible to see 'heroic' descriptions of modern leadership in a better perspective.

One advantage of using this framework is that both individual leadership behaviour profiles and organizational culture profiles can be assessed on the same dimensions, with action plans being developed at each level. Individual leadership improvement is always influenced by certain organizational-level systems, procedures or practices (e.g. teamwork needs to be recognized and rewarded). For a sustainable improvement, the interplay between the two levels needs to be kept in perspective.

The approach is now being adopted top-down throughout the company as a basis for continuous leadership development, commencing with a series of 3-day workshops in the businesses and regions.

Change agents and consultants. Hundreds of 3-day Centurion sessions and hundreds of town meetings have been held since early 1991. Nearly all these have been facilitated by an outside consultant or by an internal staff or line manager. A small 'core faculty' from prominent European and US Business Schools provided a strong intellectual input, experience of other companies' change processes and facilitation for top-level meetings. One of the main reasons for choosing people from business schools was the accent we wanted to place on *learning*, though in an *action* mode. The selection of appropriate people for this role was mainly done through personal contacts or recommendations.

In addition a firm of consultants was brought in to provide worldwide advisory and facilitation skills for organizing the Centurion sessions and town meetings in the product divisions and national organizations in several languages. Careful selection of individual consultants was done centrally by the Corporate Training Department, who coordinated the whole operation. The criteria for selection were the possession of good facilitation and presentation skills, experience of major change processes, emotional balance and personal integrity. Internal facilitators were drawn from various staff departments where possible. However, it was not easy to find people with the right combination of skills, especially the ability to confront senior managers and to bring in appropriate external experience.

'Change Agents Training' workshops lasting 2–3 days were given to over 400 line and staff people in several countries, to create an 'army' of internal 'change agents' to continue the change process. The content was primarily focused on the design and facilitation of Centurion sessions and town meetings. A survey showed that the success rate was disappointing, and that only a few were being really effective. There were simply too few people with the right combination of skills on whom senior managers could rely. Gradually line managers have been facilitating their own change meetings and processes.

The Road Ahead

The achievements are:

- Improved profitability.
- Restored pride and confidence in Philips …in the financial world and internally.
- 'Financial space' has been gained (debt/equity).

■ A basis has been created for a new managerial culture with these characteristics:
  ● Customer focus
  ● Town meetings, people involvement
  ● Philips quality approach
  ● Dialogue across levels of management
  ● Asset management
  ● Cross-boundary cooperation
  ● Values and behaviours
  ● Better business focus
  ● Respect for process
  ● Bench marking, focus on winning

■ A higher stock market value for Philips.

The new phase we are now entering involves:

■ An accent on *growth:* new and current products; new and current markets and regions. As an example, the opportunities in multimedia have been thoroughly analysed by a top-level task force set up in Silicon Valley, the results of which are being implemented worldwide.
■ Revitalization of the workforce.
■ Unrelenting attention to efficiency.

The key behaviours required for the new phase will be:

■ entrepreneurship
■ empowerment
■ risk taking
■ motivation
■ creativity
■ no bureaucracy
■ imagination
■ unorthodox behaviour

The competencies required for this growth phase will be very different, and this will provide a continuing challenge for Operation Centurion. The attention to the themes of the first phase, cost control and restructuring, will also continue.

References

1. G. Hamel and C. K. Prahalad, Strategy as stretch and leverage, *Harvard Business Review*, March–April (1993).
2. R. E. Quinn, *Beyond Rational Management: Mastering the Paradoxes and Competing Demands of High Performance*, Jossey-Bass, San Francisco, CA (1988).
3. R. Hooijberg and F. Petrock, On cultural change: using the competing values framework to help leaders execute a transformational strategy, *Human Resource Management* **32** (1), 29–50 (1993).

6

Corporate Strategies for the Asia Pacific Region

Philippe Lasserre

Western firms need to define very ambitious objectives for developing their presence in the region. Asia strategy is more than the sum of individual countries strategy; it requires specific investment effects to develop human resources, to build assets and competencies. Strategic intelligence and relationships management are the key competencies which are needed. For Western firms it implies a complete transformation of management culture and practices.

Today, nobody would challenge the view that, at least for the next three or four decades, the Asia Pacific Region is likely to remain the engine of growth for the world economy. For Western companies, whether large or small, the main issue is no longer, 'Is there a need to conceive and execute an Asian Strategy?' but rather to know 'How to do it'. In the past, Asia has often been considered by western firms as either too difficult, too risky, or too remote from the traditional way of doing business and as a consequence has not been given the necessary attention that the region deserves.

The purpose of this article is to propose a framework for organizing the architecture of an Asian strategy and to discuss the various strategic issues to be addressed at each stage of the formulation process.

Philippe Lasserre is Professor of Strategy and Asian Business at INSEAD and at the Euro Asia Centre, France.

Strategic Framework for Asia Pacific

The formulation of strategies for Asia Pacific can be organized around four types of questions:

1. *What ambition do we have for the region?* An ambition is what the firm wants to achieve both qualitatively (mission, vision) and quantitatively (specific market and finance-related objectives) during a strategic time-horizon. For Asia Pacific the definition of the strategic ambition consists of determining the expected future relative importance of the region in the corporate portfolio as compared with the existing one.

2. *How do we position the businesses?* Positioning is the selection of the businesses or market segments in which the firm wants to compete and the type of competitive profile it wants to adopt. In Asia, positioning consists in selecting the various countries in which the firm wants to operate, in which form and on what basis.

3. *What kind of capabilities need to be created?* Creating capabilities calls for three basic forms of strategic investment:

   (a) *investing in access to external resources:* how to access raw materials or components, human resources, financing, information, various types of external support (lobbying, contacts, etc.);

   (b) *investing in assets:* product development, plants, equipment, distribution networks, information systems, logistics, brand names and reputation;

   (c) *investing in competencies:* what kinds of technological and managerial know-how are required to compete in the region?

4. *How do we organize the region?* Organization covers not only the formal structure, but also the various processes and systems which will govern the distribution of power; the rules and procedures; the internal communication; the evaluation and rewards; the co-ordination mechanisms, and the management of a 'corporate culture' which fits with the requirement of the region.

These four components are depicted in Figure 1 and referred to as the 'strategic framework'. This framework can typically be applied at different levels: at the level of the total corporation or at the level of a product division. It is important, however, to consider a firm's Asian strategy or strategies as an interdependent part of its overall, world-wide strategic effort.[1]

Ambition for Asia Pacific

Taking into account both overall corporate vision and mission, and specific, long-term objectives for businesses, the first critical questions to address are:

1. How important is it for the future of the company to be a player in the Asia Pacific region?

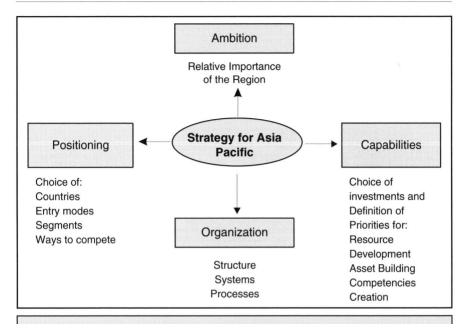

Figure 1. Strategic framework.

2. What are the key countries in Asia Pacific which play, and will play, a major role in the various industries in which the corporation is involved, in terms of markets, sources of competition, and resources?
3. What share of the businesses—expressed in terms of sales and assets—does the company want to achieve in the Asia Pacific region over the next ten years and relative to its operations in Europe and North America ?

The strategic importance of a region for a company is determined by a combination of three factors: the importance of the region as a market, the importance of the region as a resource base, and the importance of the region as a source of learning.

The Importance of Asia as a Market

In 1991, the total output of Asia Pacific was estimated at 21 per cent of total world output; by 2011 this will increase to roughly 25 per cent. In certain sectors Asia represents already more than 25 per cent of world sales and this proportion will increase over time as shown in Table 1.

However most Western firms barely achieve more than 10 per cent of their direct or exports sales in this region. Figure 2 shows the relative importance of the Asia Pacific region measured in terms of sales for selected major European and North American companies. From a global perspective, then, Asia is under-represented in the portfolio of those companies.

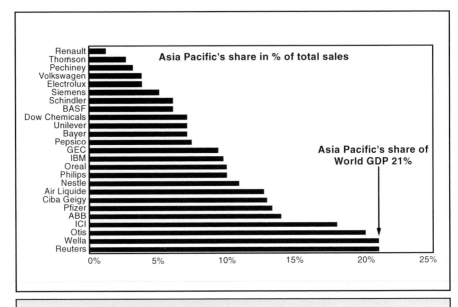

Figure 2. Asia Pacific's share in major Western firms (1991).

Companies, or individual businesses in multi-business corporations, could start their strategic thinking process by charting their position on a grid similar to Figure 3. This grid indicates where the company or the business stands internally *vis-a-vis* Asia Pacific by comparison to both the industry as a whole and to its competitors. A business positioned on the diagonal achieves sales in Asia Pacific proportional to the region's weight in the industry. Businesses above the diagonal are more involved in Asia Pacific as a region than the industry average, a rare situation for the majority of Western companies. Finally, businesses below the diagonal are the ones in which Asia is under-represented.

The advantage of such a chart is that it measures the gap between an existing position, the theoretical position represented by the industry's share in Asia, and a future industry's position (see: Figure 3 which illustrates this point with the example of the chemical industry).

This evaluation process does not imply that a firm should conduct a percentage of its activities equivalent to the weight of the Asia Pacific region in this sector. Rather, such a process is a means of encouraging managers to benchmark the company position against the industry and to reflect upon the costs and benefits of such a position in both the short and long term.

In the Asia Pacific region, the qualitative aspects of demand are as important, if not more important than the quantitative ones. Due to the demanding nature of the Asian customer, many Asian markets—especially the Japanese market—may provide Western firms with an opportunity to increase their overall corporate goodwill. For example, the fact that a Western automobile com-

Table 1. Asia Pacific's share in selected industries.

	1991			Forecast		
	World Volume	Asia Pacific share	Year	World Volume	Asia Pacific share	Sources
Vehicles (Thousand units)	42200	25.3%	1995	45800	27.0%	International motor
Cement (Million Tons}	1042	36.0%	1995	1227	40.0%	Industry
Chemicals (Billion US$)						
–Commodities	550	20.0%	2000	810	23.2%	
–Specialities	450	20.0%	2000	730	22.1%	Arthur D. Little
Bio-pharmaceuticals (Million US$)	2335	12.0% (Japan only)	1997	6930	16.3% (Japan only)	Data Resources
Telecoms (Million of lines)	526	28.9%	1994	641	31.6%	Data Resources
Advanced structural ceramics (Million US$)	1525	45.9% (Japan only)	2000	3640	57.7% (Japan only)	Data Resources
Crop protection chemicals (Billion US$)	24.1	21.7%	NA	NA	NA	Data Resources
International air traffic (Million Pax)	278	31.2%	2000	734	39.2%	IATA
Insurance's premium (Billion US$)	1072	26.6%	NA	NA		Agence Financiere
Computer hardware (Billion US$)	157	24.0%				

ponents firm is accepted as a supplier for Toyota or Nissan gives the company a reputation for quality that can be exploited elsewhere and applied to other markets. More and more companies have used a successful presence or position in Asian markets as a benchmark or reference in other countries or regions.

The Importance of Asia Pacific as a Resource Base

The Asia Pacific region offers a vast reservoir of natural, human, and techno-logical resources which can reinforce the global competitive advantages of firms. Figure 4 gives a pictorial representation of the many types of resources which can be obtained from the various countries of Asia Pacific and the type of com-petitive advantages they can reinforce.

The south-eastern part of the Asia Pacific region has been endowed with a wide range of natural resources which serve as raw materials for many mineral

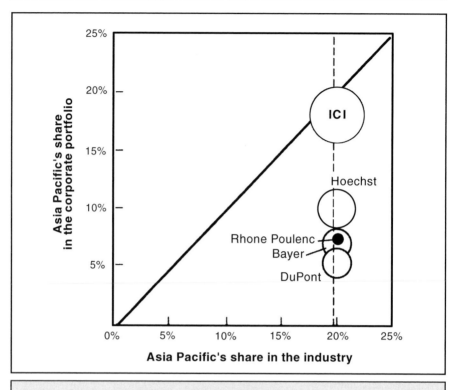

Figure 3. Asia Pacific grid in the chemical industry.

processing industries (bauxite, tin, manganese, natural gas, petroleum) as well as agro-based sectors (timber, palm oil, rubber, fisheries, cocoa, coconuts). To take the timber industry as an example by the year 2000 the region is expected to provide most of the world reserves.

In terms of human resources, Asian governments perceived the comparative advantage of their region as early as the 1960s, when they established export processing zones in order to attract foreign investment. These zones, originally established in Singapore (Jurong, Ang Moh Kio, Toa Payoh, Bedok), Korea (Mesan, Kumi, Inchon), Malaysia (Penang, Klang, Tohore) Indonesia (Batam, Surabaya, Jakarta), the Philippines (Bataan, Cebu), and Taiwan (Kaoshiung, Tsichung) served as a model for China's Special Economic Zones. In these industrial estates, foreign companies can benefit from a labour market with wages far below Western standards. The productivity and discipline of labour is variable, but these zones have generally succeeded in attracting labour intensive industries such as electronic assembly, textiles, and shoe manufacturing. To cite just one example: Matsushita Electric Industrial has different manufacturing sites in South East Asia: 14 in Malaysia, 3 in Indonesia, 3 in Thailand, 1 in the Philippines, and 8 in Singapore.

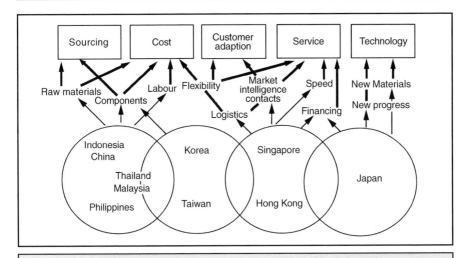

Figure 4. Asia Pacific as a resource base for competitive advantage

Western companies can benefit from low labour costs either directly through investment in manufacturing and assembly facilities, or, as is increasingly the case, through long-term components manufacturing contracts or O.E.M contracts.

Technological resources are another key resource which can be drawn from the Asia Pacific region. Until recently, Japan was the only Asian location where Western firms sought to establish R&D centres to access scientific infrastructure and capabilities. Now, a number of Asian locations have attracted the attention of Western firms as potential bases for laboratory facilities. Similar in their physical design to the industrial parks or export processing zones mentioned above, the first Scientific Park was installed in the Taiwanese city of Hunshu, followed by Kent Ridge in Singapore. Asian governments have used these parks to attract Western research laboratories by offering both infrastructure and technically skilled personnel at reduced costs.

This combination of resources availability enhances the attractiveness of the region with respect to the four major attributes of competitive advantage: cost, quality, time, and flexibility. To cite one example: a Boston Consulting Group study conducted in Singapore for an American printers manufacturer found that the productivity was 30 per cent higher, time to market 50 to 100 per cent faster, quality 10 to 15 per cent better, and the number of models 2 to 3 times higher there than in an equivalent plant in the US.[2]

The Importance of Asia Pacific as a Source of Learning

For the Western firm, the advantage of establishing and maintaining a presence in Asia Pacific does not just depend on the region's economic growth and resource potential. Advantages should also be measured in terms of the experience and competitive advantage which are to be gained by being present in one of the world's most important and fast-paced industrial battlefields. Through confrontation with talented competitors, the exposure to demanding customers, and the contact with a large variety of suppliers of components and services, Western competitors will be forced to maintain their corporate fitness and test their capabilities. Market and competitive dynamism is a source of competitive innovation and 'fitness'. In a sense, Asia Pacific is a permanent industrial Olympics where first-class competitors compete side-by-side with a wide array of newcomers and mavericks. To use the terminology of Michael Porter,[3] Asian markets can be referred to as 'global platforms' where any company which wants to be 'in the race' has to be present. Japan obviously holds first place among these 'global platforms' in a certain number of sectors, most notably new materials, opto-electronics, biotechnology or megatronics. However, other Asian countries like Indonesia for petrochemicals and process engineering, Thailand for food processing, or Hong Kong for financial engineering are also candidates. Long-term profitability cannot be secured unless a company establishes strong competitive capabilities which in turn derive from the permanent 'fitness' acquired through competition in a demanding, diverse, and constantly changing business environment like the Asia Pacific region.

Asian business philosophy and enterprise cultures and competitive approaches may force Western companies to re-evaluate and, in some cases, adapt their own traditional business strategies and concepts. Success in Asia depends to a large extent on the capacity to 'learn' new repertoires and new approaches to doing business. Operating in Asia is a learning experience—whether this takes the form of new types of relationships with suppliers, a new approach to the management of human resources, innovative ways of packaging a 'tender' to establish a long-term relationship with customers, or different ways of thinking about consumer behaviour. The example of Procter and Gamble in Japan, which after a painful experience was able to renew its approach to the design and marketing of diapers is an object lesson for other Western firms. The advantages of accumulating learning from the Asia Pacific is that lessons learned there —particularly in the domain of customer services, flexibility, total quality, and human resources management—can be transferred back to the parent company in Europe or North America.

Positioning in Asia Pacific

The Western firm's ambition for Asia Pacific determines the scope and intensity of its future business operations in the region.

This corporate ambition must be concretely reflected in a choice of products and markets. The company must also differentiate itself from its competitors both in the manner in which it chooses to establish a regional presence and in the way it carries out its competitive actions. This set of choices—referred to as 'positioning' consists of:

1. Determining whether the company is interested in accessing resources, or markets, or both.
2. Deciding on the countries in which it wants to operate.
3. Deciding on an entry mode: whether it will go it alone via wholly-owned subsidiaries, or in partnerships such as joint-ventures, licensing and franchising arrangements.
4. Defining the type of activities it plans to establish, the types of segments in which it wants to compete and a competitive approach which will differentiate it from its competitors.
5. Deciding to integrate activities regionally, strategically or country-by-country.

Resources-based versus Market-based Strategies

As indicated earlier, the Asia Pacific region offers business opportunities both in terms of its markets and its resources. The first element of regional positioning is the selection of the appropriate mix of markets versus resources.

In the case of a strategic orientation based on access to resources, the firm should concentrate its activities in the countries which have the cheapest and or best sources of supply. They should also establish sourcing offices and offshore production plants in low labour cost areas such as South China, or in raw material processing areas like Sumatra or Borneo. During the 1960s and 1970s, certain Western companies, mainly from the United States, focused exclusively on Asia's resources, setting up offshore assembly plants in the region's export processing zones. Today, however, the limits of this strategy are obvious. First, a narrow focus on resources neglects the full range of potential the region has to offer in terms of markets, learning and competitiveness. Secondly, an exclusive focus on resources is risky due to the rapid change in conditions: Asian labour costs are likely to increase, as they did in Singapore in the late 1970s. In 1976 Thomson Consumer Electronics established a factory in Toa Payoh, an industrial estate in Singapore, on the basis of the city-states low labour cost, only to find that by 1982 they were no longer as competitive. More importantly, Asian natural resource producers will most likely move quickly to fill the vacuum left in the markets by investing in downstream sectors. The evolution of the plywood industry in Indonesia illustrates this point: when in the late 1970s the Indonesian government decided to ban the export of logs, Western companies, which had relied on such supplies and suddenly found themselves without any local processing facilities or markets, were squeezed out. In practice, however, the choice Western firms will have to make is not 'either/or', between resources and markets, but on an appropriate mix of the two.

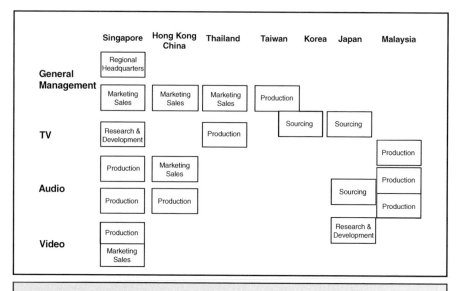

Figure 5. Thomson Consumer Electronics: Asia Pacific mosaic.

In the case of a market-based strategy, the company will set up local marketing and sometimes manufacturing activities, either wholly-owned or with local partners. The choice will depend on the market potential, the competitive climate, the government policies, and the company's competitive capabilities.

As mentioned above, a firm's regional strategic positioning should be a combination of resources and market-based orientations which will lead to a mosaic of activities spread over the region, some of them being purely resources-oriented, some of them purely market-oriented, and some of them being both. Figure 5 shows as an example the mosaic of Thomson Consumer Electronics in the region.

Choice of Countries

Country selection depends on the relative attractiveness of each country. Attractiveness is a function of three factors:

1. *Market attractiveness:* size, growth, segmentation, sophistication of demand; intensity and nature of competition.
2. *Resource attractiveness:* availability, quality and cost of raw materials, labour costs, productivity and attitudes, supplier network, quality of information, financing, buildings, general infrastructure and logistics.
3. *Political/regulatory and operational attractiveness:* political stability, monetary stability, administrative practices, operational flexibility, price and exchange controls.

Table 2. A country attractiveness assessment for a financial services company.

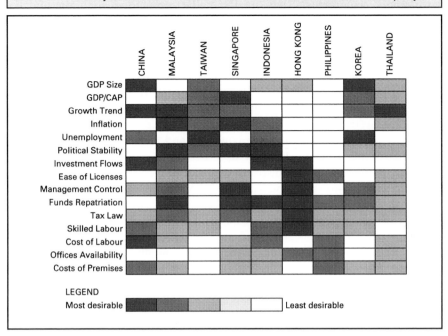

Such an assessment is obviously industry specific, and political and economic developments made some countries more 'fashionable' than others. Each company will find it necessary to design its own criteria. Table 2 shows how in 1992, a financial service company evaluated countries in the region. Such an assessment is frequently made in two steps: the evaluation of the political and regulatory climate through what is known as 'country-risk analysis'; and a business analysis which covers both market and resources attractiveness for specific business projects or business plans within a specific country.

Choice of an Entry Mode and a Pathway to Strategic Development

Entry mode decisions are concerned with the types of operations which have to be established in order to penetrate the regions and the countries which have been targeted. After entry, further decisions will have to be made in order to develop the businesses and, later on, to consolidate it.

For entering a market the typical choice is between 'going it alone' with wholly-owned operations (greenfield operations or acquisitions), or entering partnerships (joint-ventures, licensing, franchising, long-term contractual agreements, etc.). Entry mode choices for Western firms considering the Asia Pacific region should generally be determined by the following five factors: *1.* the overall attractiveness of the market; *2.* the costs; *3.* the timing and internal ability of the firm to enter and develop the necessary resources, assets, and competencies; *4. government requirements;* and finally, *5. the competitive situation,* and the political and operational risks involved.

As represented in Figure 6 one can distinguish five types of countries in Asia:

■ The *platform* countries: such as Singapore or Hong Kong which can be used at the starting phase as bases for gathering intelligence, initiating first contacts, and which can later on become the centre of regional co-ordination. Medium-sized companies for instance with no prior experience in the region could start their presence by establishing a 'listening post' in those countries.

■ The *emerging* countries like Vietnam today and Myamar (Burma) or Cambodia in the near future. The task in those countries is to establish an initial presence through a local distributor and build the necessary relationships in order to prepare the establishment of a local operation either direct or through a joint-venture.

■ The *growth* countries such as China, and the ASEAN countries, where it is becoming urgent to establish a significant presence in order to capitalize on the opportunities generated by the rapid economic development of those countries.

■ The *maturing* and established countries, for example, Korea and Taiwan, which already have significant economical infrastructures and well established local and international competitors. The task here at the entry phase is to find

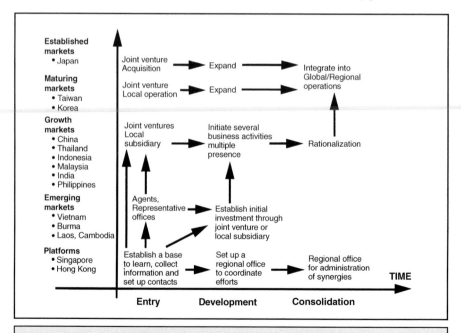

Figure 6. Entry modes and market development in Asia Pacific.

a way to acquire through joint-venture, acquisition, or through massive investment, the necessary operational capability to catch competitors up.

The particular entry and pathway to development will depend upon the company's prior experience and capabilities, and on the particular strategic attractiveness of an industrial sector in a country. However a company with limited experience will prefer to enter and develop using Singapore or Hong Kong as a platform. This was the case for Gemplus, a medium-sized French company, leader in the field of smart cards. One of the company's first moves was to set up a joint-venture with Singapore Technology. From Singapore the managing director of the joint-venture is capable of developing contacts and initiating further partnerships in the region.

Firms which have identified a potentially very attractive market not yet fully occupied by competitors would select to enter in this country and then develop their presence from this stronghold. For example, Bell and Alcatel who set up their first operation in China in the field of telecommunication equipment and are now using China as its centre of expertise for developing Asia.

Choice of Business Segments and of a Competitive Approach

Business segmentation in Asia Pacific is extremely complex, since the region can be broken down into a variety of very diverse marketing environments. At one extreme is Japan, with its extremely sophisticated and unique segmentation, and at the other is Indonesia or the Philippines, where markets are still very pyramidal with masses of consumers still living in rural economies. In the middle, Western firms will find the rapidly-growing economies of Asia's Dragons where segmentation is becoming more and more similar to the Western markets. Finally, in a category apart, are China and Vietnam, which are just beginning to shed their limitations as non-market economies, and where market segmentation is still in the infancy stage but changing very rapidly.

Traditional strategic management literature, academic scholarship, and consulting research have all advocated a dualistic approach to competitive strategy: an 'either/or' approach. Either a company positions itself as the cost leader of its particular industry, and aims to win the competitive game by under pricing its competitors, or it does so by differentiating itself and by offering better technology, quality, or services. However, this dualistic approach appears inadequate when applied to the complexity and demanding nature of Asia Pacific's markets and consumers. On the whole, Asia Pacific markets do not tend to be 'either/or' but rather 'and/and': in other words, to compete in the region a Western firm has to provide low prices and good quality, and good service, and a short response time, and proper financing, and so on. Obviously, this is a general proposition and competitive profiles will need to be designed on a case-by-case basis, but it is useful to remember that, *ceteris paribus*, Asian customers tend to exhibit a much larger repertoire of demand than Western firms are accustomed to in their traditional markets. In Japan, customers tend to be highly sophisticated and demanding in terms of certain attributes of product and service quality, while in other parts of the region, customers will try to get the best of both worlds: great price and great performance. In some countries, 'relationships' combined with indirect services will be the prime determinant of competitive approaches. The Western manager will need to demonstrate flexibility in designing competitive strategies.

Orientation: Regional versus Country-by-country

In positioning the business in the region a company will decide whether it is going to adopt a 'regional' approach or a 'country-by-country' approach. The implication of this choice is described in Table 3.

The extreme diversity of the Asia Pacific region means that there is as much difference between Japan and Indonesia as there is between Germany and Tunisia. Because of this diversity, both in terms of economic development and cultural orientation the Asia Pacific's only regional economic organization, The Association of Southeast Asian Nations (ASEAN), is still far from achieving the co-ordinated political will needed to forge the beginning of a regional common market comparable to the European Common Market. The differences in traditions, religions, public policies and government regulations have created and maintained solid barriers around country borders within the Asia Pacific region. From the perspective of the Western firm, an homogeneous or purely 'regional' approach is likely to be ineffective, and strategies should be a mix between a regional perspective and a 'country-by-country' approach.

A certain number of economic factors militate in favour of adopting a parallel 'regional' view which would serve to supplement the country-by-country approach.

Firstly, it will be argued that certain business functions—notably strategic intelligence, financial engineering, R&D, training, and specialized services — can only reap the benefits of economies of scale by servicing the whole region. Secondly, it is still possible for Western firms to achieve a regional or a sub-regional co-ordination of certain flows: most notably, components, spare parts, and semi-finished products. Thirdly, in certain industries one is obliged to serve regional customers (corporate banking for instance) and to confront regional competitors to make a regional strategy worthwhile. Finally, in many large Western corporations, managers will find that there is an internal pressure to represent the region as a whole in order to obtain an adequate allocation of investment resources. Boards of directors of large Western corporations are unaccustomed to thinking in terms of individual countries, and prefer to think in terms of aggregates: North America, Europe, etc. Therefore, many managers operating in the Asia Pacific region may find that in order to be heard they will have to present a regional perspective rather than a collection of country strategies.

Table 3. Regional vs. country-by-country positioning.

	Region	Countries
Innovation	Regional or global research Co-ordination of technological intelligence	Local laboratories Global research at HQ
Production	Specialized plants serving the world and/or the region High level of intra-regional flows	Plants tailored for national markets Little intra-regional flows
Marketing	Marketing research co-ordinated by the region Co-ordination of marketing programmes Local marketing programmes	Marketing research for local markets
Financing	Regional pooling of cash flows Regional financial engineering	Local borrowing Local cash flows
Human resources	Regional careers Regional training	National careers Local training

Creating Capabilities Through Investments in Resources, Assets and Competencies

The most critical part of any strategy process comes when the corporate ambition is confronted with the required investments needed to transform it into reality. In the Asia Pacific region it is not so much the quantitative aspect of the investment effort, but the qualitative aspect which is important. The diversity of enterprise cultures in Asia Pacific, the tenacity of certain cultural traditions and ways of doing business, make this qualitative dimension both more complex and more crucial to the success of Western ventures in the region.

Research and Western business experience in Asia Pacific have shown the most salient characteristics of doing business in the region to be the following:[4]

1. Marketing and strategic information are difficult to obtain, either because it is sparse or because it is unreliable. Consequently, forecasting market demand, assessing competitors and finding local partners is clearly perceived by Western managers to be more difficult in Asia than in the USA or Europe.

2. Building contacts and relationships is a prerequisite to any strategic development in the region. But relationship building and networking in Asia

requires time, effort and perseverance beyond what Western managers and corporations are used to.

3. Success requires long-term effort and commitment and the ability to invest cash, time, people, and management attention with the expectation that the pay off will come beyond what is considered a 'normal' time horizon in Western countries.

4. Asian business practices and enterprise culture is often difficult for Westerners to understand, either because of the complexity of cultural norms or due to the inaccessibility of ethnic or informal networks.

As a consequence Western firms will need to build capabilities in the Asia Pacific region which will demand additional and specifically tailored strategic investments in resources, assets and competencies as illustrated in Figure 7.

Resources Development

In practice there are six major strategic resources which constitute the basis of competitive advantage: finances, people, supplies, information, location, and sponsorship.

Table 4 lists the advantages and disadvantages of Western firms *vis-à-vis* local Asian firms in terms of access to those six types of resources. There is evidence

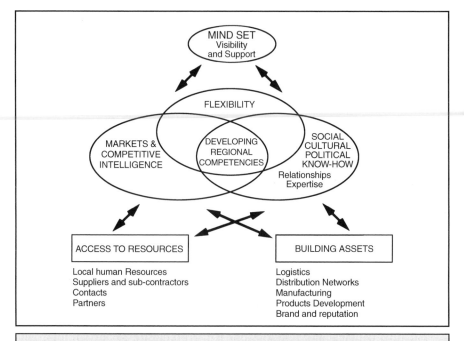

Figure 7. Strategic capabilities required in the Asia Pacific region.

Table 4. Advantages and disadvantages of western firms in accessing resources in Asia Pacific.

Resources	Western Firms	Asian Firms
Finances	Reliance on central Headquarters Access to offshore financing based on corporate credit rating Influence of Western stock markets on cost of capital Constraints on local borrowing in some cases	Japanese firms supposedly benefit from cheaper cost of capital Korean firms benefit from subsidized funds Most local governments tend to give preferential treatment to local firms
Human resources	Western firms often lack the public visibility needed to attract the best local talents Difficulties in creating loyalty among local employees	In some cases local graduates prefer to work for local firms Loyalty is stronger
Supplies	At par for international supplies Some difficulties penetrating local networks Some advantages derived from a multinational network	In certain countries, like Japan or Korea, local firms have privileged access to some suppliers
Information	Weak information base Lack of insider's sources	Long standing information network Implicit information
Sponsorship	Some Western governments subsidise exports and foreign investments Very often lack of commitment from central headquarters	Governments encourage national champions Granting of privileges

that Western firms operating in Asia Pacific are at a relative disadvantage in all six of the above-mentioned categories, the most critical being people and information. The development of these resources requires a continuous and systematic investment in the 'soft' areas of business: links to schools and universities, time spent cultivating relationships with journalists and gathering contacts and information, lobbying, general promotional efforts such as the financing of scholarships and the sponsoring of social and cultural events, the compilation and updating of 'intelligence' reports, etc. All these activities constitute cash outflows for which it is quite difficult to estimate a 'return' and for which 'results' take a long time to materialize.

Western companies sometimes complain that they are also at a disadvantage in the Asia Pacific region due to the biased treatment they receive from Asian governments, who tend to favour and protect local companies. In a 1992 Euro-Asia Centre survey on the competitive climate in the Asia Pacific region, the majority of respondents, with the exception of those Western executives based in Singapore and Hong Kong, agreed with the statement that 'local governments grant preferential advantages to local firms'. It is important, however, not to exaggerate the frequency of this preferential treatment. It is understandable, at least in the less developed Asian countries, that governments will extend incentives to local enterprises. Western firms can often compensate for this bias by taking advantage of subsidies and preferential treatment accorded by their own governments in the form of export credits, political support, tax exemption, etc.

In terms of financing, the major issue is more a question of internal commitment than of cost of capital. One may occasionally find that a local or Japanese competitor has privileged access to cheap financing. This has to be balanced with the fact that Western firms, in many instances, benefit from government subsidized loans.

Building Assets

The building up of tangible and intangible assets is the bread and butter of any strategic development in Asia, just as it is in any other area of the world. However the specific demands of operating in the Pacific arena necessitate a focus on two key areas: the transfer of technology and the building of marketing assets.

Establishing a presence in the Asia Pacific region requires a *transfer of technology* to the local operation, whether it is a fully-owned venture or a partnership. In the developing part of the Asia Pacific region, this aspect is a critical one. The aspects of this process which require particular attention are: the down scaling of operational infrastructure; the adaptation of the technology to local conditions; and the need to emphasize the software part of the investment. Down-scaling is often crucial because the size of individual Asian markets is generally far smaller than the world efficient scale. As mentioned earlier, the Asia Pacific region is far from being a single market, a reality that makes it difficult—and at times impossible—for Western firms to specialize plants, and hence to benefit from large economies of scale. A case in point was the late 1970s investment of a Western aluminium producer, ALCAN, in a Malaysian rolling mill. The size of the Malaysian market, even taking into account its considerable growth potential, was insufficient to justify an investment in a 'state-of-the-art' plant. The Western aluminium company encountered great difficulty in designing a small-scale plant because all the engineers in North America and Europe were used to 'thinking big'. Finally, after 18 long months of internal struggle, a down-sized plant was designed by engineers brought from the parent corporation's Indian subsidiary.

Marketing assets are commonly the most difficult of assets to accumulate and develop, particularly good will and distribution networks. Goodwill, in the consumer segments depends upon both image and reputation for quality and services, while in the industrial segments it depends upon the quality of the relationships with customers. Asian consumers are acutely sensitive to image and services; as a consequence, Western firms will have to exert a long and consistent effort to develop the kind of reputation that Asian markets require. The complexities of building distribution networks and personal relationships are linked to the fact that Asian markets have already been widely cultivated by local and multinational traders, Japanese and Western industrial and services firms who began investing in the region in the 1970s and 80s.

Creating Competencies

The role of 'competencies' in strategic capabilities has been described as one of the most powerful in creating competitive advantage.[5] This is probably more true for the Asia Pacific region than anywhere else. In addition to the classic competencies required according to the type of industry in which the firm is operating such as project management, time-to-market or system integration, three sets of competencies are of particular importance for success in the Asia Pacific region:

- *Intelligence building:* the ability to invest in decoding the particularities of the business, political and sociological environment and to translate it into meaningful business recommendations
- *Flexibility*: a type of decision-making process adapted to analysing problems and coming up with solutions which may be specific to Asia and at variance with the core organizational norms or accepted practices of the corporation.
- *Networking:* the ability to 'partner' and manage relationships with Asian firms and in different cultural contexts.

Those three sets of competencies can be derived from a whole range of investments:

- *Investment in cultural understanding:* language, history, sociology. Asian cultures are at the crossroads of a variety of cultural streams: Confucianism, Buddhism, Taoism, Islam, Shintoism, Hinduism, and Christianity. The Chinese heritage with its 50 centuries of documented history, not to mention Japan, Korea, Thailand, and the Indonesian islands with their very rich traditions and social norms, have always fascinated Western traders, poets, and warriors. Diplomatic services in the UK and France had a specially trained force for 'oriental' postings. However, modern, professionally trained business executives, coming from schools of engineering or business schools, very often lack the cultural sensitivity and multicultural background necessary to understand and operate effectively in such a culturally complex region. One of the problems is that managers are often recruited from students with the requisite foreign language capabilities, but who often lack the technical or business training needed to support the businesses. The task of developing an appropriate Asia-sensitive corporate culture—mixing cultural, technical and business skills —depends on the leadership of the corporation. This is a dual task: first the firm must develop in its managers specific competencies for the region; then the firm must create an organization-wide understanding and respect for these competencies so that Asian strategies will be accepted by corporate and business managers at headquarters.

- *Investment in information gathering:* The paucity and unreliability of publicly available sources of information virtually forces firms to invest in intelligence. This requires more than the purchase of a database or the subcontracting of market research. It requires the constitution of a network of contacts and a systematic cross-checking of unstructured information which calls for both an investment of time and a physical, representative presence.
- *Investment in relationships:* Doing business in Asia Pacific requires, perhaps more than any other region in the world, a unique set of competencies in developing partnerships, and creating and managing a network of contacts. Building relationships with suppliers, distributors, partners, officials, and other contacts is often a slow process, particularly in Asia, where great importance is attached to the personalization of business contacts. Building competencies in relationships is not only a matter of individual talents, it relies also on the capability to 'institutionalize' a relationship's culture. This requires time and an appropriate personnel development policy as well as the creation of an internal regional network of communication and co-operation among managers operating in various countries.

Organizational Capabilities

When Western firms come to the point that they need to translate strategic decisions into the proper organizational mechanisms for the region, the following questions are likely to arise:

- What is the proper organizational structure: geographical, global or regional?
- Should the company set up a regional headquarters?
- Should Asia Pacific as a region be represented at board level?
- What degree of autonomy should country managers enjoy in product, production, and marketing decision-making processes?
- To what extent should planning, budgeting, and performance evaluation systems be adapted or transformed to fit the regional specificities?
- How should local Asian managers be recruited and trained?
- How should expatriate managers be managed?

It can be argued that the weakness of Western companies in Asia stems from a lack of proper organizational mechanisms.[6] Given the small percentage of Western business activities currently carried out in Asia (see Figure 2), it is not difficult to conclude that top Western management is unfamiliar with the region.

This is not surprising, considering that top managers have traditionally come from businesses and countries which are heavily weighted in the corporate portfolio. It is also likely that corporate norms, systems, and procedures have not been properly adapted to the Asian business and cultural contexts. Therefore, vicious circles have tended to develop: a relatively weak, low profile presence fails to lead to cumulative internal knowledge of the region, and tends to perpetuate *ad hoc* and inappropriate business systems which in turn fail to generate adequate institutional and financial support for the region at corporate headquarters. This circle inevitably perpetuates a weak, low profile presence. 'Organizational facilitators' should be designed for implementing Asian strategies. Such facilitators include:

- The appointment of a senior, powerful top executive in charge of the region.
- The creation of a 'regional orientation' through regional networking and sometimes, although not always, the establishment of one or more regional headquarters.
- The development of a 'regional spirit', sometimes referred to as the 'missionary spirit', an orientation which encourages managers to build and act on a sense of mission in a particular country or region.
- Most importantly, the capability to operate a complete transformation in the way corporations structure problems, make and implement decisions.

Asia Pacific Requires a Complete Transformation of Organizational Practices

In managing businesses across borders, companies are confronted with three kinds of problems:

- One set of problems can be qualified as problems of adaptation. Making sure that local operations develop the skills and attitudes to adapt strategies to local contexts: to fit with local legal requirements, to adapt business practices to local social norms and to 'translate' corporate language into a local one. For instance, a British company setting up an operation in China will feel the need to adapt its literature to the Chinese language and to encourage its managers to follow the social codes of the Chinese business establishment.
- Another set of problems are the ones of modification. To develop different business 'paradigms' or mental models. Modifications are required when the conceptual distance between the dominant business logic of the corporation is very much distant from the one required in the host country. For instance a British firm setting up a subsidiary in India may not find the contextual adaptation too difficult, language wise or even institutionally but may need to change fundamentally its business approach.
- When combined, the need for adaptation and for modification require a transformation. That is to say, a complete overhaul of management practices

and business logic. Asia Pacific countries would typically fall into this category where Western firms have not only to 'speak' differently but also to 'think' differently (see Figure 8).

Asia Pacific, as a region, requires more than just an adaptation to different cultural contexts; it requires a 'paradigmatic transformation'. It is no longer enough for Western firms and managers to learn how to speak Japanese to become a player in the Japanese market. Increasingly, Western firms are having to learn how to 'play Japanese' in a Japanese game and according to a strategic logic which is often at odds with the prevailing business philosophy or strategic logic of their parent company. A good example of such a transformation is provided by Procter and Gamble (P&G) in Japan. Procter and Gamble had successfully developed and marketed products in the USA and Europe during the 1960s and the 70s. P&G core competencies were undoubtedly based on the mastery of market research, consumer analysis, mass merchandising, and product launch. For a marketing manager, having worked for P&G was a guarantee of future job offerings. When P&G entered Japan, after a period of unsuccessful trials with a joint venture partner, it installed a local subsidiary and started to apply the P&G marketing expertise. The results were so catastrophic that P&G

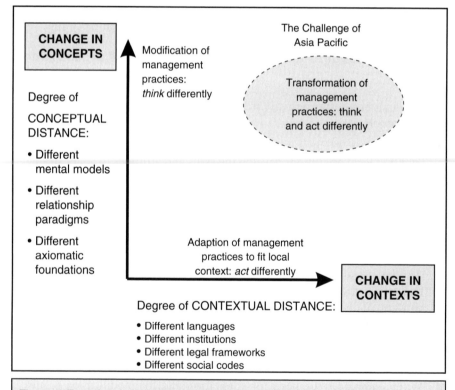

Figure 8. Transforming management practices to achieve success in Asia.

was forced to consider the complete cessation of its Japanese operations. After transforming its approach, P&G Japan became extremely successful and is now a model of innovation and a source of profit for the whole group.[7]

Interviews with Western expatriate managers based in Japan and other Asian countries support the view that the prevailing rules of the game inside both North American and European companies are ill-suited to the requirements for success in the Asia Pacific region. Similarly, it can now be argued that the competitive edge of the emerging Asian global competitors, although still primarily Japanese, has been their ability to create new, highly flexible strategic capabilities which, when compared to traditional Western corporate strategy, are better suited to the shifting and fast-paced Asian competitive climate.

This flexibility is one of the core competencies Western firms will need to learn and deploy in order to operate efficiently in the region. As they formulate strategies for Asia Pacific, Western managers should look carefully and realistically at their firm's accepted norms and business practices.

Conclusions: Putting a Strategy for Asia into Action

Time runs out very rapidly and already all signals indicate that the world has entered the Asia Pacific century. Western firms have to increase rapidly the speed of their business development into the region if they want to survive and prosper in this new global business environment.

For those companies already established in Asia, the challenge is to move faster in order to cope with the growth of the region. For companies like ABB, Siemens or GEC-Alsthom the challenge is to be able to participate on a large scale in the construction of the electrical infrastructure required in the whole region. In China alone over the next decade there is a need to build the equivalent of Switzerland's electrical power generation every year!

Practically it means for a company:

■ *A strategic mandate for the region.* The framework proposed here can be usefully adopted for designing such a mandate. It is more than the simple addition of a strategy for a particular country or countries. It is the expression of an overall corporate ambition for the region, supported by the appropriate resource allocation needed to create the enhanced strategic capabilities.

■ *A proactive mind set.* Gone is the time of the old colonial houses where young men were sent to the exotic 'Orient' to manage the imperial trading posts. Nowadays, Asia is part of the global battlefield and requires the mobilization of all corporate capabilities. No longer marginal, the region becomes a central part of the corporate strategic effect. At Asea Brown Boveri this is translated into a sentence: 'Winning the Battle of Asia'.

■ *A special emphasis on human resources development.* The game is no longer to send the maverick expatriate speaking the local language into the 'Far East', but to create a multi-layered managerial population capable of human resources capabilities are needed: Firstly the identification, selection, and appointment of those international managers able to 'pioneer' the business development in Asia: building networks of relationships, recruiting local talent, generating business opportunities. Secondly the rapid development of local managers capable of learning the corporate culture, who in the future will manage the local operations and a certain number of whom will become part of the core of international corporate managers. Thirdly the 'de-marginalization' of the region for international careers. A posting in Asia for a product manager, a plant manager, a technician, etc., should be welcomed and considered a normal pathway for a career evolution, and no longer seen as an 'exotic' appointment. Finally, even for the rest of the managers in the corporation who are not posted in the region there is a need to be convinced about the strategic importance of the region and to become acquainted with the Asian region, its business practices and logic, so that those managers will understand and support Asian related activities in their business or functions. In the same manner as a general manager needs to understand 'finance', 'marketing', or 'leadership', there is a need to understand 'Asian business'.

References

1. In most instances managers use the concept of 'strategic planning' to describe the frameworks and the processes by which strategy is formulated. One should make a clear distinction between this formal aspect of strategy formulation which is nothing more than a methodology and the concept of a strategic framework used here. While it is critical to have a strategic framework, it may not be necessary to have formal strategic plans in the Asia Pacific region. Academics like Richard Pascale (*Managing on the Edge*, New York, Simon and Schuster, 1990) and Tom Peters (*Thriving on Chaos*, New York, Alfred Knopf, 1987) argue that strategic planning hampers real strategy formulation by its excessive focus on quantitative aspects. Henry Mintzberg (*Mintzberg on Strategy*, Free Press, New York, 1990) advances similar arguments. In an earlier article, one of the authors developed the argument that a formal approach to strategy formulation in the developing countries of the Asia Pacific region was inappropriate (see Philippe Lasserre, Strategic Planning in South East Asia: does it Work?, *Euro Asia Business Review* 2 (2), 37–41 (1983)).
2. Competition in Asia, *Asian Business*, October, 4 (1992).
3. Michael Porter, *Global strategies*, Harvard University Press, New York.
4. The characteristics indicated in the figures come from two surveys done with European executives operating in the region. See Ph. Lasserre and J. Probert, Competing on the Pacific Rim: High Risks and High Return, *Long Range Planning* 27 (2), 12–35 (1994); and Ph. Lasserre, Gathering and Interpreting Strategic Intelligence in Asia Pacific, *Long Range Planning* 26 (3), 56–66 (1993).
5. Hamel and Prahalad, The Core Competence of the Corporation, *Harvard Business Review*, May–June, 79–91 (1990).
6. Lasserre Philippe, Why Europeans are Weak in Asia?, *Long Range Planning* 21 (4), 25–35 (1988).
7. Procter and Gamble in Japan, Harvard Business School case study 391 (1990).

7

Whose Company Is It? The Concept of the Corporation in Japan and the West

Masaru Yoshimori

This article examines the differences in the concept of the corporation and their possible implications for corporate performance, between Japan on the one hand and the United States and Europe (Germany, UK and France) on the other. The Japanese concept is used as the standard against which the other models are compared. The concept of the corporation is defined here as the answer to the question: 'In whose interest should the firm be managed?'[1] This is the foundation on which corporate governance and the monitoring system for the CEO is built. The analysis is focused on large publicly-held corporations with widely diffused ownership.

Three Concepts of the Corporation

Available evidence seems to suggest that in terms of corporate governance countries may be divided into three groups: with monistic, dualistic and pluralistic concepts of the corporation. The monistic outlook is shareholder-oriented and looks at the firm as the private property of its owners. This concept is prevalent in the United States and the UK. The dualistic concept also puts a premium on the shareholder interest, but the interests of employees are taken into account as well. This is an adapted form of the monistic concept and is

Dr. Masaru Yoshimori is Professor of Business Administration at Yokohama National University, Yokohama. His eight books on comparative management include *Les entreprises japonaises* (The Japanese Company), a Que sais-je? book.

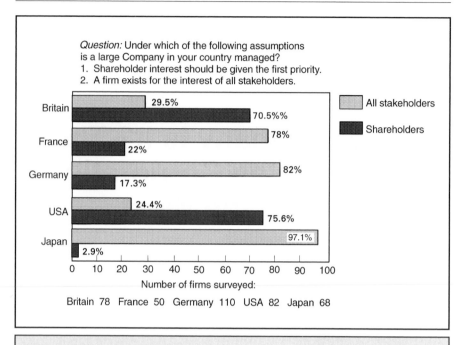

Question: Under which of the following assumptions
is a large Company in your country managed?
1. Shareholder interest should be given the first priority.
2. A firm exists for the interest of all stakeholders.

Britain — 29.5% / 70.5%%
France — 78% / 22%
Germany — 82% / 17.3%
USA — 24.4% / 75.6%
Japan — 97.1% / 2.9%

All stakeholders
Shareholders

Number of firms surveyed:
Britain 78 France 50 Germany 110 USA 82 Japan 68

Figure 1. Whose company is it?

widely shared in Germany and to a lesser degree in France. The view that the firm is a social institution where people develop themselves freely, ranked first among six alternative definitions, according to Albach's survey of leading German companies in 1975, though it slipped to the third rank in 1991.[2]

The pluralistic approach assumes that the firm belongs to all the stakeholders, with the employees' interests taking precedence. This is the concept specific to Japan which manifests itself in the form of long-term employment for employees and long-term trading relations among various other stakeholders (the main bank, major suppliers, subcontractors, distributors), loosely called *Keiretsu*.

This three-part categorization is supported by the results of a mail survey undertaken by the author with managers and executives in the five countries under review (see the Note at the end of the article for details of the survey). The shareholder-centred Anglo-American outlook starkly contrasts with the employee-centred Japanese perspective, with Germany and France in between but significantly more oriented towards 'shareholder value' than Japan. The findings on Japan are consistent with the results of other studies. For instance, a survey carried out in 1990 by *Nippon Keizai Shimbun* on 104 employees of large corporations showed a majority of 80% replying that the company belongs to its employees. 70% believed that the company exists for the benefit of society as a whole. The concept that the firm is the property of shareholders ranked third with 67%.

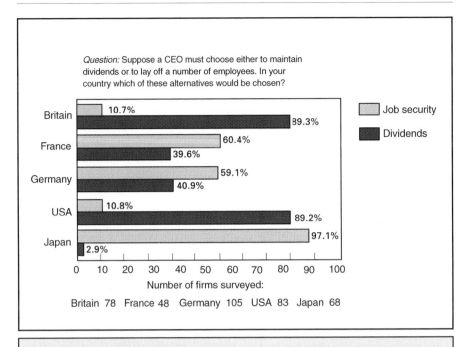

Figure 2. Job security or dividends?

Clearly Japan puts the interest of employees before that of shareholders. Her current unemployment rate of around 3% even in a prolonged recession is a testimony to this. Though increasingly challenged, job security is still defended as the mainstream ideology, as two major spokesmen of the Japanese business community recently proclaimed: Fumio Sato, Chairman of Toshiba Corporation, said that to discharge employees is 'the most serious sin' a president can commit and Takeshi Moroi, Chairman of Chichibu Cement, said that job security is the 'responsibility of the corporation'.

Key Implications of the Different Approaches

Cohesion Among the Stakeholders

The central characteristic of the Japanese pluralistic concept is the alignment of the company's goals and interests with those of the stakeholders. This leads to a higher degree of cohesion between the firm's stakeholders, i.e. shareholders, management, employees, the main bank, major suppliers and distributors. They pull together toward a common purpose: the company's survival and prosperity. They share the implicit consensus that their respective interests are realized and promoted through their long-term commitment and cooperation with the firm.

Maximization of general benefit, or the firm's 'wealth-maximizing capacity', as Drucker puts it, and not self-interest, is the name of the game.[3] Michael Porter characterizes such relationship as 'a greater community of interest' and categorizes it as 'quasi integration', that is an intermediate form between long-term contracts and full ownership. According to Porter, this type of interdependent relationship among the stakeholders combines some of the benefits of vertical integration without incurring the corresponding costs.[4] Suzuki and Wright argue that a Japanese company, though legally independent, should be regarded rather as a division of a big conglomerate.[5] This 'network structure' provides a system of collective security in time of crisis, as will be illustrated later.

Roles of the CEO

Within the Japanese concept of the corporation, the company president is the representative of both the employees and the other stakeholders. The source of legitimacy of the president is derived primarily from his role as the defender of job security for the employees. This is understandable given the fact that the employees constitute the most important power base for the president, as Figure 3 indicates. His secondary role is as the arbitrator for the divergent interests of the stakeholders so that a long-term balance of interests is achieved.

In contrast, under the Anglo-American 'monistic' concept where shareholders' interests are given primacy, the CEO represents the interests of the shareholders as their 'ally', according to Abegglen and Stalk, though their respective objectives may diverge at times. Understandably other stakeholders also seek to maximize their respective interests. In this 'zero-sum game', the firm ends up as a mere vehicle by which to satisfy the self-centred needs of the different stakeholders. The company then becomes an organization 'external' to the interests of its stakeholders, as Abegglen and Stalk point out, with no one caring about the long-term destiny of the firm itself.[6] This makes a turnaround process more difficult, once a firm is confronted with financial difficulties, as is shown later.

The Relationship Between the Firm and Its Main Bank

In the Japanese *Keiretsu* the main bank assumes a pivotal role owing to its monitoring and disciplinary function based on its financial and equity claims. The main bank is not to be confused with the *Zaibatsu** institution, as any bank,

---

Zaibatsu is a prewar conglomerate under family ownership and control. Mitsubishi, Mitsui, Sumitomo, and other *Zaibatsu* controlled a majority of Japan's large industrial, financial and service firms before World War II. They were broken up by the Occupation forces after the war. Today the firms of a former *Zaibatsu* form a loose federation based on their common tradition and business relationship.

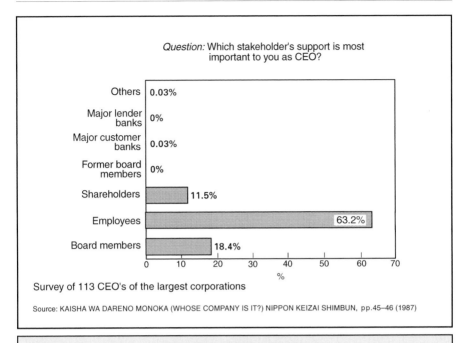

Question: Which stakeholder's support is most important to you as CEO?

Others | 0.03%
Major lender banks | 0%
Major customer banks | 0.03%
Former board members | 0%
Shareholders | 11.5%
Employees | 63.2%
Board members | 18.4%

Survey of 113 CEO's of the largest corporations

Source: KAISHA WA DARENO MONOKA (WHOSE COMPANY IS IT?) NIPPON KEIZAI SHIMBUN, pp.45–46 (1987)

Figure 3. The Japanese CEO's most important power base.

whether *Zaibatsu* or non-*Zaibatsu* in origin, can assume this role. The firm's main bank relations are characterized as follows:

- The main bank is typically the largest or one of the largest providers of loans and makes available on a preferential basis long-term and comprehensive financial services covering deposits, discounting of notes, foreign exchange transactions, advice in financial planning, agents on other loans, etc.
- Cross-shareholdings and interlocking directorships result in information sharing through official and personal contacts.
- The rescue of a client firm is attempted when it is targeted in a hostile takeover bid. Thus none of the hostile takeover attempts by a well-known raider, Minebea, were successful. An attempt to acquire Janome, a sewing machine maker, was thwarted by its main bank, Saitama Bank, another raid on Sankyo Seiki was frustrated by its main bank, Mitsubishi Bank who later arranged for an equity participation by Nippon Steel (*Nippon Keizai Shimbun,* June 21, 1989).
- Direct intervention in the turnaround process occurs in case the borrower company faces serious financial distress.

This main bank support is the most important motivation for Japanese firms to have a main bank. Typically the bailout measures range from the provision of emergency finance at an early stage in the crisis to, if the situation becomes more

serious, the reduction of or exemption from interest payments, the engineering
of a financial reorganization, the bank sending its own executives to supervise
the reorganization, and finally the replacement of ineffectual management, the
reorganization of the assets and an arrangement for an alliance or merger with
another firm. According to Sheard, the intervention by the main bank may have
effects similar to an external takeover. [7]

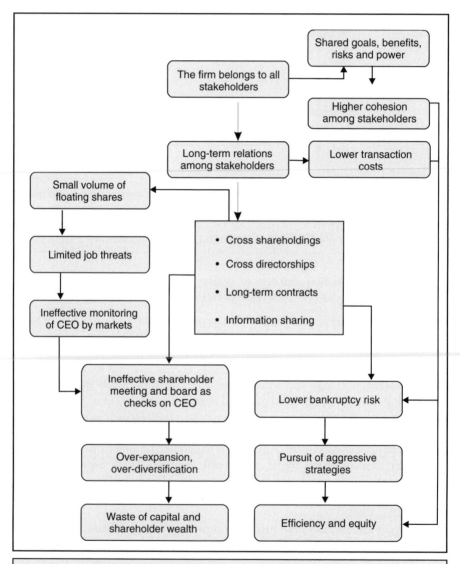

Figure 4. The Japanese pluralistic concept of the corporation—its advantages and
disadvantages.

A recent mail survey of 305 listed companies excluding financial corporations suggests that 70% of them believe that their main bank would provide them with support in case of a crisis.[8] The results of another poll of 354 corporations of Nikkeiren (The Japanese Federation of Employers' Associations) published in August 1994, indicated that 81.6% are in favour of maintaining the main bank system.[9]

A Japan–US Comparison of Stakeholder Relations—the Toyo Kogyo and Chrysler Cases

The relations among stakeholders in Japan, in particular the firm–main bank relations, may be better understood when a firm faces a crisis. The turnaround processes of Toyo Kogyo, manufacturer of Mazda passenger cars, and of Chrysler are contrasted. The following summary of the Toyo Kogyo case is based on a detailed analysis by Pascale and Rohlen and that of Chrysler on Iacocca's own account and on a book by Reich and Donahue.[10–12]

Toyo Kogyo

In 1974, Toyo Kogyo was confronted with a financial crisis due to its large stockpile of unsold cars. Mazda cars powered by Wankel rotary engines were less fuel efficient, a serious disadvantage after the first oil crisis of 1973. Sumitomo Bank, the main bank, played a vital role in the bailout operations.

■ Sumitomo Bank made a public assurance to stand by the distressed company, and a commitment to carry any new loans.
■ Sumitomo Bank sent a team of seven directors to control and implement the reorganization process.
■ Sumitomo Bank replaced the president with a new, more competent successor.
■ Sumitomo Bank coordinated negotiations with the other lenders to establish a financial package.
■ Sumitomo group companies switched their car purchases to Mazda and bought 8000 vehicles over 6 years.
■ No lay-off of employees but factory operators joined the sales force.
■ The suppliers and subcontractors agreed to extend payment terms from 189 to 210 days, resulting in estimated savings in interest payments of several billion Yen.
■ They also agreed to price reductions of 14% over 2 and half years. Joint cost reduction programmes were also implemented, with cost reductions of 123 billion Yen over 4 years.
■ The employees accepted rescheduling of bonus payments, contributing 4 billion Yen in increased annual cash flow. They also agreed to restraints in wage and bonus increases.

Chrysler

In the turnaround process at Chrysler, the stakeholders—the banks, the union, and the dealers—distrusted each other, were afraid of being stuck with an unfair burden and shunned responsibility for saving the firm. Its lead bank, Manufacturers Hanover Trust, did not or could not make an assurance to bail Chrysler out, although the bank's chairman had been on the Chrysler board for years. The chairman declared that he would approve no more unguaranteed loans to Chrysler because of its fiduciary responsibility to its shareholders and depositors. Lack of solidarity of the lenders and other stakeholders made the turnaround process dependent on government guarantees. As Iacocca sarcastically wrote, 'it took longer to get $655 million in concessions from the four hundred lending institutions than it did to get the loan guarantees of $1.5 billion passed by the entire US Congress'. For him, 'the congressional hearings were as easy as changing a flat tire on a spring day, compared to dealing with the banks'. Such financial concerns occupied top management for most of one year.

- Manufacturers Hanover Trust arranged for an agreement on a $455 million revolving credit with 80 American banks.
- Manufacturers Hanover Trust's chairman pleaded in Congress for a Federal loan guarantee for Chrysler.
- Manufacturers Hanover Trust urged its colleagues to accept Chrysler's packages of concessions.
- The Labour union agreed to a wage restraint and curtailment of paid days off.
- Suppliers agreed to price reductions.

Legal Restrictions on Banks in the United States

Contrary to Japan and Germany, the United States traditionally put a premium on investor protection by insisting on complete and accurate disclosure of company information, portfolio diversification and on a sharp line of demarcation between investor and manager roles. Thus the Glass-Steagall Act, the Bank Holding Company Act of 1956, the Investment Company Act of 1940, the ERISA Act of 1974 and finally the rules against insider trading all combine to prohibit or inhibit investing funds of banks and pension plans in the stock of any single corporation, and participation in the management of the portfolio and borrower companies. This legal framework coupled with banks' preference for liquidity over investment has made the US financial market the most transparent, fair, efficient, liquid and low-cost in the world. The downside is fragmented equity holding, and arm's length or even antagonistic relations between shareholders and management, as Bhide, Roe, Coffee and other US scholars have pointed out.[13-15]

The Roles of the German 'Hausbank'

In Germany where the Hausbank has a similar role to the Japanese main bank, many firms regard it as a kind of 'insurance, bearing appropriate premiums in good times and offering corresponding protection when things go less well', according to Schneider-Linné, a member of the Management Board of Deutsche Bank.[16] German main banks do take initiatives to reorganize their client firms in financial distress. Their part in rescuing companies, however, seems to be more limited in scope and commitment than that of Japanese main banks. The most significant difference is that the German main bank does not get directly involved in the management of the distressed firm and that the rescue concept itself is usually left to management consultancy firms, according to Edwards and Fischer.[17] The German bank usually confines itself to rescheduling interest and principal payments or reducing interest charges and debts, giving advice to management and bringing in suitable new management, according to the same authors.

The Flaws in the Japanese Concept of the Corporation

Needless to say, Japan's close-knit, inward-looking concept of the corporation has its downsides. The most serious one is inefficient monitoring of top management. Indeed, there has been practically no control exercised over top management except through the product market. Through cross-shareholdings, cross-directorships and long-term business relations, Japanese managers have isolated themselves from takeover threats and shareholder pressures and thus have been able to pursue expansionist strategies throughout the post-war period, particularly during the high-growth period up until the mid-70s. Certainly their growth-oriented strategies have been beneficial to companies, as many Japanese firms rose to dominant positions in the international market. In the process managers have not generally sought to maximize their personal income as in some other countries. The remuneration level of Japanese top executives is much lower than international levels.

But the potential risk of ineffective monitoring of top management was inherent in the Japanese governance system, as it is also in Germany. This flaw became apparent in the second half of the 80s in horrendous wastes of capital through reckless and unrelated diversifications and investments, and illegal or unethical behaviour of many large firms. We now examine major dysfunctions of the Japanese monitoring system.

Ritualized General Meeting of Shareholders

The Japanese general meeting of shareholders is without doubt the least effective among the countries under review as a monitor over management. It has degenerated into a mere formality, as nearly everything is decided between the management and the major shareholders before the meeting takes place.

A mail survey carried out in June 1993 by the Japan Association of Statutory Auditors on 1106 public corporations revealed that nearly 80% of their general meetings of shareholders ended in less than half an hour including recess time. Less than 3 % last for more than an hour. At the meeting not a single question was posed by shareholders in 87% of the companies studied, not to speak of shareholder proposals which were not made at all in 98% of the companies.[18]

Limited Monitoring Power of the Chairman of the Board

Unlike in Anglo-American and French companies, board chairmanship and presidency of Japanese corporations are seldom assumed concurrently by the same person. At first sight, therefore, the supervisory function of the chairman and the executive function of the president seem to be clearly separated. Theoretically the chairman is expected to exercise control over the president. But this is not the case, because the Japanese board chairmanship is usually an honorary, symbolic or advisory position, the last step on the ladder before retirement from the company after having been president for several years. The chairman rarely interferes with the day-to-day managerial activities of the president, though his advice may be occasionally sought on major strategic decisions or on the appointment of key managerial positions. He spends most of his time representing the firm at external functions and activities, such as meetings of trade and economic associations, government commissions etc. This 'half-retired' position of the chairman of the board is well illustrated by the fact that in 96% of the firms the president, not the chairman, presides over the general meeting of shareholders.

Board Members Are Appointed by the President

The fundamental cause of the board's dysfunction is that in most large firms nearly all of the board members are appointed by the president and naturally pledge their allegiance to him. In addition there are no or very few outside directors. If any, they are typically representatives from affiliated companies such as suppliers, subcontractors, etc. with little influence on the president. There is no distinction, therefore, between directors and officers. The board members are supposed to monitor the president who is their immediate superior, with obvious adverse consequences.

Boards Are Too Large

The average board in Japanese companies is larger than in any of the other industrialized nations examined here. Sakura Bank, second largest bank in revenue in 1993, is the champion with 62 Board members. The average board size for the top 3 construction firms is about 52, for the top 3 trading companies close to 50, and for the 3 largest automobile and banking companies around 43.[19]

This inflation of board sizes is due to the fact that board membership is often a reward for long and faithful service or major contributions to the company. The title of board member is useful to obtain business from major customers. In short, the Japanese board of directors has been transformed into a motivating and marketing tool. With such a large board with most directors engaged in day-to-day line activities, it is practically impossible to discuss any matter of importance in detail, let alone advise and sanction the president.

Ineffective Statutory Auditors

Large listed corporations are legally subject to two monitoring mechanisms: statutory auditors and independent certified public accountants. Neither is functioning properly. The primary auditing function of statutory auditors is to prevent any decisions by the directors to be taken or implemented which are judged to be in violation of laws or articles of incorporation, or otherwise detrimental to the company. Statutory auditors thus perform both accounting and operating audits to protect the interests of the company and the stakeholders by forestalling any adverse decisions and actions before it is too late. On paper they are given powerful authority, including the right to suspend illegal actions by a board member. But actual use of this power is unheard of. The root cause of the lack of monitoring by the statutory auditors is that they are selected by the president whom they are supposed to monitor.

A study conducted by Kobe University reveals that 57% of statutory auditors are selected by the president and 33% by directors or the executive committee and endorsed by the president. This shows that 90% of the statutory auditors are indeed chosen by the president for perfunctory approval at the shareholders' meeting.[20]

Flawed Corporate Governance in the West

Nor do the monitoring capabilities of Western boards function perfectly due firstly to the CEO assuming the board chairmanship (except in Germany where this is legally prohibited), secondly due to the psychological and even economic dependence of outside (non-executive) directors on the CEO/chairman, and lastly due to multiple directorships.

CEO/Chairman Duality—USA, UK, and France

These three countries share the same problem as expressed by the chairman of Delta Metal; 'The problem with British companies is that the chairman marks his own papers'.[21] In the United States, 75% of large manufacturing companies are run by the CEO-chairman, according to a survey by Rechner and Dalton.[22] CEO duality is also prevalent in the UK where in 60% of large firms including financial corporations the chairman is also the CEO, according to a Korn Ferry International survey.[23] In France firms can opt either for the conventional single board or the two-tier board system inspired by the German model. An overwhelming majority of large firms have the traditional single board where in most cases the chairman is also the CEO, as the title Président Directeur-géneral indicates.

In Germany the separation between the supervisory board and the management board is legally assured as no member of the one board is allowed to be a member of the other at the same time. Theoretically, the German system precludes the power concentration on the CEO-chairman as seen in other countries, thus assuring independent monitoring by the chairman of the supervisory board over the management board. But the reality does not altogether reflect the intention of the legislation. According to an empirical study by Prof. Gerum on 62 large firms, this monitoring mechanism functions effectively only in firms whose supervisory board is dominated by one or more blockvote holders. The study shows that in a majority of 64% of the sample firms the management board influences the supervisory board. Only in 13% of firms does the supervisory board discharge its oversight functions over the management board. In the remaining 23% of firms, the supervisory board is strongly involved in the decision making of the management board, a power concentration similar to the Anglo-American, French and Japanese situations. The researcher concludes that this represents 'pathological traits' in the light of the objectives sought by the law.[24]

Lack of Neutrality of Outside Directors—USA and Europe

In the United States the board chairman (who is often also the CEO as mentioned already) recommends candidates for outside directors in 81% of the 600 firms surveyed by Korn Ferry International.[25] In the UK 80% of the non-executive (outside) directors are selected from among the 'old-boy network', reducing their monitoring potential, as reported by Sir Adrian Cadbury.[26] A similar situation is observed in France where new candidates for board membership are recommended by the CEO-chairman in 93.5% of the firms controlled by owner-managers, and in 92% of firms under managerial control, according to a study by Profs. Charreaux and Pitol-Belin.[27] In Germany, no hard data are available, but the preceding findings of Prof. Gerum on the dominance of the management board over the supervisory board leads us to infer that in a majority of large firms it is the managers on the management board that effectively determine who will be the members of the supervisory board.

Multiple Directorships—USA and Europe

This is a phenomenon that does not exist in Japan. All the Western countries reviewed here share this convention. In the United States 72% of the CEOs of the largest 50 corporations serve on the board of other firms and 50% of them have more than 6 outside directorships, according to Bassiry and Denkmejian.[28] In Germany the maximum number of board memberships is set at 10 without counting directorships in subsidiary companies. Bleicher's study of directors shows that 36% of his sample assume directorship in more than three corporations.[29] Whenever there is spectacular corporate mismanagement, further reduction in the maximum number of directorships is urged, often to five. In the UK 58% of directors assume non-executive directorship positions in other companies and 81% of them hold two to four directorships.[30] In France the legal limit is 8 directorships plus 5 at subsidiary firms. 47% of 13,000 directors have one to thirteen outside director positions, 2% have 14 to 50 positions, according to a survey by Bertolus and Morin.[31]

The question is to what extent they can be counted on to be an effective monitor and advisor. They surely have enough problems in managing their own company. They do not have in-depth knowledge or information on the business and internal problems of the other companies where they serve as outside directors.

Which System Will Win Out?

The inevitable and tempting question which follows from this kind of international comparison is which system has superiority, if any at all, over the other in the long run in the light of two fundamental criteria: efficiency and equity.

Efficiency Perspectives

As for efficiency we have limited evidence but one of the first empirical studies revealing a positive correlation between efficiency and the pluralistic concept of the corporation was offered by Kotter and Heskett.[32] They report that firms with cultures that emphasized the importance of all the stakeholders (customers, stockholders, and employees) outperformed by a huge margin firms that did not (See Figure 5). If sufficient similar evidence is accumulated, we may conclude that the pluralistic concept does enhance a firm's efficiency.

Equity Perspectives

The pluralistic concept seems to be more conducive to an equitable distribution of the firm's income, and fairer sharing of risk and power among the stakeholders. This will increase organizational cohesion and survivability, as we have

11-year growth	Firms emphasising value to customers, shareholders & employees.	Other firms
	%	%
Revenue	682	166
Workforce	282	36
Stock prices	901	74
Income	756	1

Study carried out between August 1987 and January 1991 with 202 US firms.

Based on: John P. Kotter and James L. Heskett *Corporate Culture and Performance*, p.11 (1992).

Figure 5. The pluralistic concept may bring better performance—a US study.

seen in the comparative case studies. Under the monistic concept of the corporation, employees tend to incur a disproportionately higher risk, as their job security is jeopardized in favour of shareholder/manager interests. They are usually the first to bear the brunt of poor decision-making by top management, even if they are not responsible for it. This makes it difficult to expect a high commitment from them, under normal conditions or in crisis situations.

Applicability of the Pluralistic Concept

The pluralistic concept of the corporation may find wider applicability in countries outside Japan and may be a more viable and universal way for the modern corporation to promote efficiency and equity. It is not an ideology unique to Japan. An almost identical concept of the corporation was put forward in 1917 in Germany by Walther Rathenau and in the United States by Adolf Berle/Gardiner Means in 1932, and by Ralph Cordiner in the 50s.

Germany—Walther Rathenau

Walther Rathenau, who was to become Foreign Minister later, succeeded his father as the CEO of the electric engineering firm AEG. In an influential article in 1917 he asserted that 'a big business is not only a product of private interests but it is, individually and collectively, a part of the national economy and of the whole community'.[33] This thesis is believed to have been instrumental in the later development of the concept of 'the firm itself' (*Unternehmen an sich*), which is close to the pluralistic approach. It paved the way for a dilution of shareholder rights, the protection of management positions, the post-World War II co-determination, and the justification of 'hidden reserves' and shares with multiple votes.

USA Adolf Berle/Gardiner Means and Ralph Cordiner

Most probably influenced by Rathenau (quoted twice in their seminal work), Berle and Means conclude their book with exactly the same proposition. In the last chapter titled 'The New Concept of the Corporation', they suggest: 'neither the claims of ownership nor those of control can stand against the paramount interests of the community.... The passive property right (i.e. diffused ownership).... must yield before the largest interests of the society. It is conceivable indeed it seems almost essential if the corporate system is to survive that the 'control' of the great corporation should develop into a purely neutral technocracy, balancing a variety of claims by various groups in the community and assigning to each a portion of the income stream on the basis of the public policy rather than private cupidity'.[34]

A similar ideology was espoused by Ralph Cordiner, CEO of General Electric in the 50s who advocated that top management, as a trustee, was responsible for managing the company 'in the best interest of shareholder, customers, employees, suppliers, and plant community cities'. This concept of the corporation did not last, however, primarily because of the rise of the hostile takeover in the late 1970s, according to Peter Drucker.

Emerging Convergence

The concept of the corporation is firmly rooted in the historic, economic, political and even socio-cultural traditions of the nation. Each approach has its own positive and adverse sides. It would be improbable nor would it be necessary, therefore, that any one concept should drive out another at least in the foreseeable future. Through the cross-fertilization process, nations will be correcting the flaws in their systems, while retaining the core norms. In the process different concepts of the corporation may slowly converge, but certainly not totally. Some signs of such partial convergence are already discernible.

Japan

Japan and Germany are edging towards the Anglo-American model for increased openness and transparency, emphasis of shareholder interest and short-termism. In Japan the traditional emphasis on job security is being eroded and the process seems to be irreversible in the long run for various reasons: firms' tendency to place merit before seniority, perspectives of low growth economy, the changing industrial structure, competitive pressures from the rapidly developing Asian countries, the increasingly detached attitude of young employees to their company, and so on.

Yotaro Kobayashi, Chairman of Fuji Xerox, for instance, made an almost unprecedented declaration for a Japanese executive to the effect that Japanese management giving top priority to employees was no longer tenable. Several companies recently announced their target return on equity to show their emphasis on shareholder wealth. Mitsubishi Corporation has declared that it will raise ROE from currently 0.6% to 8% by the year 2000. Other listed corporations such as Marubeni, Omron, Daikin, etc. are following suit.

The amended Commercial Code came into force on October 1, 1993, albeit under the usual (salutary) pressure from the United States. Every large company is now required to increase the minimum number of statutory auditors from two to three. The newly introduced 'stockholders' representative action' makes it easier for shareholders to bring lawsuits against company directors as the court fee has been fixed at a flat rate of only ¥8,200 per case, regardless of the size of the claim. The number of shareholders eligible for access to confidential financial documents has been expanded to those with at least 3% ownership, down from the former 10%. This revision may be a small step forward but it is still progress.

USA

In the United States, conversely, the traditional restrictions on concentration of funds in a single investment and of board representation at portfolio companies are breaking down. Anti-takeover regulations have been introduced in a number of States, so that the interests of the company i.e. all stakeholders and particularly employees, are taken into account. Employees are regarded as a major stakeholder and are involved in small group activities and share ownership. Long-term business relations are being introduced notably in the automobile industry between subcontractors and assemblers.

Germany

In Germany legislation against insider trading is finally being passed. The US style audit committee is advocated by senior executives (e.g. Schmitz of Deutsche Bank, Mohn of Bertelsmann, etc.) and by scholars (Profs. Luck, Bleicher, etc.) as one of the effective remedies to ensure the proper monitoring of the supervisory board.[35–37] Shareholder activism by Anglo-American institutional shareholders as well as domestic individual shareholders is increasing. In an unprecedented move the CEO and CFO of Metallgesellschaft were simply fired for their responsibility in the alleged mismanagement of oil futures business. Increased reliance on the New York capital markets and the future location of the EU's central bank in Frankfurt am Main will certainly accelerate the Anglo-Americanization process. Disclosure by Daimler Benz of its hidden assets to conform to the SEC regulations for listing on the New York Stock Exchange is symbolic.

Conclusion

The business organization is one of the few social institutions where the deficit of democracy is pronounced, compared with the national governance system. Lack of consensus as to whose interest the company should be promoting, and insufficient checks and balances among various corporate governance mechanisms are some of the evidence. As Prof. Rappaport of the Northwestern University stresses, corporate governance is 'the last frontier of reform' of the public corporation.[38] This reform is a daunting challenge, but it will determine the economic fate of any industrialized nation in the next century.

Appendix

Figures 1 and 2 show the results of two mail surveys. The first was carried out between October and December 1990. The questionnaire in Japanese was sent out to 257 Japanese middle managers of manufacturing firms listed on the First Section of the Tokyo Stock Exchange. The same questionnaire in the English version was sent to 232 French middle managers working in manufacturing and financial sectors in France who are graduates from INSEAD. The usable responses were 68 for the Japanese (a response ratio of 26.5%) and 51 for the French sample (a response ratio of 22%). The project was financed by Cartier Japan. The second mail survey took place January–March 1992 on German, UK, and US samples, middle management in manufacturing and financial sectors. All are graduates from INSEAD. The number of usable responses was 113 for Germany, 80 for the UK, and 86 for the US. The latter project was financed by the International University of Japan while the writer was working there.

References

1. Georg Schreyögg, Unternehmungsverfassung, In H. Corsten (Hrsg.), *Lexikon der Betriebswirtschaftslehre* (1992).
2. Horst Albach, Wertewandel deutscher Manager, In Albach (Hrsg.), *Werte und Unternehmensziele im Wandel der Zeit* (1994).
3. Peter Drucker, Reckoning with the Pension Fund Revolution, *Harvard Business Review*, March–April (1991).
4. Michael E. Porter, *Competitive Strategy* (1980).
5. Sadahiko Suzuki and Richard W. Wright, Financial Structure and Bankruptcy Risk in Japanese Companies, *Journal of International Business Studies*, Spring (1985).
6. James Abbeglen and George Stalk, *Kaisha, the Japanese Corporation*, (1985).
7. Paul Sheard, The Main Bank System and Corporate Monitoring and Control in Japan, *Journal of Economic Behavior and Organization* **11** (1989).
8. Keimei Wakasugi *et al.*, An Empirical Study on the Attitudes toward Cross-Shareholdings, *Shoken Analyst Journal*, May (1994) (in Japanese).
9. Asahi Shimbun, August 6 (1994).
10. Richard Pascale and Thomas P. Rohlen, The Mazda Turnaround, *Journal of Japanese Studies* **9–2** (1983).
11. Iacocca, *Iacocca* (1984).

12. Robert B. Reich and John D. Donahue, *New Deals—The Chrysler Revival and the American System* (1985).
13. Amar Bhide, Efficient Markets, Deficient Governance, *Harvard Business Review*, Nov–Dec (1994).
14. Mark J. Roe, A Political Theory of American Corporate Finance, *Columbia Law Review* **91** (10) (1991).
15. John C. Coffee, Liquidity versus Control: The Institutional Investor as Corporate Monitor, *Columbia Law Review* **91**, 1277 (1991).
16. E. R. Schneider-Linné, Corporate Control in Germany, *Oxford Review of Economic Policy* **8** (3) (1992).
17. Jeremy Edwards and Klaus Fischer, *Banks, Finance and Investment in Germany* (1994).
18. The Japanese Institute of Statutory Auditors, The Results of a Survey on General Meeting of Shareholders, *Kansayaku*, September (1994) (in Japanese).
19. Toyo Keizai Shimposha, *Yakain Shikihou* (Directory of Directors) (1994) (in Japanese).
20. K. Ito, The Current Situation and the Tasks of Corporate Governance, *Kigyo Kaikei* **46** (2) (1994) (in Japanese).
21. R. L. Tricker, *Corporate Governance* (1984).
22. P. L. Rechner and D.R. Dalton, The Impact of CEO as Board Chairperson on Corporate Performance: Evidence vs. Rhetoric, *The Academy of Management Executive* **III** (2) (1989).
23. Korn Ferry International, *Board of Directors—UK* (1991).
24. Elmar Gerum, Aufsichtsratstypen Ein Beitrag zur Theorie der Organisation der Unternehmensführung, *Die Betriebswirtschaft* 6 (1991).
25. Korn Ferry International, *Board of Directors* (1986).
26. Michael Cassel, Blueprint for Good Boardroom Practice, *Financial Times*, 28 October (1991).
27. Gérard Charreaux and Jean-Pierre Pitol-Belin, *Le Conseil d'administration* (1990).
28. G.R. Bassiry and Hrair Denkmejian, The American Corporate Elite: A Profile, *Business Horizons*, May–June (1990).
29. Knut Bleicher, *Der Aufsichtsrat im Wandel* (1987).
30. Tom Nash, Bit Parts and Board Games, *Director*, October (1990).
31. Jean-Jérôme Bertolus and Françoise Morin, Conseil d'Administration, *Science et Vie Economie* **33**, November (1987).
32. John P. Kotter and James L. Heskett, *Corporate Culture and Performance* (1992).
33. Walther Rathenau, *Vom Aktienwesen, eine geschäftliche Betrachtung* (1923).
34. Adolf A. Berle and Gardiner C. Means, *The Modern Corporation and Private Property*, Transaction Publishers (1991).
35. Ronald Schmitz, Aspekte der Aufsichtsratsverfassung im Lichte der Krise der Metallgesellschaft, Paper presented at the Handelsblatt Conference on Aufsichtsrat in Frankfurt am Main on 12 September (1994).
36. Wolfgang Lück, Audit Committee–Eine Einrichtung zur Effizienzsteigerung betriebswirtschaftlicher Überwachungssyteme?, *Zeitschrift für Betriebswirtschaftliche Forschung* **12** (1990).
37. Interview with Reinhard Mohn in *Manager Magazin* **8** (1993).
38. Alfred Rappaport, The Staying Power of the Public Corporation, *Harvard Business Review*, Jan–Feb (1990).

8

Partnership with an Asian Family Business—What Every Multinational Corporation Should Know

P. Narayan Pant and Vasant G. Rajadhyaksha

The family-controlled firm and the state-owned enterprise are the most common ownership structures in Asia. Foreign firms seeking local joint venture partners in Asia will, of necessity, face the prospect of allying with family-controlled firms. Family control in firms creates special concerns that alliance partners should anticipate. Signs of family stability, well-laid succession plans and clearly demarcated professional decision-making represent attractive characteristics for foreign partners. This article will examine the implications of these and other features for alliance partners, using case studies from Indian business. It will also suggest useful sources from which potential partners can obtain information on family-controlled firms.

Many people believe that countries in the Asian region will lead global rates of growth well into the next century. Asian consumers with their increasing share of world purchasing power are only part of the picture. Skilled and relatively

Dr P. Narayan Pant is Lecturer in Business Policy at the National University of Singapore. Vasant G. Rajadhyaksha is an ex-Chairman and CEO of Hindustan Lever, the Indian subsidiary of Unilever, and a former member of the Indian Planning Commission.

inexpensive workforces are rapidly converting Asian locations into important hubs in global networks of production and R & D. This has prompted several multinational firms to enter different countries in the region.

Alliances with local firms provide multinationals with cost-effective platforms for entering these new countries.[1,2] Local partners can provide foreign firms with valuable skills needed to operate in their markets. In return, foreign firms provide access to international markets and technologies not always available to local firms.

The dominant non-governmental business structure in Asia is the family-controlled firm.[3–5] Hence, in alliances between foreign and Asian firms, the Asian partner will often be a family-controlled firm. Family control creates special features that affect alliance success.[6,7] Family firms are particularly susceptible to ambiguity in succession mechanisms.[8,9] The intrusion of family roles into the professional sphere,[10] poor demarcations of responsibility and the resultant lack of clarity about where decisions get made[11–13] create problems for family firms.

This article takes a look at the particular concerns that Indian family-controlled firms present for their foreign partners. Similar issues could also affect family firms in other parts of Asia. Indeed some peculiarities of family firms, such as their poor record at managing succession, are the same all over the world. Even so, cultural differences in areas such as inheritance norms and differential treatments of male and female children restrict the generalizability of some of the points made here.

The next section reviews issues pertinent to the management of family businesses anywhere. The third section looks at the consequences of these issues for firms proposing to ally with family firms in India. Next we discuss an additional issue—the process of allying, suggesting that how firms enter an alliance affects the alliance's success. The penultimate section suggests sources of information on family firms and is followed by a brief conclusion.

Key Issues in the Administration of Family Businesses

Authors disagree about the definitions of family businesses or family-controlled firms. A recent study argued that a family firm was any firm in which the owners could transfer ownership and control to subsequent generations of their own families.[14] In India in particular, and Asia in general, majority ownership is not always a prerequisite for control to pass from one generation to another of the same family. For instance, the Tata family does not hold majority shares in all firms linked by the Tata name. Yet effective control over the Tata group has rested in the hands of a Tata for the greater part of a century. Hence we will view a family-controlled firm or group as one where effective control rests in the hands of a group of individuals related by family ties.

The Succession Issue

Poor succession management potentially affects all firms, not just those which are family-controlled.[15] Few organizations possess transparent succession policies which enjoy widespread credibility.[16] The rare firms that do possess credible succession plans receive consistent shareholder approval.[17]

In family-held firms poorly managed succession often leads to failure.[18] Two-thirds of all family firms in the USA fail to survive the transition to new management.[19] Leaders refrain from planning their succession, or from announcing their succession plans, creating tremendous uncertainty for all stakeholders. Anointed successors may prove unable, unwilling or be denied the opportunity to perform their task. Family disgruntlement over the choice of successor also militates against their success.

In Family Firms Familial Relations May Override Competence

Family-controlled firms usually do not have clearly understood rules for promoting family members.[20,21] For instance, Liem Sioe Liong's son Anthony Salim was only 'understood' to be his father's successor in Indonesia's giant Salim group, but held no formal position.[22]

This apparent disregard for professionalism sparks the concern that family ties rather than capabilities will determine appointments in family firms.[23,24] However, the relevant issue is not so much a concern that family firms employ family members, but the issue of how they employ them.

India's changing competitive environment has prompted several prominent business families to send members of younger generations for professional training. Far-sighted leaders have even seen appropriate training as reason to bypass traditional succession patterns. G. D. Birla of India's Birla group left the business to his grandson rather than to anyone in the immediate generation. Similarly the younger Shrenik was chosen to head the Lalbhai group rather than older brother Siddharth. Hence even traditional family firms are placing greater emphasis on capability as they appoint family members to important positions.

Authority Does Not Always Coincide with Position

Formal titles can be poor indicators of where decision-making authority resides in the family firm. Even when senior family members retire from formal positions of authority, they may continue to wield substantial influence and even control. Non-family members credited with expertise in specific areas can command the trust of family members, also without occupying formal positions in their organizations.

The prevalence of informal lines of authority and decision-making in family firms means that the real decision-makers are not always obvious to outsiders.

Foreign partners need to ensure that family members negotiating with them enjoy the support of the real power brokers in the family.

The foregoing issues have often been addressed in the literature on family-controlled firms. However, unique conditions in different parts of the world demand unique responses. The following paragraphs highlight ways to deal with these issues in alliances between family-controlled firms in India and partners from other countries.

What to do About These Issues Before Allying with a Family Firm

The importance of the following factors will clearly vary depending on the nature of the potential association. A one-off transfer of technology in return for a fee will not ordinarily be critically dependent on stability in the leadership of the purchaser. Not all longer associations are critically dependent on the local partners either. When the role of the family business is limited to providing access to local contacts, making infrastructural arrangements or local equity contributions, leadership stability will not be critical. Only when the family-controlled partner becomes responsible for operational issues such as marketing, finance or production does stability in leadership become critical for survival.

Often, the leadership of a family business is the business and the expertise manifested in the leadership is the very reason for the association with the firm. In such instances foreign partners should ensure that the leadership is stable and unlikely to topple at short notice. Since no leader lasts forever, they should also convince themselves that their proposed ally possesses adequate succession plans. Finally, succession plans themselves are not much use if the potential candidates do not appear promising.

Ensure that the Current Leader is Stable

Any alliances concluded with a weak family chief will be suspect. Leadership in India is often absolute. Heads of families have the final say in all decisions pertaining to the group of companies they control. A new family head will normally review all agreements concluded by the former family head, sometimes purely as a means of establishing his authority over the family. The following factors influence the stability of the family leader.

1. *How Much of the Business is Owned by the Family Leader?* A leader who owns a significant portion of a family group's businesses will be immeasurably more powerful than one who must rely on the support of other shareholders to govern. The latter situation will become increasingly common as family firms age and family shareholdings are divided among several individuals. A large share in the family business is often the strongest factor legitimating a

leader. Leaders who do not enjoy this advantage must rely on other attributes to shore up their legitimacy.

2. *How Direct is the Leader's Connection to the Founder of the Business?* A more appropriate lineage can also legitimate a leader. Families often evaluate contending claims to leadership as if they were evaluating claims to a throne. Consequently, individuals with a more direct connection to the founder bypass more capable managers. Even when a capable manager secures the leadership, the presence of more direct descendants could pose an ongoing threat to the leader. The potential successor in the case study in Box 1 will, therefore, continue to face a leadership challenge from others who feel they have a legitimate claim to his position.

3. *How Long has the Current Leader Been in the Position?* Endurance is a good proxy for managerial experience. Leaders survive for longer periods often

---

Box 1
My father was closer to granddad than your father

A scion of a wealthy Indian family founded a financial services firm in the early 1930s. One of the first of its kind in the country, the firm thrived and grew steadily through the 1940s. The founder had children of his own, as well as several nephews and nieces and was the undisputed leader of the extended family. He observed the progress of various family members through school and college and spent some time discussing the business with them.

When the time came to choose a successor, the founder chose a younger nephew rather than any of his own sons or daughters. Nonetheless all the cousins had significant stakes in the business and the chosen leader depended upon the support of all in order to run the business. The business was still small relative to the family's wealth and its dividends represented a small part of their income.

The new leader, or Managing Director (MD), proved to be a very successful manager and nurtured the firm to become one of the largest in India in its specialized area of financial services. As the firm grew, the other income of the family shrank. By the late 1970s, the dividends of the firm became the family's most important source of income. The power and the perks enjoyed by the MD began to generate jealousy and resentment amongst several male family members. Their rancor increased when many perceived the MD's son to be the most competent member of the next generation and an obvious successor. Some members of the family then attempted to break up the company so as to obtain a larger share in its running for themselves. They failed because the strong general consensus in the family still favored the MD and his son.

After this aborted breakup, the company has seemingly settled back into its successful trajectory. The apparent resolution of the succession issue has attracted several Indian and foreign firms who have offered to contribute to the company's capital base.

because they possess the capability to weather organizational and environmental crises. In family concerns endurance also indicates the ability to manage divergent family interests, often a more difficult task. Leaders who have endured longer, therefore, will receive greater legitimacy both within and outside their organizations.

At least two variables substitute for length of tenure as a legitimating factor. The first is the support given by a past leader with great legitimacy to a less experienced successor. Such support helps provide new leaders the respite needed to acquire legitimacy of their own accord. Secondly, the degree of success attained by the new leader can also substitute for length of tenure. The case study in Box 2 describes just such an instance where an unorthodox successor succeeded in acquiring legitimacy, first through the support of the earlier leader and later through his own success.

4. *How Well Trained is the Current Leader?* Formal training or experience in a given industry is not always the most important or even a necessary criterion in a partner. Given the brevity of industrial history in many parts of Asia, such experience may be hard to come by. However, since the final say-so on most issues in family businesses rests with the head, leaders with more appropriate training present more attractive alliance prospects than others.

Box 2

He may be young but he's got what it takes

An older son of a textile firm's founder distinguished himself as an outstanding entrepreneur, building one of the larger industrial empires in India. As long as he lived, this second generation entrepreneur was accepted by the entire family, including his siblings who had substantial stakes in the company, as the ultimate decision maker in the group.

This leader felt that his most capable relative was a grandson, a young man in his twenties, and he left the largest collection of firms in the group in the grandson's charge. The remaining firms in the group were formally divided among other family members. Such was the respect commanded by the architect of the group that no family member questioned his decision.

Things could have changed after the old man's death. The nature of intercorporate investments in the group meant that other family members owned a large stake in the group of companies run by the grandson. However, the grandson fully lived up to his grandfather's expectations and even his uncles and cousins acknowledged him as the ablest manager of all. The confidence of the family in his leadership has extended to his appointment of successor—his son, a young man in his late twenties.

This family group's ability to make such enlightened decisions has helped generate an enviable track record. Coupled with a credible succession plan, the group today presents an attractive opportunity for future foreign collaboration.

How Stable are the Succession Processes?

Even though the proposed project may be of short duration, potential partners need to be clear about what might happen were the current leader of the organization to leave suddenly. Several variables influence the stability of the likely succession process.

1. *How Many Potential Successors are There?* More than one clear contender for the leadership will create turmoil at the time of transition. Potential contenders come from several groups in family firms.

   At the first level, all managers at the level reporting to the incumbent leader could consider themselves potential replacements. Most family organizations work with the understanding that non-family members, including those who attain high levels of responsibility, are not eligible for the top job. However, where such understanding is absent, even non-family members may entertain hopes of leading the organization.

   Sometimes, family members not involved in the business during the time of the incumbent leader may present themselves as potential candidates for, if not the top job, at least key roles in management. The case study in Box 3 describes how members of a family which owned significant stock in a company attempted to lay claim to operational control that they had never had, once their company started to perform well.

   Although less common in India, and indeed in Asia, even female family members could choose the uncertainty surrounding transition to assert their claim to involvement in the business. Spouses or daughters who bore responsibilities of leadership informally while the incumbent was present, could seek to formalize their roles once the incumbent departed.

   The greater the number of potential contenders, the more turbulent will be a family firm's passage across a leadership transition.

2. *Are the Potential Successors Arranged in a Hierarchy?* The more ambiguous the relative positions of potential successors to the chief executive, the greater the problems they will present at the time of transition. Potential successors arranged in a hierarchy are more likely to be sanguine about the individual at the top replacing the incumbent leader. The case study in Box 4 contrasts two companies, one with a hierarchy among successors and one with no hierarchy. The company with no hierarchy had to go into arbitration before the succession could be resolved. The company with a hierarchy, though unorthodox, fared much better.

   Custom may decree the absence of hierarchy in some family businesses. Where the custom among families is that of primogeniture, hierarchies may exist and indeed prove a stabilizing factor during transition. In other communities where such imperatives are absent, firms may rarely survive in their original shapes after a transition in leadership.[25]

3. *How Credible is the Chosen Successor?* Overt choice of a successor by an incumbent helps the latter establish legitimacy. However, the credibility of the choice affects the ease with which the successor actually makes the transition. Once again, the factors that enable an incumbent leader to maintain legitimacy—extent of shareholding, performance, lineage, training—will play similar roles in establishing the credibility of the successor.

Box 3

Biding your time to 'claim what is yours'

A foreign firm and a local Indian entrepreneur founded an engineering firm as a joint venture in the 1940s. The Indian partner had neither the ability nor the desire to actively manage the joint venture. In time the firm became very successful in its particular niche. Restrictive policies toward foreign investment in the 1960s and 1970s forced the foreign partner to withdraw from India, and they offered their majority share to the Indian partner at a very reasonable price. However, the Indian partner possessed neither the resources to purchase the firm nor the desire to run it, and the management began looking for an external buyer for the foreign partner's share.

The CEO of the firm enjoyed the confidence of his management and employees. As a result, when he proposed that the employees should buy out the foreign partner, they concurred and in effect became the majority shareholders of the company. Senior managers were appointed to the Board as full-time directors and the most senior was appointed MD. An older member of the original Indian partner's family, who continued to hold a minority share in the firm, was named part-time Chairman with no operational role. After the departure of the foreign partner, the company flourished and became one of India's largest and best run firms in its industry.

In time, male members of the next generation of the founding family began to demand a greater role in the daily management of the company. They felt that their family's shareholding entitled them to seats on the Board as well as executive responsibility comparable to that held by other full-time directors. Most others felt that the current lot of family members was unfit for executive responsibility. This difference of opinion threatened to end up in the courts, but the family desisted upon discovering that it would lose the case.

This attempt by the family to re-establish their claim over the running of the company prompted the MD to ensure that it could not happen again. He strengthened the Board with an external non-executive chair and eminent professionals as part-time directors, thus squelching further dissent from the family completely. The company has since collaborated successfully with engineering firms in the USA and Europe, exploiting opportunities in India and elsewhere.

How Ready is the Next Generation?

Several family businesses do survive transitions in leadership. The most common price paid for survival is the breakup of a conglomerate entity into several components controlled by different family members. This is not, however, the

---

Box 4

The importance of clear hierarchies at succession time

Case A

A large family-owned and -run group started businesses in textiles and sugar. Until the mid-1970s a strong patriarchal figure led the group, taking it into areas such as fertilizers, synthetic fibres, inorganic chemicals and even consumer durables. The founder died without either nominating or building up a credible successor.

Upon the founder's death quarrels broke out between several potential contenders for the leadership post. This generated bitterness and infighting that lasted for over a year. Eventually the group agreed to accept the decision of an external arbitrator whose job it would be to carve out companies held by the group and award them to contending factions. The awards made by the arbitrator were to be final. The arbitrator chosen was a friend of the founder and his sons, and occupied a position of some eminence in industry in his own right. After much consultation the arbitrator arrived at an award that seemed to divide resentment among all aspirants as equally as possible.

The costs of this hiatus in the functioning of the group were severe. The period of infighting coupled with the wait for the arbitrator's decision meant that the group collectively experienced no growth for over 2 years. Several companies in the group went into the red from which they have as yet to emerge. Though some stronger companies in the group have recovered, the group as a whole enjoys a mere shadow of its earlier respect and market presence.

Case B

The founder of a small chemical company started in the 1930s decided that one of his younger sons showed the greatest potential to follow in his footsteps. In the late 1940s, he sent the chosen son to the USA for post-graduate studies in business, an unusually progressive step among Indian business families of that time.

When the son returned to India his father encouraged him to take a starting managerial position in a well-known multinational operating in the same industry as the family business. Soon thereafter, he left the multinational to rejoin his family business as its MD. An elder brother became non-executive chair with the implicit understanding that his role was to be titular only, and that the MD would make all operational decisions. The founder died shortly afterwards. A few years later the family consolidated the MD's position by appointing him to chair the Board.

Today the company is one of the largest players in its segment of the Indian chemicals industry. Two multinational world leaders recently vied with one another to enter a joint venture with this Indian company. The firm has formed a new venture with one of its suitors, agreeing to share equity equally but retaining management control with the Indian CEO. Keeping with tradition, the MD has further designated as his own successor an individual generally accepted to be the most qualified to take over the family business.

end of their concerns. Their chances of survival will depend upon the following key characteristics of their new leaders.

1. *Their Training.* Average levels of formal education have risen dramatically in Asia. Therefore, later generations of leaders in family businesses will likely possess more formal education than earlier ones. Formal education itself does not indicate more than a family's ability to spare a child from productive employment until after they complete their education. With the proliferation of educational institutions in India, the most expensive aspect of a college degree is its opportunity cost rather than its direct cost.

   However, specialized education is often a credible indicator of a family's commitment to a field. A family with a business in manufacturing may encourage its next generation to acquire specialized education in some aspects of engineering. Part of their justification may be to reduce their dependence on outsiders with specialized knowledge. However, the presence of several such highly and appropriately trained people among potential successors to a leader speaks strongly of family commitment to the business.

2. *Their Business Experience.* Experience that might ease a successor's transition to leadership comes in several forms. Some incumbents have non-family senior managers train chosen successors, avoiding problems arising from a confusion of family and professional roles. Others prefer to give potential successors complete responsibility for some unit of the business. Others require potential successors to 'work their way up' the organization, performing apprenticeships in different branches of the family's business. There may not be much to choose between these various modes of experience. However, the seriousness that families expect apprentices to bring to their training—always hard for an outsider to evaluate—will ultimately determine its utility.

Other Questions to Ask

How one enters an alliance with a family firm can often be as important as with whom. The following paragraphs expand briefly on implications of different modes of initiating an alliance.

Who Invited You or Whom Did You Approach?

The identity of the first contact within a family firm says a lot about the seriousness with which a family will view a proposed project. By the very nature of family organizations there are several individuals in the organization with impressive sounding titles who do not necessarily enjoy the confidence of the family. A title such as Director (Special Projects) could imply only that the individual with the title has no operational responsibility. Consequently, a proposal presented via such an individual may risk not attracting the serious attention it might merit.

Although foreign partners have little control over their first contact, they do have control over what follows. They should seek details of the structure of their proposed partners' organizations. Knowing the relative power of different branches of the family, and hence the implications of going into business with one branch rather than another, will help an informed decision. Often different branches of families may even operate under the same name while enjoying varied levels of expertise, reputation and capability.

If Not the Family Head, Then How is Your Contact Connected to Him?

Initial contacts will rarely be through the heads of organizations, nor should partners expect early negotiations to involve them. However, the identity of the individual assigned to liaise with the partner indicates the seriousness with which the family takes the project. The closer an individual is in the hierarchy to the head of the family, the greater the importance probably accorded to the project.

Again, the individual concerned does not have to be a blood relative of the head, nor even a family member. In some instances, particularly when the leader of a family group is young, potential successors may not merit important responsibilities such as negotiating with foreign partners. In such instances the job could fall to a trusted lieutenant or long-time aide. What is important in such an instance is to attempt to establish how close the individual is to the head of the concern.

Will Other Members of the Family be Adversely Affected?

When a family comprises several branches, a project sponsored by one branch often will not receive the unqualified support of other branches. The case study in Box 5 describes a situation where two brothers carried their mutual hostility to a point where one ended up helping the other's competitors.

In less dramatic instances, issues such as relative prestige may be at stake. Family branches raise or lower their relative prestige and consequent ability to attract uncommitted family resources, along with the degree of success enjoyed by the enterprises they manage.

Succession to the leadership may also depend on how well various contenders perform. The current head may formally or informally create the perception that his successor will be the individual who shows the greatest promise, based on past success. Then, the success of a particular individual may reflect poorly on competitors for the top job. While dramatic acts of sabotage may be unlikely when all members of the family benefit from one branch's success, the project will not receive the support of individuals adversely affected in a leadership contest.

Box 5

Family feud

An engineering firm started business in the early 1970s, assisted by equity participation and technological assistance from a well-known foreign firm. It began manufacturing a range of machines far superior in quality and service to any then made in India. By the early 1980s its name had become synonymous with that class of machines. Liberalization of economic policy in the early 1990s saw a surge in competition, with several joint ventures set up in India featuring the best international names. Also customs duties fell drastically, dramatically raising the competitive climate overnight.

To make matters worse, the company's foreign collaborator was acquired by a firm who subsequently showed no interest in the Indian joint venture and sold its shares to a large Indian business house. This new partner, unlike the original foreign promoters, began to take an active interest in running the business and within months had ousted the founder. The founder's considerable experience and reputation helped persuade another large foreign firm—one of the biggest names in the field—to set up a new joint venture with him.

During the turbulent times when the founder was trying to retain control over his firm, his two sons quarreled and the father openly supported the older brother. When the new joint venture was formed, different parts of the business were divided among the two sons. A separate company, controlled by the younger son, was to run one of the joint venture's three factories supplying needed components at an agreed transfer price.

The bitterness between the two brothers escalated to the point where the younger attempted to become independent of his elder brother's joint venture by selling his products to competing firms. The costs of this defection were severe since the younger son took with him valuable knowledge of manufacturing techniques, acquired when he was technical director of his father's first company. Not only did bad blood cause one family firm to lose an important supplier, but the supplier's knowledge effectively strengthened the competition.

What is the Culture of Your Potential Partner?

Industries established a long time ago, such as jute and cotton textiles, often show little change in their organizational cultures from the time they were established. As a consequence, the working environment that a foreign partner would face in such an old firm is likely to be more alien than the average working environment in India. The case study in Box 6 describes an instance of a company where the leadership appears capable, and indeed possesses the will and support for change. However, the deeply rooted culture of an old and traditional organization poses barriers to change.

Box 6
When culture resists change

A family firm started manufacturing textiles in the early 1920s and prospered due to the entrepreneurial skills of its founder. In the 1960s the firm successfully diversified into a range of chemicals and engineering products. Some of the new businesses were managed almost entirely by foreign firms, their largest shareholders. These latter firms adopted highly professional cultures in contrast to the older ones that were still run traditionally, with decisions taken solely by the founder or, later, by his eldest son.

The companies managed by foreign partners performed very well for the next 20 years. The others did too except during recessions when losses were greater than necessary. The Indian licensing system effectively stifled competition and protected weak firms. Once licensing and other controls were removed and trade barriers lowered in the early 1990s, the traditional companies in the group began to flounder. Decades of personalized management had created layers of deadwood that made it difficult to run the companies successfully.

Recently the family's next generation acquired control of the group. A direct descendant of the founder, a young man with training in corporate management at Harvard, inherited the largest portion of the group of companies. His uncles had separated from the group previously, each taking a few companies with him.

The new CEO has set about trying to bring about the necessary managerial transformation in the group of hitherto traditionally run firms that he has inherited. The degree of success he has obtained has enabled him to attract internationally renowned partners. However, the age profile of managers in the older firms in the group and their deeply rooted traditional cultures, prevent the companies from doing as well as they could.

Getting Information—the Hardest Part

We have suggested several different concerns relevant to a foreign partner allying with a family business in India. Information addressing some of these concerns might not always be available in the public domain.

When potential partners are publicly listed, statutory information provides broad structural details and little more. Rarely, however, is detailed shareholder information available and it is this information that might indicate who possesses the real power in a family.

Ultimate control may also be exercised through a family dominated holding group, and information on such groups is rarely available publicly. Even when it is, the information may only be able to suggest the identities of important family decision-makers. It is unlikely to reveal details about trusted aides and other key advisors. Finally, the nature of the succession plans envisaged by the organization, if any, need not be common knowledge, even within the organization.

Alternative sources of information include formal and informal sources. Sometimes family members who approach potential partners may themselves be quite forthcoming about where the true authority in their families reposes. The information they provide can be corroborated in at least three ways.

The business press in many parts of Asia has acquired considerable sophistication. Almost always, family disputes and disagreements provide grist for its mills. Computer-based searches of past issues of publications are often possible and yield substantial information. Information obtained from the press requires careful handling since many countries in Asia do not possess or enforce libel laws with as much rigor as do western countries. Consequently journalists receive greater license with their stories than they would elsewhere. As with information received from family members, information from the press also requires corroboration.

Stock-brokers and market-makers in the stocks of a given family group will often possess information about them that may not be publicly available. Merchant bankers, financial lending institutions and company solicitors are other useful sources. In addition, commercial banks headquartered in the country of the foreign partner who have branches in the host country will usually provide companies from their home country with useful information. Informality and discretion in such data-gathering are essential, naturally, since the knowledge that a group is the target of negotiations with a foreign partner is likely to be valuable to interested parties.

Finally, local management consultants are good sources of information on the workings of family groups. They often have access to information privy to the local business community and not commonly available outside.

Conclusions

This article began with two premises. It argued that Asian markets will attract increasing interest from western firms who see them as part of a larger global strategy. Since alliances with local firms constitute cost-effective modes of entry into untried markets, the predominance of family control in Asian firms will lead to western firms allying with Asian family-controlled firms.

Using the example of India, we suggested that family control requires potential western partners to be cognizant of special factors in the family groups with which they propose to do business.

The identity, strength and support enjoyed by the chief executive of the group will directly influence the likely success of projects sponsored by the group. The existence of succession plans, the number of potential successors and their levels of training and experience constitute other factors that influence a family group's attractiveness as partners. Obviously, some of these factors override others in this array of contingencies, and strong positives on some grounds might be a reason to ignore some negatives.

We also observed that the mode through which a given proposal enters an organization is important to its likely success. The identity of the family member who transmits the proposal and the individual assigned to negotiate indicate the importance given to the project and hence its likely success. Information on these and other issues relevant to alliances is now increasingly available from multiple sources.

References

1. B. Kogut, The stability of joint ventures: reciprocity and competitive rivalry, *The Journal of of Industrial Economics* **38**, 183–198 (1989).
2. C. Oliver, Determinants of interorganizational relationships: integration and future directions. *Academy of Management Review* **15** 241–265 (1990).
3. T. T. Chau, Approaches to succession in Asian business organizations, *Family Business Review* **4**, 161–179 (1991).
4. S. R. Clegg, S. R. and S. G. Redding, *Capitalism in Contrasting Cultures,* Walter de Gruyter, New York (1990).
5. C. F. Yang, Familism and development: an examination of the role of family in contemporary China Mainland, Hong Kong, and Taiwan, In D. Sinha and H. S. R. Kao (eds), *Social Values and Development,* pp. 93–123, Sage, New Delhi (1988).
6. R. Beckhard and W. G. Dyer Jr, Managing change in the family firm—issues and strategies, *Sloan Management Review* **24** (3), 59–65 (1983) .
7. K. M. File, R. A. Prince and M. J. Rankin, Organization buying behavior of the family firm, *Family Business Review* **7**, 263–272 (1994).
8. W. C. Handler, Succession in the family business: a review of the research, *Family Business Review* **7**, 133–157 (1994).
9. J. A. Sonnenfeld, *The Hero's Farewell: What Happens When CEOs Retire,* Oxford University Press, Oxford (1988).
10. P. C. Rosenblatt, L. de Mik, R. M. Anderson and P. A. Johnson, *The Family in Business*, Jossey-Bass, San Francisco, CA (1985).
11. P. Alcorn, *Success and Survival in the Family-owned Business*, McGraw-Hill, New York (1982).
12. M. Harvey and R. Evans, Life after succession in the family business: is it really the end of problems? *Family Business Review* **8**, 3–16 (1995).
13. J. R. Mancuso, and N. Shulman, *Running a Family Business*, Prentice Hall, New York (1991).
14. J. L. Ward, *Keeping the Family Business Healthy*, Jossey-Bass, San Francisco, CA (1987).
15. Heirs and races, *The Economist* **69**, 9 March (1991).
16. C. Getty, Planning successfully for succession planning, *Training and Development* **47**, 31–33 (1993).
17. W. N. Davidson lil, D. L. Worrell and Dutia D., *Journal of Management* **19**, 517–533 (1993).
18. R. Beckhard and W. G. Dyer Jr, *op. cit.* (1983).
19. E. Davis, Long live the business, *Small Business Reports* 17, 30–40 (1992).
20. P. Alcorn, *op. cit.* (1982).
21. R. Fritz, *The Entrepreneurial Family*, McGraw-Hill, New York (1992).
22. A. Rowley, Birth of a multinational, *Far Eastern Economic Review*, 44–56, 7 April (1983).
23. C. E. Aronoff and J. L. Ward, Rules for nepotism, *Nation's Business* **81**, 64–65 (1993).
24. M. F. R. Kets de Vries, The dynamics of family controlled firms: the good and the bad news, *Organizational Dynamics* **21**, 59–71 (1993).
25. T. T. Chau, *op. cit.* (1991).

9

Strategic Alliances in Fast-moving Markets

Victor Newman and Kazem Chaharbaghi

The pace of technological change and market shifts is forcing organizations to reconsider their strategies for creating sustainable competitive advantage. Strategic alliances focused on destabilizing market values are currently the most effective source of sustainable competitive advantage. The purpose of this article is to explain how successful strategic alliances can be arranged in fast-moving markets.

The myths surrounding strategic alliances in fast-moving markets are embedded in the problem of language and metaphor. Whereas new ideas are often perceived as the equivalent of the Emperor's new clothes, the literature on strategic alliances seems to make a virtue of everyone, not just the emperor, walking around naked. Like the millenarian doctrine,[1] it suggests that business heaven on earth might be achieved through some form of brotherhood and sharing.[2, 3] This confusion is compounded by the mistaken use of the marriage metaphor to represent alliance partnerships which is often linked with myths of the virtual enterprise and the problem of inflexible organizational mindsets fastening onto

Dr. Victor Newman is the Head of Organization Development at the CIM Institute, Cranfield University, UK. Dr. Kazem Chaharbaghi leads Strategic and International Management at East London Business School, University of East London, UK.
*The models and frameworks developed in this article are the product of knowledge gained through consulting work in developing partnership alliances for British Aerospace, Moog Controls International and General Motors (Europe), the application of thinking about learning organizations and recent Ph.D. research at Cranfield into the nature of the relationship between product innovation and process efficiency.

the complementary nature of strategic alliances. In other words, if organizations can create a complementary alliance they will not have to change themselves, making a virtue out of their weakness.

The danger of focusing on optimizing existing organizational processes instead of concentrating on developing the ability to deliver product innovation is being increasingly realized. The optimization mindset has led organizations to restructure in order to protect markets by combining new competencies or adopting defensive strategies. As a result, organizations have distanced themselves from innovating which is the real source of delivering new market values. The problem with the optimization mindset therefore lies in an unwillingness to understand that sustainable competitive advantage is the result of continually engineering instability into market values through innovating. In other words, the real competitive strategy is about doing new things rather than focusing on optimizing the way things are currently done. The prevailing misconception concerning strategic alliances has been to see them as the opportunity to optimize existing generic and stable products instead of the creation of new market values. Strategic alliances are often used as the next step for survival. That is, if the organization cannot compete effectively then it has to become partner dependent. Although this approach may prolong life, it will not lead to sustainable competitive advantage. The risks are considerable in the long term and include the potential erosion of knowledge leadership and loss of mobility through being tied to allies who can grow into competitors. The search for sustainable competitive advantage is a necessary illusion in providing the psychology of direction to drive and respond to change. The problem for optimizers is to bury the optimization mindset and to learn how continually to destabilize market values in order to sustain competitive advantage. Strategic alliances are purely a mechanism for managing this destabilization process and not an endgame.

Purpose of Strategic Alliances

A key driver for creating and sustaining strategic alliances will be a shared perception of opportunity, potential impact on market values, high returns and low exit barriers. Strategic alliances happen because they have to happen, with each party having something to offer which makes a marked difference. They also take place because they deliver focus without stretching each party's resources. They are effective when each party is not threatened and when they do not limit freedom for future moves. Alliances collapse when the conditions that supported working together change.

As shown in Figure 1, strategic alliances can be located along a continuum where extremes represent defensive and offensive competitive strategies. The former focuses on stabilizing existing market values while the latter aims at destabilizing and thus creating new market values. The defensive strategy often

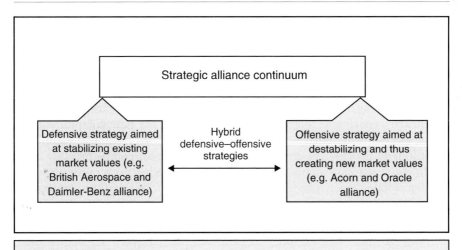

Figure 1. Strategic alliance continuum.

takes the form of protection of existing capacity and markets, exemplified by the proposed alliance of British Aerospace with Daimler-Benz in the field of military aircraft production.[4] Such an alliance provides a powerful catalyst for creating a European defence industry that can compete both economically and politically with its American counterpart, avoiding the need for further rationalization and cost cutting at British Aerospace and Daimler-Benz. Politically it will imply that European governments will find it more difficult to buy equivalent military aircraft from non-European manufacturers, thus protecting their capacity and markets. Strategic alliances can also take an offensive form, particularly in fast-moving markets. Offensive alliances are driven both by speed and by the need to integrate disparate knowledge resources to create new market values where the resulting product has to combine different forms of knowledge which could not possibly be owned by a single organization. In other words, it is a necessity. A prime example is the alliance between Acorn and Oracle[5] threatening Microsoft and Intel's dominance in desktop computing through the development of network computing, shifting the users away from desktop computers towards easy to use programmes transmitted over the Internet or corporate computer networks.[6] Between the two extremes of the continuum in Figure 1 numerous examples can be found which combine both aspects of offensive and defensive alliances with some being closer to defensive than offensive strategy and vice versa. An example of hybrid defensive–offensive alliance is that of Rover and Honda[7] where Rover developed from being a weak, state-owned enterprise into a successful one through a systematic learning programme from Honda which was seeking to exploit its superior knowledge in other markets. Such an alliance resulted in Rover significantly improving its performance and halving its defect rate, while substantially accelerating its product development cycle. In this way Rover managed to protect its markets while becoming a marketable asset subsequently purchased by BMW for £800 million. Another example of hybrid defensive–offensive alliance refers to Siemens and Motorola planning to build a chip plant in the USA with the aim of producing 64-megabit memory chips.[8] LG Semicon is also planning a similar move with Hitachi to start commercial production in Malaysia in 1998.

In fast-moving markets alliances are becoming a norm as the level of conflict is minimized by partners recognizing that they are the only vehicle for minimizing risk associated with market and technology uncertainty. Alliances enable organizations to provide the necessary connectivity across complementary capabilities to create new market values without stretching each party out of its existing competencies. The fundamental question for industrialists still remains whether their organization should lead the market or follow the leaders. In fast-moving markets only one choice will prevail—to lead. This is because

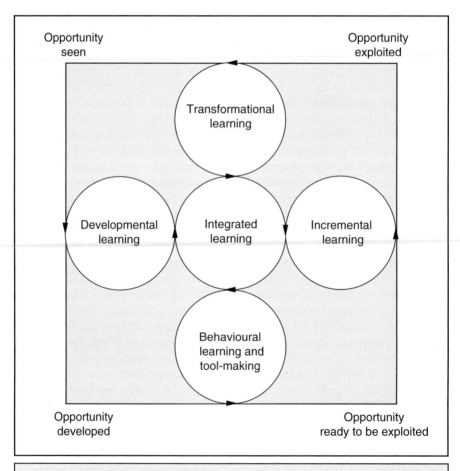

Figure 2. Integrated learning model.

opportunities are short-lived in fast-moving markets. As a result strategic alliances are driven by the creation and exploitation of opportunities before someone else does and are terminated as soon as the opportunity ceases to exist. The integrated learning model[9] captures the way in which business opportunities are created and exploited. This model which is shown in Figure 2 represents a continuously evolving process integrating four learning cycles. The transformational learning cycle relates to generating breakthrough ideas in order to develop the new market values. The developmental learning cycle will create the prototypes and define the delivery system. The behavioural learning and tool-making cycle is concerned with configuring and implementing the delivery system. Incremental learning takes place through running and improving the delivery system. Although the creation and exploitation of new business opportunities requires all four cycles of the integrated learning model, success does not have to come from the knowledge developed within the organization. Success is often the result of a ruthless ability to exploit knowledge developed elsewhere.[10] Faster integrated learning to exploit the briefest of opportunities whilst maintaining knowledge leadership is the reason why organizations make alliances.

Fast Strategic Alliances

There are four underlying concepts shaping successful strategic alliances in fast-moving markets: increasing returns, destabilizing market values, chain of timely ideas and the three dimensions of competition. Figure 3 integrates these four concepts in a way that explains how sustainable competitive advantage is realized in fast-moving markets.

The principle of increasing returns[11] suggests that the more an organization sells, the easier it becomes. This is based on the supposition that advantage in the market is dependent on setting the standard which determines the market value against which all competing products will come to be judged. This is in direct contrast to the principle of diminishing returns which considers that the more an organization sells, the harder it becomes. This is because attractive markets encourage emulating entrants, eroding the organization's advantage in the market. Both these principles point towards the same conclusion which is that sustainable advantage in a market requires the constant creation of new market values through superior knowledge, constantly setting new standards. The ability continually to introduce new standards and destabilize market values is the product of understanding the requirement for a chain of timely ideas which are introduced both to succeed existing products and destabilize existing market values embodied within them. Any discussion of deliberately setting out to destabilize market values, increasing returns and the chain of timely ideas needs to consider the question of the speed at which movement is planned and introduced. In other words how fast can a market be moved? High speed for the sake of being fast is pointless. The speed at which an organization moves its

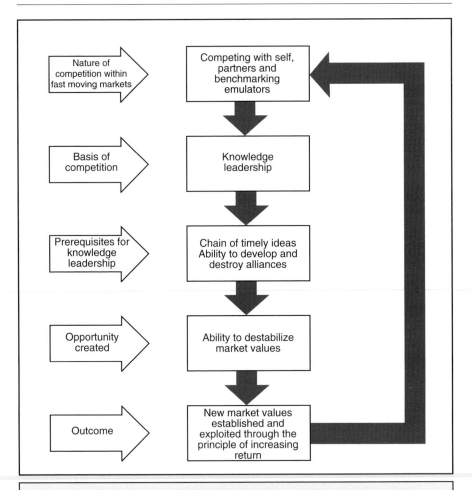

Figure 3. A connecting model for sustainable competitive advantage.

market should be based on maintaining knowledge leadership. This requires creating and sequencing a chain of ideas and timing their release into the market. In this way the organization can choose to accelerate or slow the market down, depending on the proximity of competitors and the relative advantage it commands. Any threat to erode the advantage in the market is fought by an accelerated release of ideas. Accordingly, the organization can decide to kill products already in the market in order to increase instability and take market values in a new direction.

There are three dimensions of competition surrounding the creation of new market values, and together they combine to determine just how fast is fast: competing with self, partners and benchmarking emulators. An organization is its own competitor because all markets are finite, and the organization has to compete with its own sold products in order to create new demand. An organization also competes with its alliance partners because they will learn the organization's capabilities and can potentially erode its knowledge leadership and ability to create and exploit new opportunities. An organization competes with benchmarking emulators who may even develop new capabilities which take them past the organization. Sustainable competitive advantage is therefore a form of monopoly achieved through creating and banking ideas, and deliberately not introducing them until the competitive benchmarkers have managed to emulate the organization's last idea. A major implication of the timing of ideas is the concept of fantasy benchmarking for competitive advantage which enables new competitors to escape the logical development of existing approaches and products and jump ahead. The concept of fast alliances is a natural, logical progression from the chain of timely ideas, making it possible to develop relationships with outside organizations without risking losing the market advantage. The organization will deliberately choose partners to do the hard work, and move on before they can learn how to emulate its existing capabilities. This fast alliance concept requires learning how to work with strangers; in a way this means the organization becomes even more skilled at partnering whilst remaining fit for its purpose.

Implications for Organizations

From the preceding analysis it is apparent that knowledge leadership must be the primary goal of organizations. A framework for distinguishing knowledge leadership is presented in Figure 4, based on strategic impact which is described in terms of the advantage the organization has in the market and its sustainability. If knowledge is too accessible and of low strategic impact, then such a knowledge has passed its sell-by-date and hence is of no use to the organization. If the organization identifies knowledge owned by others and of high strategic impact, this knowledge becomes the reason why an organization pursues an alliance. Similarly, if the organization owns knowledge which is of low strategic impact in its product markets but of high strategic impact for others, this also represents an opportunity for an alliance. However, knowledge of high strategic impact owned by the organization must constantly be developed and protected as the wealth creation capacity of the organization is dependent on this knowledge leadership. There is a continuous transition of private knowledge of high strategic impact losing its value and eventually becoming public domain. As a result, the focus of organizations must be continuously to develop private knowledge while seeking the knowledge of others in order to develop the knowledge leadership which enables constant creation and exploitation of new market values.

As knowledge leadership becomes the primary goal of organizations, the role of traditional financial and economic models for measuring the value of an

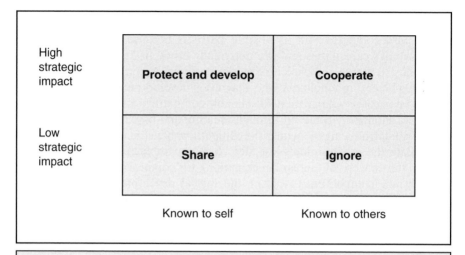

Figure 4. A framework for distinguishing knowledge leadership.

organization will diminish because these models only serve to confuse and prevent organizations from learning how to achieve sustainable competitive advantage. The core of organizations operating in fast-moving markets will be concentrated around the creation of the new organizational wealth which is knowledge leadership.

Conclusion

There is a series of prevailing unstated assumptions which obscure organizations from realizing the real benefits and risks of strategic alliances. These are:

- There are sufficient stable, generic products and processes which can continue to be optimized indefinitely to sustain the existing nature of the organizations.
- There is a formula for business success through alliance partnerships which enables organizations to escape from their weaknesses without ever having to innovate or learn how to change themselves.
- Partners will remain partners. They will not divorce or grow into competitors.

The nature of alliances was different before and will change in the future. In slow-changing markets many industrialists and researchers treated alliances as a marriage within an optimization framework aimed at stabilizing market values, protecting capacity and market share. The problem is how continuously to create new products which create new market values within a global market rather than optimizing generic, standard products and processes indefinitely. By concentrating on the marriage paradigm, post-rational models have been developed which seek to explain the nature of what has happened but have a limited predictive use. These models are the result of observations of successful alliances at work. They have included a community of shared interests working together in harmony to pursue a single goal. As a result they have concluded that a successful alternative to competition is co-operation and not conflict. The consumers of these post-rational models have applied this formula with mixed results. What these post-rational studies have missed is the reason why strategic alliances happen in the first place. As a result, the consumers of post-rational alliance models are continually attracted and confused. Attracted by those aspects of the post-rational models that seem to be recognizable and confused by those contradictory elements that are new and alien.

This article suggests that strategic alliances in fast-moving markets can only take the form of a one night stand. Alliances happen because they have to happen and are engineered because they are the only way organizations can create and exploit new opportunities rapidly. The key parameters surrounding strategic alliances are opportunism, necessity and speed. Their ultimate aim is to maintain knowledge leadership whilst minimizing time to market in exploiting the briefest of business opportunities. Too much dependence on alliances can result in partners growing into competitors while limiting future strategic choices for the organization. The key question that must be asked before entering into a strategic alliance is whether the organization will be able to sustain their competitive advantage and continue to determine their own future destiny. This will require a new set of competencies which include:

- Managing and exploiting the timing of new market values.
- Building and destroying alliances.
- Working with strangers so that organizations do not civilize each other through developing a unitary culture (i.e. alliance partners are only valuable through their complementary capabilities).

The degree to which the views presented in this paper will be shared depends on whether strategic alliances continue to be treated as a marriage based on love and mutual esteem, rather than a temporary relationship based on lust and convenience.

References

1. N. Cohn, *The Pursuit of Millenium: Revolutionary Millenarians and Mystical Anarchists of the Middle Ages*, Paladin, London (1984).
2. R. Moss Kanter, Collaborative advantage: the art of alliances, *Harvard Business Review*, July–August, 96–108 (1994).
3. E. R. Stafford, Using co-operative strategies to make alliances work, *Long Range Planning* **27** (3), 64–74 (1994).
4. C. Schofield and R. Gribben, BAe in talks with Daimler-Benz, *The Daily Telegraph*, 25 July, p. 20 (1996).

5. P. Taylor, Acorn computer moves to tap Internet market, *Financial Times*, 22 May, p. 28 (1996).

6. P. Taylor, Clash of the software titans, *Financial Times*, 22 May, p. 25 (1996).

7. J. Bleeke and D. Ernst, Is your strategic alliance really a sale?, *Harvard Business Review*, January–February, 97–105 (1995).

8. Siemens in US Chip Venture, *Financial Times*, 22 May, p. 7 (1996).

9. K. Chaharbaghi and V. Newman, Innovating: towards an integrated learning model, *Management Decision* **34** (4), 5–13 (1996).

10. K. Chaharbaghi, Development of new technology-based organisations as a dynamic concept, *Proceedings of the 4th Annual High Technology Small Firms Conference* (1996).

11. J. Eatwell, M. Milgate and P. Newman, *The New Palgrave: a Dictionary of Economics*, Macmillan, London (1987).

10

The ICI Demerger: Unlocking Shareholder Value

Carol Kennedy

Britain's biggest manufacturing company has made the historic decision, conditions permitting, to demerge into two separately quoted businesses by floating off its 'biosciences' operations—pharmaceuticals (the present company's profit leader), agrochemicals, seeds and specialities—while leaving ICI itself to comprise heavy chemicals, paints, and explosives. The decision is the fruit of lengthy restructuring and strategy-making, which started well before the Hanson Group raised the shadow of takeover in 1991. How ICI's strategists reached their solution in the light of increasing pressures and rationalization in the global chemical industry, and how the synergies between ICI's varied businesses were rethought, are explored in tracing the evolution of what will undoubtedly be a key industrial transformation of the 1990s.

In the spring of 1993, if market conditions allow, ICI will formally demerge into two companies by floating its pharmaceuticals and other biotechnology-based businesses on the stock market. The 'old' ICI that is left will continue to bear the historic name born of the original four-company merger in 1926: the new biosciences group, contrary to first expectations, will emphasize its ability to thrive independently with an entirely new identity.

In bulk chemicals, the 'new' ICI plc will enjoy world leadership in two key areas—paints and explosives; in biosciences it will have a high global ranking in seeds and agrochemicals and the opportunity to build its profitable pharma-

---

Carol Kennedy is Executive Editor of DIRECTOR magazine.

ceuticals business, perhaps by acquisition. Analysts have speculated that the premium rating usually accorded by the market to drugs companies should enable it to raise equity more easily than when this jewel in the crown was part of a diversified chemical company. Capitalization figures put on the two ICI companies as at 30 July 1992, based on splitting the existing assets:

ICI (bulk chemicals, paints, explosives)	£2.5 billion
ICI Bio, now renamed Zeneca	
(pharmaceuticals, agrochemicals, seeds, specialities)	£6 billion

This may have been the strategy in Lord Hanson's mind when the Hanson Group took its controversial 2.5 per cent stake in ICI in May 1991, throwing the chemical group's top management into high gear on restructuring plans. Whether or not Hanson intended to bid in order to unlock more shareholder value—the stake was sold a year later—the company has now taken its own bold step into the unknown. The months of secret background planning can now be told.

The Trigger

The seeds of Britain's biggest industrial demerger were sown in an early-morning call to ICI's chairman, Sir Denys Henderson, in Phoenix, Arizona, in the autumn of 1989. This was fully 18 months before the predatory shadow of Lord Hanson fell across the chemical giant's boardroom. Although ICI has now done what Hanson might have been expected to do had he taken over the company—and presumably thereby pre-empted any similar predator—the benefit is accentuated by hindsight. Several other elements were converging from late 1989 on in favour of the demerger proposal, when it finally hit Henderson's desk in early 1992.

The telephone call to Arizona was from ICI's then finance director, Alan Clements, who had disturbing news about the third-quarter results for 1989. The full-year results would actually turn out to be ICI's best, but the third-quarter figures were about £100m less than expected, and what seriously concerned Henderson was that the shortfall came in areas on which the company had pinned much of its strategy, such as speciality chemicals and advanced materials.

Henderson had what he calls a flash of 'instant vision' that undermined all his assumptions about the repositioning and refocusing of ICI's businesses throughout the 1980s, with acquisitions that had taken it to world No. 1 in paints and explosives and world No. 2 in agrochemicals, while reducing costs and improving efficiency. He realized with a shock that the company's claims for being both leaner and more robust were not as sustainable as they had believed.

Henderson's flash of insight that autumn day in Arizona has to be seen against the postwar evolution of ICI, which after a long period of comfortable, even complacent growth had been jolted into radical change at the start of the 1980s. Since its enormous burst of invention and production during and after the Second World War, the company had been slow to take advantage either of the opportunities in the U.S., the world's largest market for chemicals, or in the fledgling European Common Market, though that was an inevitable by-product of Britain's own lackadaisical attitude to the converging Continent, and in fact ICI was more ahead of the game than many large British corporations in building up in Europe in the 1960s.

The neglect of America was more puzzling. Since the famous anti-trust verdict of 1951, when an American judge had decreed that ICI could no longer work its amicable hand-in-glove arrangement with DuPont to regulate competition, the company had been served notice that it had to get bigger in the U.S. on its own account—yet hardly any moves were made until 1972, when Atlas Chemicals was acquired.

Re-structuring

At home, ICI was seen as a national institution, a 'slumbering giant', as Anthony Sampson described it in *Anatomy of Britain* in 1960. Through the 1960s and 1970s, the company's proud divisions like Mond, which had been crucibles of invention, saw themselves at the leading edge of technology, but marketing was an alien concept. The unconventional Sir John Harvey-Jones, who came in as chairman in 1981, stripped out layers of management, set the divisions free to manage themselves as business centres (and deprived them of their champions on the board) and changed the company's ethos to 'inventing into the market-place'. Directors no longer acted as advocates for divisions; all were now a team judging strategy and tactics for all the businesses and for the group as a whole.

The groundwork for reform had been laid by Harvey-Jones's predecessor, Sir Maurice Hodgson. In the late 1970s, after a decade in which the switchback sequence of oil price rises and collapses had left the industry reacting to rather than planning for events, Hodgson set the company four targets:

■ reduce the numbers employed—though this had been a trend for some years;
■ improve energy utilization—essential with oil costing up to $34 a barrel;
■ improve the capital productivity of new plants;
■ reduce working capital.

As a result of this programme, when the economy turned up in 1983–1984, ICI was well placed to benefit from recovery. Labour costs were halved in the U.K. during the 1980s, with numbers employed cut from around 90,000 to 50,000 by the end of the decade.

Strategy for Recovery

Henderson had been appointed to the ICI board in 1980 after 23 years working his way through various divisions, and he became involved in planning under Harvey-Jones. The two worked out a clear strategy, in which the leading priority was to get bigger in overseas markets. In pursuit of that, Henderson helped to set up an acquisitions unit, aimed principally at the world's richest market for chemicals, the United States.

'We had a very clear view', says Henderson now, 'that you had better be in the top two or three in your particular businesses, and not down at 11 or 12'. This strategy produced the acquisition of Glidden Paints in 1986, which took ICI to world No.1 in paints, the purchase of Stauffer Chemical Company in 1987, which made ICI No. 2 in agrochemicals, and Atlas Powder Company in 1990, which established it as global leader in explosives. (The acquisition of Beatrice Chemicals in 1985, intended to establish substantial new markets for advanced materials in the aerospace and defence industries, was overtaken by history and the 'peace dividend', and ICI has since cut its losses in that area.)

The second part of the strategy analysed the future of heavy chemicals and found it wanting. The industry was highly cyclical and petrochemicals and plastics—a merger of divisions carried out in the 1970s—was making losses. The board decided to maintain the operations that could be made profitable, but to start building up the higher added-value speciality chemicals.

As a result, through the 1980s ICI radically changed its portfolio. Between 1980 and 1990, while group sales more than doubled from £5.7bn to £12.9bn, the share of pharmaceuticals, agrochemicals and seeds, paints and other 'effect' products, grew from 34 to 56 per cent. Geographically, sales in the Americas grew from 16 to 29 per cent and in Continental Europe from 19 to 26 per cent, while the U.K. share was cut from 42 to 22 per cent. The strategy appeared confirmed in its success with pretax profits peaking in 1989 at £1.5bn.

Another Recession

However, the alarming third-quarter dip in 1989, highlighting weaknesses in areas that ICI had thought strategically soundly based, was enough to provoke Henderson's conviction that immediate action was needed to reduce costs throughout ICI and to review two areas in particular, specialities and fertilizers. Fertilizers had been a pillar of ICI since the group was welded together out of Britain's four leading chemical companies in 1926, but in Henderson's words it was now 'falling downhill'.

Around the summer of 1990, Henderson also got what he describes as 'a nasty feeling in the pit of my stomach' about the direction in which the world economy was headed. The first of a series of restructurings was put in train, together with a pullback on capital expenditure and further economies in manpower. In July it was announced that the fertilizers business would be sold and a new, reorganized ICI Specialities business established. The Beatrice business, for which many analysts considered too high a price had been paid in 1985, was put under the microscope in the light of geopolitical developments affecting the defence industry—the so-called 'peace dividend'—and recession hitting the civil aviation industry. The board decided to phase out its commitment to advanced composite materials and divest those interests in Beatrice, retaining only the speciality chemical side. Then came a move which unwittingly was to lay the groundwork for the momentous decision to split the company into heavy chemicals and 'biosciences'.

Task Forces

In September 1990 Henderson set up two Task Forces, each drawn from members of the executive team, to review the direction in which the world chemical industry was heading and determine whether the restructuring changes of the 1980s had been sufficient. The key committee, under Tom Hutchison, was charged with examining the current corporate strategy and to look hard at the individual businesses—which could be sustained in the new, more rigorous economic climate, and which could no longer justify their keep? The other group, under Ronnie Hampel, later to become chief operating officer, was asked to design the new organizational structure. Both groups were asked to highlight those businesses and territories which should have priority for resources, and to look for opportunities to simplify group structure, cut overheads and reduce management layers still further.

The committees' work was done against some bleak criteria for the 1990s, including lower growth, higher capital requirements, increasing costs for R & D and for environmental factors, The high cost of environmental protection, says David Barnes, who will lead the new biosciences company, was an important consideration in the logic which led to the demerger. Sir Denys Henderson believes that the whole chemical industry has greatly underestimated the cost of environmental management.

Barnes describes the task force's work as 'a process of intellectual fumbling around'. Hutchison's committee had by far the more difficult task of the two, as Hampel acknowledges: 'You've got to know what businesses you are in before you start talking about how to manage them.' Barnes recalls: 'As we got deeper into the exercise it became clear that we had far too many businesses to sustain them all.'

The task forces' reviews concluded that ICI's strategy was headed in the right direction, but that the company's activities were too widely spread and required a sharper focus, both on individual businesses and on territories. During repeated reappraisals and fine-tuning of options, what Barnes calls a 'cleavage' or 'fault line' between ICI's main blocks of activities became evident, although splitting the company was not seriously considered at this stage.

Another Restructuring

The two committees, working flat out at the Millbank headquarters and keeping in close contact with each other, produced their reports in 2 months, enabling the board to accept their conclusions in January 1991 and Henderson to announce

ICI	Turnover £m	Trading Profit or Loss £m
Paints	1588	118
Explosives	536	54
Materials	2037	−20
Industrial Chems	3894	132
Regional	1246	29
	8701	313

Employees at 31.12.91:   88,100

ZENECA

	Turnover £m	Trading Profit or Loss £m
Pharmaceuticals	1588	538
Agrochems/seeds	1365	144
Specialities	984	38
	3937	720

Employees at 31.1 2.91:   35, 500

Combined turnover	£12.488m
Combined profit	£1,033m
Total employees	123,600

Figure 1. Turnover and profit statistics for the two companies based on 1991 results

major restructuring changes after ICI's annual results in February 1991 (see Figure 1).

The key actions were to be:

■ Division of ICI into seven core business groupings (pharmaceuticals, agrochemicals and seeds, paints, materials, explosives, industrial chemicals and specialities including the synthetic protein foodstuff Quorn, originally produced with Rank Hovis McDougall, and Biopol, an ingenious biogradable plastic made originally from a sugar base. This had been around as a 'laboratory curiosity' since the mid-1980s, but through reformulation had found rewarding niche markets such as medical sutures, heart patches and hygiene applications. To these seven, Tioxide, a potential world leader, was later added.

■ Sharper focus on businesses which either already were global players in the major markets of Europe, North America and Asia Pacific, or had the potential to become global players.

■ A major reshaping of the group, providing £300m net of tax for further redundancies, factory closures and divestments.

■ Establishment of a materials business group.

■ Establishment of a new Policy and Performance Committee. This would bring the heads of ICI's eight core businesses (including Tioxide) into quarterly discussions with executive directors about the group's results and strategy. In September 1991 Ronnie Hampel was appointed chief operating officer, to whom all business heads would report directly.

Geographically, the group would focus more closely on Europe and the U.K., the Americas and Asia-Pacific (where producers of basic chemicals were gaining in volume and would be exporting by the end of the 1990s), and would trim its commitments elsewhere in the world. Divestments, closures and redundancies were expected to reduce the workforce by a further 20,000 by 1993.

The restructuring was announced at the year-end results in February 1991. Henderson observed that it was a 'once in a decade' event. An organization, he remarked, was a hardy plant, 'but one shouldn't pick it up by the roots too often'. However, the board was continuing to look at wider-ranging possibilities, including flotation of parts of the company, and the chairmen's report to shareholders in March 1991 noted that ICI would pursue reshaping 'still more radically'. Just over a year later, he would be announcing plans to consider the complete demerger of the company.

Hanson Buys ICI Shares

1991 was to prove one of the most unsettled years in ICI's history. In mid-May the Hanson Group dropped its bombshell, buying £240m worth of ICI shares, 2.8 per cent of the company's equity. Alarm bells rang. Could Hanson, whose speciality was acquiring low-tech businesses and making their assets sweat, be contemplating a bid for Britain's biggest and most R & D-intensive manufacturing group? Henderson and his board decided, although no bidding intention was ever made known, that they should act as if Hanson would bid, and if that happened, they should not assume that institutional investors would reject it, or that if it were referred to Brussels, that would save the company's independence.

The business world, including Lords Hanson and White, was to be jolted by ICI's aggressive defence strategy, which caused Hanson's credentials to be closely scrutinized and questioned in the financial pages. At the same time, the board moved swiftly to implement its restructuring plans and let the world know that it could improve its own performance and shareholder value without benefit of outside interference. Henderson had had a defence plan prepared since he became chairman in 1987, and one of the scenarios addressed by Tom Hutchison's task force was the vulnerability of ICI to a possible predator. Several organizational models had been studied, one of them being a full demerger—the pharmaceuticals business having multiplied sixfold since 1980—but this was not pursued at that time. The prevailing view was to concentrate on the restructuring and get that right to meet the external economic circumstances.

During the weeks and months of preparing for a possible Hanson bid, a kind of war cabinet met at ICI's Millbank headquarters early each morning—chairman Henderson, deputy chairman Frank Whiteley, chief operating officer Ronnie Hampel, and finance director Colin Short. In the course of putting together ICI's defence for the—in fact non-forthcoming—bid, the core management looked intensively and in great detail both at its own organization and at Hanson. By October, it had concluded that sufficient problems were being exposed at Hanson Group, and question marks posed over its strategy, for a bid to be extremely unlikely, though it did not entirely relax its guard, aware that any serious falling-off in performance might still leave room for a pounce.

A Demerger?

Studying the task force findings again, it became increasingly clear that the synergy between ICI's businesses—publicly touted as a strong reason for keeping the company intact—was developing down two tracks. David Barnes describes the phenomenon as a 'fault line', either side of which could be discerned two businesses that could theoretically stand alone, roughly divided between industrial chemicals and biological businesses. Another analogy Barnes used is that of Siamese twins who had reached the point of development where their individual systems could sustain a separate life. At this point Henderson decided to call in a lateral thinker to look at the businesses from outside. He telephoned Sir David Scholey, head of ICI's merchant bank S. G. Warburg, and asked him to recommend a candidate. Scholey chose John Mayo, a 36-year-old director of Warburgs. Those who met him at ICI describe him as highly able, quite abrasive, very confident of his own ability. ICI's database was unlocked for him, and he was given complete freedom of action within the company, responding personally to the chairman. 'I didn't want him to talk to people and be influenced by subjective views. I wanted him to look at the numbers', said Henderson.

Mayo took 6 weeks over the task, then spent the best part of a day closeted with Henderson going through the options. He had identified a possible dozen plans for reorganizing ICI and reduced them to one—demerger. It was a daunting prospect for a company of such national significance, though there was an encouraging, if smaller-scale precedent in the Courtaulds demerger of 1990. In this, the textiles side had been separated from the newer chemicals side, and both had prospered. Sir Christopher Hogg, Courtaulds' chairman, had lunched with Henderson at the time of the announcement, and had spoken of a great release of management energy into both companies. Henderson was to be particularly influenced by this memory as he debated with himself over Mayo's proposal, though Hogg had been able to implement his strategy over several years and ICI's 'hiving down' would have to be done in months. The BAT 'unbundling' under threat of takeover from Sir James Goldsmith also gave encouraging signals, though Henderson has always maintained that the demerger motive was 'business-driven'. Undoubtedly, however, the once-unthinkable possibility that Hanson put in play did concentrate minds in a way that might otherwise not have happened.

The demerger proposal, codenamed Project Dawn, began to be discussed under conditions of the highest confidentiality, by the executive teams in March 1992. A high-level core group, nicknamed the Dawn Patrol, was formed comprising chairman Henderson, deputy chairman Frank Whiteley, chief operating officer Ronnie Hampel, finance director Colin Short, and David Barnes, the director responsible for North America who had also had extensive experience in ICI's pharmaceuticals business. Two others—ICI's general manager, planning, and the group secretary and solicitor—completed the tight-knit team. Later, for security reasons, Project Dawn became Project Mortar and the team controlling it was humorously dubbed the Mortar Board.

This main core of high executives had a support staff of around 30, but it was inevitable that more and more people had to be drawn into the secret. By the time it was made public in July 1992, the number was riskily large, close to 200.

The Mortar Board established a number of expert task forces and project teams to look at all the implications of demerger on a worldwide group of some 400 companies in 150 countries—financial and tax implications, the impact on employees, on pensions and profit-sharing schemes, on synergies of research and development, communications, and a myriad other aspects. At this point too, although the biosciences group had received a working title—at first 'Phab Labs', later 'ICI Biosciences'—it was decided to search for a replacement name that would establish the new company's credentials as an independent entity. (Courtaulds, though successfully demerged as Courtaulds PLC and Courtaulds Textiles, was said to have regretted not going for two distinctive names.) In both pharmaceuticals and agrochemicals, the argument runs, it is the specific brand name that counts—Tenormin or Paraquat, rather than the corporate logo. As well as the massive 'hive-down' programme discussed during the 4 months of secret meetings, a great deal of ingenuity went into diversionary tactics to ensure that nothing unusual was suspected within the company. Meetings were called around agendas that would soon be redundant; strategies were discussed that would be overtaken by events; contingency plans were drawn up for statements to the press in the event of a leak. It was also essential that top management knew of all key executives' movements during the holiday season, as it became increasingly certain that an announcement would have to be made in the summer.

In April Henderson convened a Chairman's Strategy Conference (when ICI's directors meet in an informal mode, to talk strategy but not to make decisions) to allow the whole board to evaluate progress. Having decided that he must give a strong lead to the board, Henderson made an uncharacteristically long speech setting out his belief in the 'sheer business logic' of the plan. He stressed that he was not asking for a formal vote, but for the directors' verdict on whether demerger was best for the company. The verdict was favourable, with the proviso that much more needed to be done. A second, also affirmative, Chairman's Conference was held in June at the headquarters of ICI Pharmaceuticals at Alderley Park, Cheshire, when prospects for that business, the heart of any new flotation, were reviewed in depth.

Formal approval by the ICI board to consider a demerger was given on 29 July, and since further work on the many complex issues involved was unlikely to be feasible without breaching the tightly-kept confidentiality of the project, it was decided to release a public announcement on the following day. That evening, all ICI's European chief executives were summoned to a special meeting at the company's conference centre near Heathrow Airport, while simultaneously ICI directors flew out to brief senior staff in the major overseas territories. Individual letters from the chairman, enclosing copies of the press statements, were mailed to all ICI employees throughout the world, and copies of the statement went to all shareholders and pensioners.

The skill at diversionary tactics was needed to explain the mandatory summons of the European CEOs, some of whom were on their way to holiday destinations when the call came: they were told that the board required a full briefing on the quality of their latest trading figures before the interim results were declared.

The Proposed New Companies

The announcement was greeted at first with surprise, then with enthusiasm by ICI managers. By business commentators and City analysts it was generally hailed as an inspired move, offering investors a choice between a solidly based commodities business with proven world positions and good long-term growth potential despite the cyclical aspect of some businesses, and a potential market star set free to exploit all ICI's knowledge bank in biotechnology processes. A particular benefit, it was speculated, would be the additional resources that could be released to bolster the capital-intensive industrial chemicals side, while the new biosciences company should find it easy to replenish its own coffers with an early rights issue. At the time of demerger, for each ICI share held, it was proposed that a shareholder would also receive a share in the biosciences company.

Henderson, musing later in his holiday deckchair, thought further about the strategy for each company beyond demerger. He formulated a sort of mission statement in an acronym he called PREGNANT: both companies (of which he would remain joint chairman at the Millbank headquarters until his retirement in 1995) should be:

Profitable, Rewarding to shareholders and employees, Exciting, and Growing.

As the holiday season ended, work began intensively on the 'hive-down' separations, to be ready by the end of December so that the new company could be registered on 1 January and group assets allocated. The task was particularly daunting on the biosciences side as 'long-form' reports, in due course to be condensed down into the new company's prospectus, came in from every business, all requiring verification by independent accountants.

Meanwhile the search for a new company name went on. The consultancy Interbrand produced a list of 1000 possibilities, which was down to 35 by mid-October. Within a month, a short list was presented for every ICI director to make a choice. The final selection—Zeneca—was announced in late November. David Barnes, the new company's CEO-designate, knew it would be an 'emotional decision' and predicted: 'Everyone will hate the name when they hear it. Six months later it will have an image of its own.'

Basic Chemicals

As 1992 drew to an end, the speculative prospectus for each company looked promising. The new 'basic' ICI offered a group of global businesses with good long-term yield prospects: leading positions in paints, explosives and titanium dioxide and in materials with enormous ranges of applications such as polyurethanes, acrylics and polyester film; with global strengths in polyester intermediates, surfactants and catalysts. There was also the potentially world-class business of CFC substitutes being developed at Runcorn, in which ICI has chosen to go directly for two HFC products, KLEA 134a and KLEA 32, rather than the easier intermediate HCFC, which still has some ozone-depleting risk.

Most of these businesses have similar needs in chemical engineering and capital project management; share a strong technology base in polymer sciences, colloid science, materials and composite technology, and are skilled in operating complex chemical plants with sophisticated process technology.

Biosciences

The biosciences company (Zeneca) will inevitably focus on ICI's internationally renowned ethical pharmaceuticals business, the world's fourth most profitable with a number of potential star products in the pipeline to replace Tenormin, the betablocker now phasing out of patent, and also with some long-running successes such as Hibitane, the world's best-selling hospital antiseptic since the 1950s. But it also includes a cluster of technologically exciting speciality businesses such as biodegradable polymers and the world's No. 2 agrochemicals business. The seeds business is a growing attraction for international chemical groups (Ciba-Geigy, for example) and at ICI has been nurtured since the mid-1980s with special investment. It offers revolutionary possibilities for self-regulating plant breeding, among which is the successful trial marketing among U.S. ketchup manufacturers of the 'non-squashy tomato', able to resist premature decay and

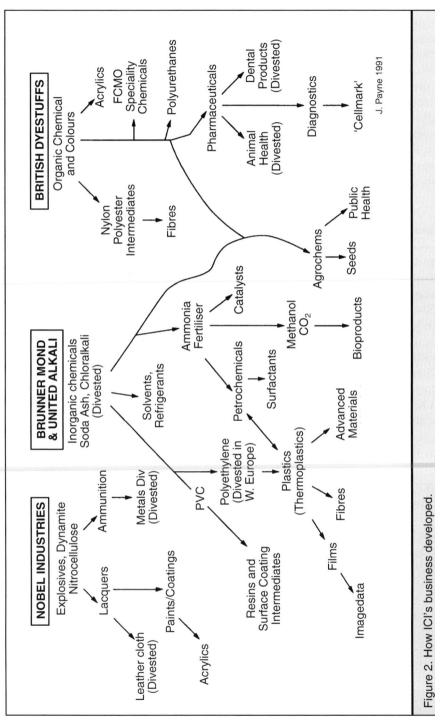

Figure 2. How ICI's business developed.

with great richness of texture and flavour. Interestingly, ICI's famous DNA 'fingerprinting' technique, marketed through Cellmark Diagnostics and most in the public eye through its foolproof method of catching criminals, offers its greatest real value in 'gene-mapping' for the seeds business; enabling plant breeders to grow precisely and consistently to the characteristics required.

These businesses, all research- and technology-intensive, share extensive international development and marketing skills and have a strong common science base as well as sharing scientific software systems and other infrastructure. Historically, much R & D had been shared between pharmaceuticals (which itself sprang out of the dyestuffs business in 1936) and agrochemicals, for example. In total size, Zeneca on 1991 sales will be just smaller than Roche, bigger than Pfizer.

Given the persistence of the recession, there might never be an ideal time for the demerger, but in late 1992 most analysts expected it to be in April or May 1993 (Henderson and the board had watched the Wellcome float, a critical pointer). 'Despite today's difficult trading conditions, I am sure it is right for us to consider a strategic move of this kind now', said Henderson at the time of the announcement. The grouping of core businesses would enable each company, post-demerger, to respond better to economic circumstances and to the great shifts and rationalizations likely to come in the international chemical industry.

Some months later he said he hoped that the market, in capitalizing both companies, would 'make one and one more than two. People forget that ICI Pharmaceuticals is a bigger, and I believe a better-quality business than Wellcomes, for example, in terms of size and profitability. But it undoubtedly suffered from its association with the heavy chemicals, or from not being sufficiently visible.'

'Both these businesses will be well up the Fortune 500 . . . People are going to be forced to concentrate on areas where they have real strengths and skills, where they have real global muscle, and where they will have a competitive edge. Being seventh, eighth or ninth in the world just won't be good enough.'

PART II: WHAT HAS NOT CHANGED?

11

Creating a Sense of Mission

Andrew Campbell and Sally Yeung

Mission is still a relatively neglected area of management, and there is no clear agreement on what it encompasses. The Ashridge Strategic Management Centre conducted a 2-year research project designed to fill this gap. The research found that if mission is more clearly defined it can be managed better, and it developed a model of mission that includes four elements—purpose, strategy, behaviour standards and values. The project identified companies where, in addition to strong links between these elements, employees also showed an emotional commitment to their company which Campbell has called a 'sense of mission'. This commitment was deepest when there was a match between the employee's values and the company's values.

Many managers misunderstand the nature and importance of mission, while others fail to consider it at all. As far back as 1973, Peter Drucker[1] observed: 'That business purpose and business mission are so rarely given adequate thought is perhaps the most important cause of business frustration and failure'. Unfortunately, his comment is as true today as it was then.

Understanding Mission?

The reason for this neglect is due in part to the fact that mission is still a relatively uncharted area of management. Most management thinkers have given mission only a cursory glance, and there is little research into its nature and importance.

Andrew Campbell is a founding Director and Fellow of the Ashridge Strategic Management Centre. He is co-author of *Strategies and Styles*, *A Sense of Mission*, and *Mission and Business Philosophy*. Sally Yeung is a Research Associate at Ashridge Strategic Management Centre and co-author with Andrew Campbell of *Do You Need a Mission Statement?*

What research there is has been devoted to analysing mission statements and attempting to develop checklists of items that should be addressed in the statement.[2] Indeed, a major problem is that mission has become a meaningless term—no two academics or managers agree on the same definition. Some speak of mission as if it is commercial evangelism, others talk about strong corporate cultures and still others talk about business definitions. Some view mission as an esoteric and somewhat irrelevant preoccupation which haunts senior managers, while others see it as the bedrock of a company's strength, identity and success—its personality and character.

Despite the diversity of opinion about mission, it is possible to distinguish two schools of thought. Broadly speaking, one approach describes mission in terms of business strategy, while the other expresses mission in terms of philosophy and ethics.

The strategy school of thought views mission primarily as a strategic tool, an intellectual discipline which defines the business's commercial rationale and target market. Mission is something that is linked to strategy but at a higher level. In this context, it is perceived as the first step in strategic management. It exists to answer two fundamental questions: 'what is our business and what should it be?'

The strategy school of mission owes its birth to an article, 'Marketing Myopia', which appeared in the *Harvard Business Review* in 1960.[3] The author, Ted Levitt, a Harvard marketing professor, argued that many companies have the wrong business definition. Most particularly, companies define their businesses too narrowly. Levitt reasoned that a railroad company should see its business as moving people rather than railroading, an oil company should define its business as energy and a company making tin cans should see itself as a packaging business. Managers, Levitt argued, should spend time carefully defining their business so that they focus on customer need rather than on production technology.

Most recently, it has become common for companies to include a statement of what their business is in the annual report. The cover of the 1988 annual report of Redland, a roofing, aggregates and construction materials company, is an example. It reads:

Spanning the
Roofing
World with
Aggregates
Construction
Bricks
Materials

The first page of the 1989 annual report of British Telecom reads: 'British Telecom's mission is to provide world class telecommunications and information products and services and to develop and exploit our networks at home and overseas'.

Corning Glass states: 'We are dedicated to the total success of Corning Glass Works as a worldwide competitor. We choose to compete in four broad business sectors. One is Specialty Glass and Ceramics, our historical base, where our technical skills will continue to drive the development of an ever-broadening range of products for diverse applications. The other three are Consumer Housewares, Laboratory Sciences, and Telecommunications. Here we will build on existing strengths, and the needs of the markets we serve will dictate the technologies we use and the range of products and services we provide'.

In contrast, the second school of thought argues that mission is the cultural 'glue' which enables an organization to function as a collective unity. This cultural glue consists of strong norms and values that influence the way in which people behave, how they work together and how they pursue the goals of the organization. This form of mission can amount to a business philosophy which helps employees to perceive and interpret events in the same way and to speak a common language. Compared to the strategic view of mission, this interpretation sees mission as capturing some of the emotional aspects of the organization. It is concerned with generating co-operation among employees through shared values and standards of behaviour.

IBM seems to subscribe to the cultural view of mission. The company describes its mission in terms of a distinct business philosophy, which in turn produces strong cultural norms and values. In his book, *A Business and its Beliefs*, Thomas J. Watson Jr. described these beliefs, many of which were established by his father, and insisted that they have been the central pillars of the company's success. Watson asserted: 'The only sacred cow in an organization should be its basic philosophy of doing business'. For IBM, 'the basic philosophy, spirit and drive of the business' lies in three concepts: respect for the individual, dedication to service and a quest for superiority in all things. The importance of other factors which contribute to commercial success, such as technological and economic resources, is 'transcended by how strongly the people in the organization believe in its basic precepts and how faithfully they carry them out'.[4]

Is it possible to reconcile these two different interpretations? Are they conflicting theories or are they simply separate parts of the same picture? We believe these theories can be synthesized into a comprehensive single description of mission. We also believe that some of the confusion over mission exists because of a failure to appreciate that it is an issue which involves both the hearts (culture) and minds (strategy) of employees. It is something which straddles the world of business and the world of the individual.

In the pages that follow we outline a framework that defines mission. The value of this framework is that it helps managers to think clearly about mission and, more importantly, it helps them to discuss mission with their colleagues. Previously, managers have had an intuitive understanding of mission. Intuition is not, however, enough. Mission needs to be managed and it can be managed better if it is clearly defined.

Building a Definition of Mission

We have developed our theory of mission both through an intellectual, top down process and through discussions with managers and employees. Through this approach, we have tried to build an understanding of mission that is firmly grounded in the day-to-day realities of corporate life (see Table 1).

We focused on managers in companies with a strong sense of purpose and a strong culture. We wanted to know why they were committed to their organizations, and if they had a sense of the company's mission. They responded by telling us about the behaviour patterns and behaviour standards in their companies.

They brimmed with stories about why their companies were special. In Marks and Spencer, a retailer known for its high quality and value for money, employees talked about quality and value. They described the high standards they demanded of themselves and their suppliers. One manager commented: 'The M & S standards were much higher than those I had worked with before. It appealed to me and I became hooked. Before I had set my standards to conform to the group of people with whom I associated. I was fairly lazy. I found at M & S I had to work harder than I had ever worked at school, but it was attractive because the standards that were set were so high and to fall short of them would be letting myself down'.

They enthused about good human relations and visible management: 'I have had 27 years in Marks and Spencer. What was it that appealed to me when I joined? It was that the senior levels were real people and real personalities, even for me in a relatively low position. It wasn't that I spent a lot of time with them but rather it was the apocryphal stories that were handed down to me that made me feel I had met them. The organization had a strong personality and I could identify with the policies, people and practices of the business. The Board have enough visibility so that I have a good idea of what they want from me.'

At British Airways, staff spoke of the new pride and professionalism among employees as the result of the effort in the 1980s to build a service culture: 'I feel proud to work for BA', said one individual. 'People outside BA recognize the achievement, especially when they travel on the airline.'

Pride and dedication were also evident in Egon Zehnder, an executive search firm. Consultant after consultant spoke of concepts and values which the company holds dear: the primacy of the client's interest, teamwork and the 'one firm' concept. Mark Weedon, former managing director of the London office, explains: 'We are not a group of separate profit centres. The objective is to maximize the whole. We shy away from measuring productivity. You're selling the firm, not the individual or the office. We are very different from the average search firm. It's a sort of subjugation of self.' Said another consultant: 'There are very few arguments here. Because? Because we all depend on each other. We're not selfish in generating work... We recognize each other's skills and we'll switch assignments or work as a team.'

Table 1. The research approach

A research team from the Ashridge Strategic Management Centre approached 42 companies that expressed an interest in the project. These companies are listed below. Initially we asked them how they had developed and used their mission statements. However, we soon discovered that a number of the companies in our sample had a strong sense of purpose, or a strong culture, or both.

We therefore identified from the original group of companies four businesses that seemed to have a strong sense of purpose supported by a strong sense of culture. These companies were Bulmers, manufacturers of cider and soft drinks; Egon Zehnder, the Swiss-based international executive search consultancy; Marks and Spencer, the international retailing business; and Royal U.S., the American arm of a British insurance company.

Finally, we examined four cases where senior managers had set about developing a new mission and philosophy. One of these cases, Shell (U.K.) Refining, has been well documented by a variety of different researchers and we relied on their evidence. We also relied on published data for Borg-Warner, a diverse multinational corporation, since the company's efforts to create a mission have been developed into a Harvard Business School case. The Burton Breweries story has been described in a book, *By GABB and by GIBB*, published and edited by former managing director David Cox, and we tested its evidence through a number of interviews. In the other company, British Airways, we interviewed many managers and employees at different locations.

Detailed Interviews
Carried Out

Bulmers
Egon Zehnder
Marks & Spencer
Royal U.S.

Full Case Studies

Borg-Warner
British Airways
Ind Coope Burton Brewery
Shell U.K. Refining

Personal Experience Discussed

Akzo	Gencor	Price Waterhouse
Ashridge Management College	Grand Metropolitan	Prudential
	Hanson	Rank Xerox
BBA	ICI	Royal U.K.
BOC	LIG	Shell International
The Body Shop	Lloyds Bank	W.H. Smith
British Petroleum	Richard Lochridge Associates	Tarmac
BUPA		TI Group
Burmah Castrol	Mars	Trusthouse Forte
Burson Marsteller	McKinsey & Co.	Valmet
Courtaulds	Metropolitan Police	Wellcome
First Chicago Bank	Northern Ireland Electricity	
Ford	Portsmouth & Sunderland Newspapers	

An employee in a large manufacturing company spoke of emotional commitment and sense of purpose. For her, the company's high standards of behaviour are epitomized by the chairman's example. She commented: 'He believes that all people are equal. He's a bit paternalistic for my way of thinking but he insists on human decency and he is consistent... The company believes in treating people like human beings. There is too little of that in my life—look at the way people push past you in the street...' To this woman, working for her company is one way of supporting 'human decency', a concept she values strongly.

In these companies the commitment and enthusiasm among employees seem to come from a sense of personal attachment to the principles on which the company operates. To them mission has more to do with living out behaviour standards than with achieving goals. To the managers we spoke to, their mission appeared to be to follow the standards and behaviours their companies ask of them. From this flow pride and enthusiasm. Employees are not simply conforming to peer pressure or suffering from corporate indoctrination—they are giving their personal endorsement and commitment to these standards and behaviours.

To understand why, we tried to push interviewees to articulate their feelings further. We asked questions such as: 'Why are you attached to these standards? Why is the one firm concept important to you? Why is treating people well so important to you?' The answers were the same—in the blunt words of a director of Bulmers, the U.K. brewery and drinks business, 'because it's right'. Interviewees were making strong value judgements, arguing that the values and practices of their companies are morally correct. In other words, they make a connection between their own personal values and the beliefs of their companies. When these reinforce one another, people feel a deep satisfaction.

But the sense of rightness these employees feel is not restricted to a personal or moral realm. When pushed even further, some also articulate a commercial rationale. They assert that their behaviour is more effective than their competitors. They argue that their way of working is not only more personally satisfying but also superior to that of their competitors.

A consultant at Egon Zehnder explained the commercial rationale behind the Egon Zehnder philosophy: 'The philosophy means you're more dedicated to the client. One has a different attitude from what you might have in another research firm . . . The firm bends over backwards to encourage sharing, giving advice, helping other offices around the world . . . In the long term, the approach produces better quality search work.'

Another consultant from Egon Zehnder reinforced the link between the commercial rationale and moral rationale, showing how the two can become intertwined. 'When you first come here, you get exposed to a lot of strong hype and ethics. At first it seems a bit heavy . . . Then you start to believe it, and that worries you, until you realize that you have to have it because of the way we try to present ourselves and our belief in quality, in confidentiality, the process of clearing with the client—that's all fundamental to ensure that you operate

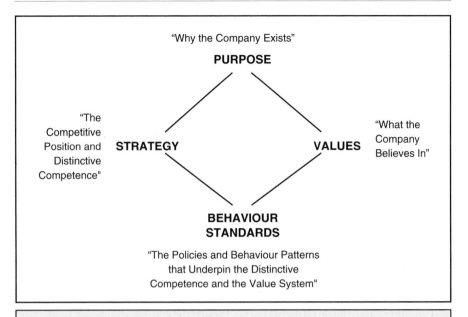

"Why the Company Exists"
PURPOSE

"The Competitive Position and Distinctive Competence"   **STRATEGY**   **VALUES**   "What the Company Believes In"

BEHAVIOUR STANDARDS

"The Policies and Behaviour Patterns that Underpin the Distinctive Competence and the Value System"

Figure 1. The Ashridge mission model.

efficiently . . . I was interviewing this morning and I found myself becoming Messianic about the firm because you really believe it. I do believe it because I need it.'

We were hearing managers talk primarily about the standards and behaviours in their companies and why these are important to them. They gave two reasons. They are committeed to the standards because, to them, they are worthwhile and elevating. They are also committed to the standards because they can see the practical good sense behind them; they can see that the standards add up to a superior business strategy.

We have attempted to make sense of these responses by developing a definition of mission. Our definition, which we have illustrated in Figure 1, includes four elements—purpose, strategy, behaviour standards and values. A strong mission, we believe, exists when the four elements of mission link tightly together, resonating and reinforcing each other.

Purpose

What is the company for? For whose benefit is all the effort being put it? Why should a manager or an employee do more than the minimum required? For a company these questions are the equivalent of a person asking 'why do I exist?'. The questions are deeply philosophical and can lead boards of directors into heated debate. Indeed, many companies do not even attempt to reach a conclusion about the nature of their overall purpose.

However, where there does appear to be an overall idea of purpose, companies fall into three categories. First there is the company that claims to exist for the benefit of the shareholders. For these companies the purpose is to maximize wealth for the shareholders. All decisions are assessed against a yardstick of shareholder value. Hanson, a conglomerate focused on Britain and the U.S.A., is one example. Lord Hanson repeatedly states, 'The shareholder is king'. Unlike many companies whose chairmen claim to be working primarily for the shareholders, Lord Hanson believes what he says and manages the business to that end. Hence Martin Taylor, a director, feels quite free to say: 'All of our businesses are for sale all of the time. If anyone is prepared to pay us more than we think they are worth we will sell. We have no attachment to any individual business.'

Most managers, however, are not as single minded as Lord Hanson. They do not believe that the company's only purpose is to create wealth for shareholders. They acknowledge the claims of other stakeholders such as customers, employees, suppliers and the community. Faced with the question: 'Is your company in business to make money for shareholders, make products for customers or provide rewarding jobs for employees?', they will answer yes to all three.

The second type of company, therefore, is one that exists to satisfy all its stakeholders. In order to articulate this broader idea of purpose many of these companies have written down their responsibility to each stakeholder group. Ciba-Geigy is an example.

It has published the company's business principles under four headings—the public and the environment, customers, employees and shareholders. Under the heading of the public and the environment it has five paragraphs describing principles such as: 'We will behave as a responsible corporate member of society and will do our best to co-operate in a responsible manner with the appropriate authorities, local and national.' For customers there are three paragraphs, employees eight paragraphs and shareholders five paragraphs.

A less detailed statement of the company's commitment to its stakeholders is given by Monsanto: 'Monsanto's continuing success requires customer enthusiasm for our products, employee dedication and skill, public acceptance of our social behaviour, and shareowner confidence and investment. Our goal is to merit their collective support and, in so doing, share with them the rewards that a truly great worldwide company can generate'.

In practice it can be argued that the multiple-stakeholder view of purpose is more a matter of pragmatism than arbitrary choice. In a competitive labour market, a company which totally ignored its employees' needs would soon find its labour costs soaring as it fought to stem the tide of rising employee turnover. But what is important is the psychology of statements of purpose. Lord Hanson is saying that he is expecting his managers to put the allegiance of employees after the interests of shareholders in their lists of priorities. Other companies say they have equal priority. For employees this makes them very different companies.

Managers in the third type of company are dissatisfied by a purpose solely aimed at satisfying stakeholder needs. They have sought to identify a purpose that is greater than the combined needs of the stakeholders, something to which all the stakeholders can feel proud of contributing. In short, they aim towards a higher idea. The planning director in one company, operating in a depressed region of Britain, explained: 'I don't get excited about making money for shareholders. I like to help business succeed. That's something I can get excited about. I believe our future depends on it—I don't just mean this company, it's about the future of the nation, even the international community—it's about world peace and that sort of thing.'

At Marks and Spencer one manager described the company's purpose as 'raising standards for the working man'. This rings true for many others in the company who felt, particularly in the early days of Marks and Spencer and after the war, that they were improving the standard of clothing available to the average person because they were able to retail high quality goods at affordable prices.

At The Body Shop, a retailer of cosmetics, managers talk about 'products that don't hurt animals or the environment'. At Egon Zehnder the purpose is to be the worldwide leader in executive search. Whether these companies have an almost moral crusade, like Marks and Spencer or The Body Shop, or whether they just aspire to be the best, like Egon Zehnder, they have all reached beyond the stakeholder definition of purpose. Each stakeholder, whether shareholder, employee or supplier, can feel that doing business with the company supports some higher level goal.

We believe that leaders will find it easier to create employees with commitment and enthusiasm if they choose a purpose aimed at a higher ideal. We have met individuals committed to shareholders or to the broader definition of stakeholders, but we believe that it is harder for this commitment to grow. Purposes expressed in terms of stakeholders tend to emphasize their different selfish interests. Purposes aimed at higher ideals seek to deny these selfish interests or at least dampen their legitimacy. This makes it easier to bind the organization together.

Strategy

To achieve a purpose in competition with other organizations, there needs to be a strategy. Strategy provides the commercial logic for the company. If the purpose is to be the best, there must be a strategy explaining the principles around which the company will become the best. If the purpose is to create wealth, there must be a strategy explaining how the company will create wealth in competition with other companies.

Strategy will define the business that the company is going to compete in, the position that the company plans to hold in that business and the distinctive competence or competitive advantage that the company has or plans to create.

Egon Zehnder provides a good example of a strategy which explains how the firm will achieve its purpose. Egon Zehnder wants to be the most professional, although not necessarily the biggest, international executive search firm. Its competitive advantage comes, it believes, from the methods and systems it uses to carry out search assignments and from the 'one-firm', co-operative culture it has so carefully nurtured. Marks and Spencer's strategy in textiles is a second example. In its clothes retailing business, Marks and Spencer seeks to offer the best value for money in the high street by providing a broad range of classic quality clothes. The company's competitive advantage comes from its high levels of service, and the low overheads generated by high sales per square foot.

Behaviour Standards

Purpose and strategy are empty intellectual thoughts unless they can be converted into action, into the policy and behaviour guidelines that help people to decide what to do on a day-to-day basis.

British Airways provides a good example of how the company's purpose and strategy have been successfully converted into tangible standards and actions. It promotes itself as the 'world's favourite airline' and declares as its aim 'To be the best and most successful company in the airline industry'. The strategy to achieve this is based on providing good value for money, service that overall is superior to its competitors and friendly, professional managers who are in tune with its staff. These strategic objectives are translated into policies and behaviour guidelines such as the need for in-flight services to be at least as good as those of competing airlines on the same route, and the requirement that managers and employees should be helpful and friendly at all times.

By translating purpose and strategy into actionable policies and standards senior managers at British Airways have dramatically changed the performance of the airline. Central to this effort was the training and behaviour change connected with the slogan 'Putting People First'.

The Body Shop, an international retailer of cosmetics, has a purpose of developing cosmetics that do not harm animals or the environment. Its strategy is to be more environmentally conscious than its competitors, hence attracting the 'green' consumer and the 'green' employee. Within the company, environmental consciousness has been translated into policies and behaviour standards, one of which was almost unique when first introduced. All employees have two waste paper baskets: one for recyclable products and one for ordinary garbage. Employees receive training in what can be recycled and what cannot. In the last year or two a number of other companies have introduced similar policies.

Egon Zehnder provides another example of the link between strategy and policies. Egon Zehnder's strategy is to be more professional than other executive search consultants. Connected with this it has a set of policies about how consultants should carry out assignments called the 'systematic consulting approach'. One of the policies is that consultants should not take on a search assignment unless they believe it will benefit the client. Another policy is that there should be a back-up consultant for every assignment in order to ensure a quality service to the client. Supporting this systematic approach are the behaviour standards about co-operation. These are ingrained into the culture rather than written on tablets of stone. An Egon Zehnder consultant willingly helps another consultant within his or her office from other offices around the world.

Philip Vivian, a consultant, explained this behaviour standard: 'Collaboration and co-operation are very important and it is unusual in this industry. It is essential that we recognize each other's skills and switch assignments or work as a team. It is also critical for international work. We have one Japanese assignment that is being coordinated from Tokyo, Milan, Paris, London and Frankfurt. So we have to work as a team. It does not always work out perfectly because of the inevitable problems of communication. But the "one firm" concept helps. We all know we are working for the same firm—no office is going to lose out if it helps another'.

The logic for the co-operation as described by Vivian is a commercial logic. The firm wants to be the best. This means being better at co-operation than its competitors. As a result it needs a behaviour standard that makes sure consultants help each other. This commercial logic is the left-brain logic of the firm.

Human beings are emotional, however, and are often driven more by right-brain motives than left-brain logic. To capture the emotional energy of an organization the mission needs to provide some philosophical or moral rationale for behaviour to run alongside the commercial rationale. This brings us to the next element of our definition of mission.

Values

Values are the beliefs and moral principles that lie behind the company's culture. Values give meaning to the norms and behaviour standards in the company and act as the 'right brain' of the organization. In Figure 2, we show how strategy and values constitute the left and right brain of companies with a mission.

In many organizations corporate values are not explicit and can only be understood by perceiving the philosophical rationale that lies behind management behaviour. For example, consultants in Egon Zehnder believe in co-operative behaviour because they are committed to the firm's strategy. But they also believe in co-operative behaviour because they feel that it is 'right'. Egon Zehnder people are naturally co-operative. They have been selected for that quality. They believe that people ought to be co-operative. 'It makes a nicer place to work and it suits my style', explained one consultant. 'And it's a better way to work', he added with the faintest implication of a moral judgement.

Egon Zehnder people can also be moral about certain aspects of the systematic approach. The policy of not taking on an assignment unless the consultant believes it is good for the client highlights a moral as much as a commercial rationale. Other executive search companies will take on any assignment, they

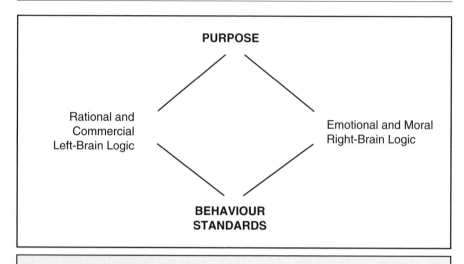

PURPOSE

Rational and Commercial Left-Brain Logic

Emotional and Moral Right-Brain Logic

BEHAVIOUR STANDARDS

Figure 2. Two reasons for action.

argue. But Egon Zehnder puts the interests of the client first and will advise the client against an assignment even if it means lost revenues. It is a professional code of behaviour. As professionals they feel a moral duty to advise the client to do what is best for the client rather than what is best for Egon Zehnder. There is a commercial rationale for this behaviour, but the moral rationale is stronger.

The same is true in British Airways. There is a good commercial reason for 'Putting People First', but there is also a moral reason: we are all people and life would be better for all of us if we took a little more care with each other. This moral rationale was put high on the agenda when 35,000 British Airways staff went on the Putting People First training programmes. The new behaviours described by the trainers were presented as a philosophy of life as much as a way of improving British Airways. Participants were asked to consider how they greeted their families when arriving home as well as how they handled customers.

A third example of the way in which values can provide an additional logic for behaviour comes from Hewlett-Packard. The HP Way describes a behaviour standard made famous by Tom Peters in *In Search of Excellence:* managing by wandering around (MBWA). Hewlett-Packard's strategy has been to succeed in high value niches of the electronics industry by being better at innovation and product development. To implement this strategy HP needs to attract and retain the best engineers and product managers. These high quality individuals do not like to be closely controlled or hierarchically managed. HP, therefore, developed the MBWA policy as a management approach suitable for these kinds of high achievers. The MBWA behaviour standard is based on good commercial logic.

But MBWA has also become a crusade of its own. Managers believe it is the right way to manage not only high achievers but all personnel. MBWA is not good behaviour only because it is good strategy but also because it is something everyone should be doing. It acknowledges the innate creativity of individuals and underlines the manager's respect for people. It has been imbued with values.

The objective observer can easily identify situations, such as captaining a ship, where MBWA would be totally the wrong style of management. Yet for managers committed to the HP Way it is almost sacrosanct. Like the systematic approach at Egon Zehnder, or putting people first at British Airways, MBWA in Hewlett-Packard is not only good strategy but 'the right way to behave'.

These three examples show how values can provide a rationale for behaviour that is just as strong as strategy. It is for this reason that the framework in Figure 2 has a diamond shape. There are two rationales that link purpose with behaviour. The commercial rationale or left-brain reasoning is about strategy and what sort of behaviour will help the company outperform competitors in its chosen arena. The emotional, moral and ethical rationale or right-brain reasoning is about values and what sort of behaviour is ethical: the right way to treat people, the right way to behave in our society.

Our definition of mission includes both these rationales linked together by a common purpose.

Creating a Strong Mission

A strong mission exists when the four elements of mission reinforce each other. This is most easily perceived by looking at the links between the strategy and the value system and whether both can be acted out through the same behaviour standards. Are the important behaviour standards central to both the strategy and the value system?

In Egon Zehnder, British Airways and Hewlett-Packard they are. We looked at only one or two behaviour standards for each company, but we would find much the same reinforcement of both strategy and values if we examined other behaviour standards. Hewlett-Packard's commercial strategy depends on attracting and keeping high quality committed employees. This means it has to demonstrate a set of values which desirable employees will find attractive. So, for example, it has an 'open door' policy that encourages dissatisfied employees to approach senior managers; a policy of high integrity and open communications with stakeholders; a belief in informality and in decentralization; a policy of promoting from within; and a commitment to teamwork. Each of these policies and behaviour standards has a rationale both in the company's strategy and in its value system. They work cumulatively to create a strong mission.

Marks and Spencer is another company where the most important behaviour standards are essential pillars of both the strategy and the value system. One of the platforms of Marks and Spencer's philosophy is good human relations. As one manager explained: 'Marcus Sieff gave many presentations both in the company and outside. But he only ever gave one speech, about good human relations'. Part of Marks and Spencer's strategy is to have employees who take more care, particularly in relation to customer service. By caring for employees, Sieff would argue, the company will create employees who will care for the company and its customers. As a result Marks and Spencer is famous for its services and support for employees, from the quality of the toilets to things like dental care. The policy of good human relations is a standard of management behaviour referred to by one manager as 'visible management'. Almost identical to Hewlett-Packard's standard of MBWA, visible management requires that managers, even at the highest level, spend time visiting stores and talking to staff and customers. As one board member explained: 'In a normal week, the 12 board members will probably between them visit about 25 stores. These are not red-letter days. We will just go in and talk with some of the management, supervisors and staff. It's about getting out and listening to the organization'.

In companies like Egon Zehnder, Marks and Spencer and Hewlett-Packard, the management philosophy and value system dovetail with the strategy so that the company's policies and behaviour standards reinforce both the strategy and the philosophy. The whole has integrity. These companies have strong missions. Strong missions come, therefore, from a clear fit between the four elements in the framework.

A Sense of Mission: The Emotional Bond

A sense of mission is an emotional commitment felt by people towards the company's mission. But even in companies with very strong missions there are many people who do not feel an emotional commitment. We were told, for example, that even at the height of Hewlett-Packard's success an employee survey revealed a large minority of employees who did not have a strong belief in the capabilities of the senior management team, implying that they lacked a sense of mission.

A sense of mission occurs, we believe, when there is a match between the values of an organization and those of an individual. Because organization values are rarely explicit, the individual senses them through the company's behaviour standards. For example, if the behaviour standard is about coop- erative working, the individual will be able to sense that helpfulness is valued above individual competition. If the individual has a personal value about the importance of being helpful and co-operative, then there is a values match between the individual and the organization. The greater the link between company policies and individual values, the greater the scope for the individual's sense of mission.

We see the values match (illustrated in Figure 3) as the most important part of a sense of mission because it is through values that individuals feel emotional about their organizations. Commitment to a company's strategy does not, on its own, constitute a sense of mission. It is not unusual for groups of managers to discuss their company's purpose and strategy and reach an intellectual agreement.

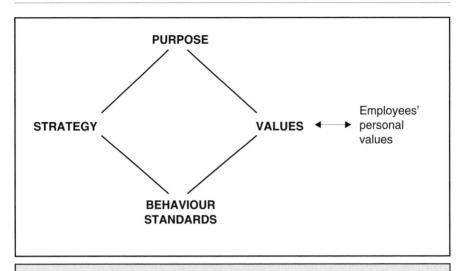

Figure 3. Meaning comes mainly from values.

However this intellectual agreement does not necessarily translate into an emotional commitment and hence the strategic plan does not get implemented. The emotional commitment comes when the individual personally identifies with the values and behaviours lying behind the plan, turning the strategy into a mission and the intellectual agreement into a sense of mission.

The source of the emotional commitment created by a values match is subtle. People are searching for meaning and for an opportunity to transcend the ordinariness of day-to-day existence. Values give meaning. Living up to one's values or joining a group of people successfully following these values helps an individual feel a sense of transcendence. In these circumstances, work becomes more fulfilling because it is filled with greater purpose. Work helps the individual achieve something that is personally important and which, therefore, gives him or her intrinsic satisfaction.

Consider a fastidious individual who has a personal bias towards tidiness and perfection and who works as a proof reader. If the organization believes fervently in accuracy and error-free work, the individual will, in all likelihood, find satisfaction in fastidiously rooting out the minutest blemish or error. He or she will also feel valued. If the organization applies these principles to other areas of the business, the person may begin to feel a warmth for the organization that gives further personal satisfaction. The employee will see the organization as a 'good' company. If, on the other hand, the organization is driven by deadlines and allows too little time for proof reading, causing books to be published with errors, the proof reader will feel frustrated, unappreciated and angry.

Working with a 'good' organization does not guarantee that employees will have a sense of mission. Consider the person who is responsible for cleaning the car park of the Boy Scouts headquarters. The organization has an elevating purpose. It has a clear strategy. It has strong values and well-grooved policies and behaviour standards. It is also highly successful, with more than 17 million members world-wide. In other words the Boy Scout movement has a strong mission. Yet the car park cleaner may or may not feel a sense of mission. It will depend on his or her personal values and the values and behaviour standards by which he or she is managed. Each individual is making a judgement: 'Does this organization care about the sort of things I care about?' If it does, then there is the potential for developing an emotional commitment. If not, then support from the individual is grudging, based on a contract of so much work for so much pay.

It is important to recognize the individual nature of a sense of mission. It is a personal, emotional feeling created by the individual relationship that the person has with the organization. If the car park cleaner is gregarious and believes more in making people happy than in dirt-free cleanliness, he is more likely to feel a sense of mission about the Boy Scouts if the office workers stop to have a joke with him in the car park and involve him in the office events. If his boss is a tidiness fanatic, he is going to feel uncomfortable and will be unlikely to develop an energetic commitment to the organization.

Recognizing the personal nature of a sense of mission is important because it has two implications. First, no organization can hope to have 100 per cent of its employees with a sense of mission, unless it is very small. People are too varied and have too many individual values for it to be possible for a large organization to achieve a values match for all its employees. Second, careful recruitment is essential. People's values do not change when they change companies. By recruiting people with compatible values, companies are much more likely to foster a sense of mission.

We have pointed out that even in companies with a strong mission, many people lack a sense of mission. This may be because they have few strong values and, therefore, feel very little for the company. It may also be because their values conflict with those of the company. These individuals may not be poor performers or disruptive but their motivation is more self-interested and their attitudes are likely to be more cynical. These individuals may give good service to the company but there are benefits to a company that only come through having individuals with a sense of mission.

We have defined the terms mission and sense of mission at some length and been at pains to draw a distinction between these two concepts because we believe managers are frequently confused by them.

Mission is an intellectual concept that can be analysed and discussed un-emotionally. Like strategy, mission is a set of propositions that can be used to guide the policies and behaviours of a company. However, mission is a larger concept than strategy. It covers strategy and culture. The strategy element of mission legislates what is important to the commercial future of the company. The values element of mission legislates what is important to the culture of the company. When the two are in tune, reinforcing each other and bound by a common purpose, the mission is strong. When there are contradictions and inconsistencies, the mission is weak.

Sense of mission is not an intellectual concept: it is an emotional and deeply personal feeling. The individual with a sense of mission has an emotional attachment and commitments to the company, what it stands for and what it is trying to do.

A company with a clear mission does not necessarily have employees with a sense of mission. Some individuals may have a sense of mission with varying degrees of intensity. Many will not. Over time the number of employees with a sense of mission will increase as the policies of the mission become implemented and embedded in the company culture. But even a company like Hewlett-Packard, that has had a clear mission for 30 or more years, will not have more than 50 per cent of employees with what we would recognize as a sense of mission.

Implications of the Mission Model

Mission thinking has implications at all levels in business as well as for those connected to business. Our greatest hope is that our research will stimulate management teams to give the subject some executive time.

We are confident that our mission model is a powerful analytical tool and we want managers to use it. It may be appropriate, therefore, to summarize why we think the model is so powerful.

First, the model states that organization values need to be compatible with employee values. This compatibility or lack of it can be analysed and measured, bringing objectivity to the discussion of culture and human resource issues. Will the members of the executive team have a values conflict with the proposed mission? Will the marketing department have a values conflict? While we recognize that the analysis of cultures and values has, in the past, proved difficult and of limited managerial benefit, we believe that values differences of the kind exposed by mission thinking can be analysed and have important management implications. Techniques for interviewing, group discussions and questionnaires will quickly expose these value differences and confront managers with the need to change the values in the mission, change the people or win the people to the new values.

Moreover, since values must be embedded in behaviour standards, values conflicts become exposed when managers or employees react to behaviour instructions. It may be hard to analyse whether the managers of the chemical laboratory believe in 'supportive management'. It is much easier to decide whether these managers are likely to implement a standard of managing by wandering around. The model's strength, therefore, is that it defines the relationship managers need to create between organization values and employee values.

Second, the model demands that strategy and values resonate and reinforce each other. It is possible to identify many values that are compatible with a particular strategy, but it is hard to analyse whether these are the right values, whether they resonate with strategy sufficiently strongly.

The mission model's emphasis on behaviour standards helps to bridge this analytical gap. By insisting that strategy and values are converted into a few behaviour standards acting as beacons of the mission, the degree of resonance between strategy and values is exposed. If it is possible to condense the mission into a few symbolically important behaviour standards, such as 'putting people first' or 'management by wandering around' then we can be confident that the strategy and the values resonate strongly. If not, if no powerful behaviour standards can be identified, then the fault almost certainly lies in a lack of resonance between strategy and values. Further mission planning, further experimentation and further insight are needed.

We can illustrate this with an example drawn from our own organization, Ashridge, whose largest activity is a management college outside London. Ashridge has identified four important planks of its future strategy: two of these are 'self-directed learning' and 'internationalization'. With the ambition of becoming Europe's best management school, Ashridge recognizes the need to become more international and to eliminate elements of its culture and product offering that have historically been focused on the British and Commonwealth market. It also feels that the best way of achieving European pre-eminence is to become more learner-centred: to focus on the needs of managers. Since different managers have different needs a learner-centred focus demands that Ashridge should develop ways of helping managers learn what they want to learn rather than what the lecturer wants to teach them.

Both of these thrusts are proving difficult to implement; not because the strategy is unclear or because there is widespread disagreement about the values, but because the policies and behaviour standards that need to underpin the new mission are hard to identify. What behaviour is required of a lecturer or a programme administrator or a member of the hotel staff to ensure that they are contributing to the themes of internationalization or participant-centred learning? We do not yet know. It will take more months, possibly even more years, to identify the appropriate behaviours and get to the point where the behaviour standards can be articulated. We have not yet found a resonance between the desired strategy and the organization's current values.

Managing mission is, therefore, a continuous, ongoing process. Few companies will be able to articulate the behaviour standards that drive their mission without working at the problem over a number of years. By being clear about the need to have a mission, the need to create a relationship between strategy and values and the need to articulate behaviour standards, managers can avoid a superficial attitude to mission and continue the analysis, thinking and experimentation for long enough to develop the mission that will build a great company.

Acknowledgement

This article is drawn from *A Sense of Mission*, Andrew Campbell, Marion Devine and David Young, Economist Publications/Hutchinson (1990).

References

1. Peter Drucker, *Management: Tasks, Responsibilities, Practices*, Harper & Row, New York (1973).
2. The main academic work on the contents of mission statements has been done by Fred David and Jack Pearce (J. A. Pearce II and F. R. David), Corporate mission statements: the bottom line, *Academy of Management Executive*, **1** (1987): D. Cochran and F. R. David, The communication effectiveness of organizational mission statements, *Journal of Applied Communication Research* (1987); Fred R. David, How companies define their mission, *Long Range Planning*, **22** (1) (1989).
3. T. Levitt, Marketing myopia, *Harvard Business Review*, pp. 45–56, July/August (1960).
4. Thomas J. Watson Jr., *A Business and Its Beliefs*, McGraw-Hill, New York (1963).

Further Reading

Andrew Campbell and Kiran Tawadey, *Mission and Business Philosophy: Winning Employee Commitment*, Heinemann, Oxford (1990).
Andrew Campbell and Sally Yeung, *Do You Need a Mission Statement?* Special Report No. 1208, The Economist Publications Management Guides, London (1990).

12

Strategic Benchmarking at ICI Fibres

Tony Clayton and Bob Luchs

Learning from comparison has two generic forms in business, at the strategic or business level, and at the level of individual processes. Most literature has discussed the 'micro' form—focused on specific practices or processes. The case of ICI Fibres shows that:
1. business performance benchmarks are just as measurable as those for processes,
2. there is a clear hierarchy of strategic/operating/micro-process benchmarks which managers need to understand,
3. effective strategic management brings together benchmarks for business strengths and benchmarks for process capabilities,
4. you cannot benchmark your way to profit with the wrong strategy.

Benchmarks and benchmarking are the topics most likely to grab the interest of business executives today. They were probably featured at more management conferences in 1993 than any other subject. Benchmarking in business is not a new concept, however. The office where we write, in the City of London, lies opposite one of the Livery Halls, whose Guilds represented the 'business standards' of medieval times, providing benchmarks for comparison to benefit customers (together with certain restrictive practices to benefit suppliers).

But benchmarking as a business management technique has come to mean something very specific. The majority of the literature on the subject which has

Tony Clayton is a Director of PIMS Associates in London.
Bob Luchs is a Director of PIMS Europe, working in Germany and the UK.

appeared over the last 2 years has focused strongly on benchmarking as a system for comparing detailed business processes or functions. It is based on pulling apart business activity into its component parts, identifying the important processes which make a business work, then searching outside for—and learning from—best practice in that process or function.[1]

Such benchmarking at this 'micro' level can be powerful. Managers like David Kearns, CEO of Xerox, who make it part of their culture, claim it is one of the most effective tools for enhancing performance.[2] The comparison process links closely to the approach of total quality management (TQM). By involving the entire workforce it motivates teams to establish precise standards for performance, and to work towards continuous improvement.

However, not all benchmarking applies to business processes. For example, Xerox benchmarks customer satisfaction, but customer satisfaction is not a process—it is the result of many processes between the expression of a customer need and the delivery of a product or service to meet it. Most of the competitive and financial measures on which businesses can be compared are the results of multiple processes which take place within a business unit—or outside it in the interaction with customers and suppliers. Since these benchmarks usually relate to the output of many processes and practices, we call them 'macro' benchmarks.

Since the 1970s PIMS (the Profit Impact of Market Strategy programme) has measured and compared businesses on such a macro basis, at the business unit level. It has examined the impacts of market attractiveness, competitive strength and resource use (and more recently of human resources and IT) on behaviour and performance of whole business systems. PIMS' contribution to benchmarking is to demonstrate that a business unit's performance can be benchmarked just as effectively as a business process. Our definition of benchmarking is therefore somewhat wider than those who focus on practices and processes. It extends to learning from all appropriate comparisons.

Managers need to understand micro and macro benchmarks, and how the two perspectives are linked, if they are to develop and implement successful strategies. ICI Fibres was an early example of this synthetic benchmarking of business potential, illustrating how a business twice used different types of benchmarks to respond to new market conditions. Before reviewing it, it is worth exploring the differences between business unit and business process benchmarks, and the links between them.

Business Processes, Business Units and Strategic Benchmarks

'Micro' benchmarking is characterized by focus on specific processes (e.g. delivery logistics or invoice processing) and linking achievement to 'best practice' functional management. Many who practice in the field have extended the comparisons they draw beyond their own industries. The work done by Xerox to improve distribution by studying LL Bean, a mail order company, is the classic example of benchmarking outside the direct competitor set, but whether inside or outside the industry the principle of comparing like processes remains the same.

Managers apply business process skills in the context of business units, and the needs of customers in their markets. Within a company, some processes are common to different business areas, while others are specific—usually related to particular customer or product needs. The example below of a soft drinks business illustrates the point.

The strategic planning process aims to establish, on the basis of competitive and market analysis, business unit strengths and weaknesses. Our definition of strategic benchmarking is the development of measures for a business unit which quantify its key strengths and weaknesses, to give some external reference to the strategic planning process. Quantification of such measures, to permit comparison with other business experience, is what justifies the term 'benchmark'.

From an understanding of business unit strengths and weaknesses, corporate managers set priorities and strategies. At this level, the list of strategic benchmarks in a corporate portfolio is relatively short. For example, Jack Welch, the CEO of GE, is clear that his company will compete only in markets where it can be number one or two. Share rank is a key strategic benchmark for GE because experience has shown that in the types of market in which it operates, being number three is usually unprofitable. Other companies use a broader range of key strategic indicators. What has become known as the 'balanced scorecard approach' attempts to put in context financial and non-financial business measures that affect future performance of units in a portfolio.[3]

The principle that key characteristics of a business determine its financial success or failure lies behind most thinking on strategy. PIMS proves that such characteristics can be measured, their effects quantified, and that the 'earning power' of a business can be benchmarked in a statistically reliable way.[4]

The concept of 'Par ROCE'—the return on capital normally associated with a business unit with specific measured characteristics, irrespective of industry —was a significant contribution to the development of strategic analysis in the late 1970s. This was, in essence, the first strategic benchmarking system. It relates 30 measures, of market structure, competitive position and resource productivity, to the ability of a business unit to earn good returns. These relationships have subsequently been proved by data covering over 22,000 years of business experience; they have been extended to cover measures for productivity and business growth. We shall see them applied in the first part of the ICI Fibres case.

While a portfolio manager's key question may be simply 'will this business make money?', business unit managers need to know 'how can we make the most of the business we've got?' Strategic targets for business managers have to be situation specific. Appropriate targets can be found in matched comparisons against the performance of other businesses in similar market and competitive situations. Through such comparisons it is often possible to gauge the potential

	Business Units		
Business processes	Mineral Water	Fizzy Drinks	Fruit Juices
Purity/analysis	X		
Procurement		X	X
Blending		X	X
Carbonation	X	X	
Bottling	X	X	
Canning		X	
Cartoning			X
Logistics/order processing	X	X	X
Formulation		X	X
Brand management	X	X	X
Channel management	X	X	X
Human resource management	X	X	X

Figure 1. Business units and business processes.

impact of innovation or quality improvement on the development of a business position, or to understand the marketing effort required to build strategic assets. This type of matched comparison was used in the second part of our work with ICI Fibres.

In recent years there has been much greater emphasis on understanding corporate capabilities and competencies as determinants of the success of strategy. John Kay draws useful distinctions between various types of know how, and 'strategic assets' of the type captured by PIMS measures.[5] Our experience suggests that managers gain important insights at the strategic level by bringing together benchmarks for business performance and benchmarks for process competence.

Strategic benchmarks for business performance are measures which set overall direction, and show managers how others have succeeded in similar circumstances. Process benchmarks, in contrast, usually indicate standards which should be achievable in day-to-day operations, given the willingness to learn. In our view of the 'hierarchy' of benchmarks, the place to start is at the top. However strong process competencies may be in a business, if they are applied in situations which normally lead to failure, they are likely to be wasted.

At the strategic level, business strategies are assessed in terms of their potential to deliver value to shareholders. Business performance measures which drive company stock market prices include sustainable ROCE and business growth at the top of the list. These in turn are driven by productivity, innovation and competitive quality capability, which can be benchmarked in their own right. Measures for each of these are vital in developing business unit strategy which gives the best prospect of adding to shareholder value.

Given the 'right strategy', business potential is realized via effective management of business processes. Moving directly from strategic to 'micro' benchmarking may, in some cases, be appropriate. In others it helps to look at 'macro' business measures which do not in themselves define strategy, but can indicate priorities for action. These 'macro' benchmarks complete our hierarchy in Figure 2. They are 'macro' measures in the sense that they apply to a combination of business processes, and are measured for the business as a whole. They can be benchmarked against appropriate comparators (i.e. other businesses), in terms of cost level or cost structure, or physical parameters.

The distinction between these three types of benchmark will be illustrated by the ICI Fibres case. Strategic benchmarking showed which areas of the business and of the wider industry presented profitable opportunities, and which did not. It also suggested essential changes in the 'shape' of business units. Macro benchmarks were used to pinpoint functions where process management was poorly aligned to strategic needs, and areas of unnecessary cost representing unrealized business potential. Micro benchmarks were derived by

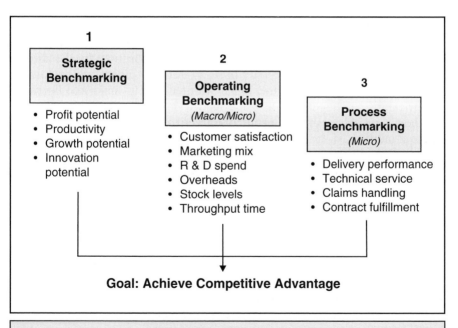

Figure 2. Hierarchy of benchmarking.

functional specialists, mainly within the business, to improve the working of specific processes.

Strategic Benchmarking at ICI Fibres: 1979–1981

Strategic benchmarking is vital when markets change, because business potential usually changes too. ICI Fibres confronted major shifts in its market boundaries over the last 20 years. First, in the period up to 1979, market barriers between the countries of the EC collapsed to create pan-European markets with new competitor dynamics. Then in 1990 these markets became global, the barriers between Europe and the rest of the world being swept away—again requiring a radical reassessment.

In each case managers needed to understand what was happening in a totally new situation. They also had to develop new benchmarks for performance to assess business potential, and to define ways of achieving that potential. The story of the first challenge is told in Sir John Harvey-Jones' book *Making It Happen*.[6] It is one occasion when the trouble-shooter came to admit that his strategic view was wrong!

Brief History to 1980

In the 1940s ICI and Courtaulds launched a version of nylon, using different technology from the world leader DuPont, but essentially entering as followers. They were successful in developing a wide range of applications for the fibre. In 1953 ICI acquired rights to polyester fibre, a UK development, and exploited it with success as the market grew. It was licensed widely, and some licensees—particularly the Japanese—invested heavily in quality development. Most suppliers were able to operate profitably, and to build positions in a number of national markets.

During the 1970s, as several producers built new capacity in both nylon and polyester, the market matured quickly. The new fibres had penetrated some market areas from which they were subsequently displaced. Severe overcapacity, coinciding with the integration of EC economies, caused competition to move to a European rather than national level. Prices fell, and all producers faced large losses.

By 1980 ICI Fibres was in crisis. It was losing cash and its traditional UK customers were being squeezed by recession. The decision process that followed is outlined in Sir John Harvey-Jones' book, seen from a 'top-down' perspective. His initial view was that cash from nylon—seen as a product in decline—should be used to revitalize polyester—the in-house success story. Systematic strategic benchmarking of sectors of the business was to prove—for the markets of the 1980s at least—that such an approach would not work.

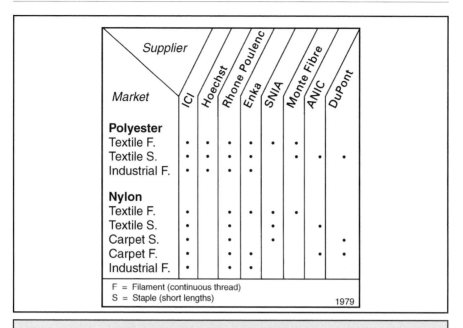

Figure 3. Who competes in which European markets?

Competition in the 'New' Market

Competitive analysis of the 'new' European market of 1979 was undertaken. Market boundaries were no longer defined by national frontiers, but by technology (polyester vs nylon) and by end use. Different areas of the market—textiles, carpet fibre, rubber reinforcement—were fought over by different producers. The strengths and weaknesses of competitors ICI had to face in each arena also varied considerably.

A review of the factors influencing long term profitability made it clear that ICI's share positions in most of the nylon businesses were still strong, and its quality in textile fibre was good enough to justify a price premium. The company possessed clear strategic assets in certain areas. Most markets were simple in terms of marketing costs and customer structure—normally a plus for long-term performance. The business was not particularly capital intensive, but did suffer from low productivity—measured in terms of value added per employee.

Evaluation of sustainable earning power (Par ROCE) from strategic benchmark comparisons showed a clearer picture of future potential than simply looking at current profits. Some nylon and some polyester businesses made current losses, and a few of each were profitable. But none of the polyester activities had the structural or competitive characteristics associated with positive long term returns. Investment in polyester, without clear plans to reposition the business in terms of quality, critical mass and innovation, would push them

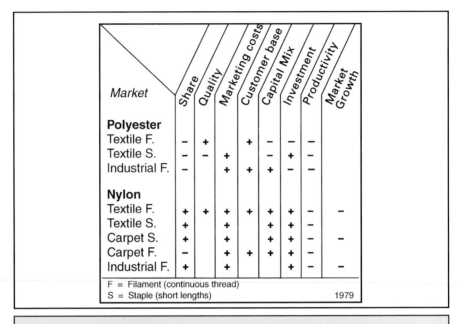

Figure 4. ICI Fibres' strengths (+) and weaknesses (−).

further into loss. For nylon, on the other hand, the picture was more promising—better share and a more attractive cost structure—so the hill to climb was much less steep. Nylon, for ICI Fibres, was a better bet for the 1980s.

In addition to (strategic) profit benchmarks, PIMS developed (macro) cost benchmarks for each market area, based on experience of similar businesses. These showed that ICI's R & D expenditure was high compared to activities with similar levels of innovation, competitive position and market demands. Either the output of R & D should be more visible, or the level of continuing investment by ICI in R & D should fall. Productivity targets for the total business were set in a number of areas, redefining overhead costs and direct employee output which would be normal for a business like Fibres.

The vital strategic conclusion of the exercise was that ICI Fibres should be reshaped round its areas of long-term strength. This could only be done by disposing of weak polyester positions, using them as bargaining chips against other producers, to build better positions in nylon.

But operational targets emerging from the study were just as important. Without the attention focused on innovation by 'macro' benchmarking it is debatable whether new nylon development would have received the boost which it did at ICI Fibres during the 1980s. A clearer market focus in development helped to cut lead times for development, cut development costs and increase the rate at which the business was capable of delivering new products to the market.

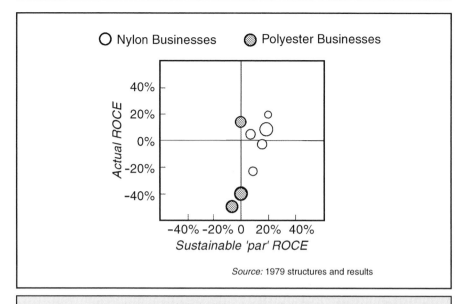

Figure 5. 1979 par and actual ROCE.

A great deal of detailed work in repositioning ICI nylon in fashion markets, to compete from a reduced cost base with other innovative fibres, paid off. To quote Sir John Harvey-Jones in 1988, 'the nylon business produced innovation after innovation and today is a world leader in its specialized fields'. Without both the cost reductions and the innovation, the restructuring which followed would not have turned the business round.

Restructuring for the 'New' Market

The conclusion reached in strategic benchmarking that ICI's polyester business was, to quote Sir John, *too far gone*, did not mean that the business had no value in the surgery which followed. Restructuring ICI Fibres was subject to cash constraints, which meant that reshaping had to be funded by disposals. There was also an obvious requirement that any new structure should generate cash in the medium term. It was therefore imperative that the portfolio shifted from low profit/high growth areas—which soak up cash—towards areas with higher sustainable margins requiring less continued investment. The cash position of other European producers made them subject to the same pressures.

It was quite clear where ICI Fibres' cash drains were likely to be—and which were the opportunities for cash generation, with strong 'Par' profits and capable of generating their own investment funds for growth. But from a competitor's point of view the picture was very different. Fibres' managers, using strategic

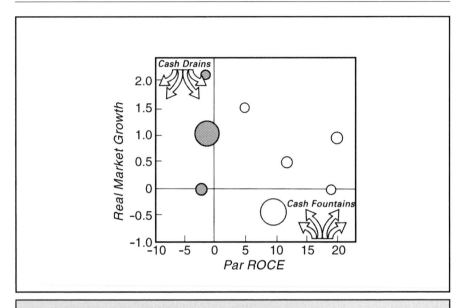

Figure 6. Portfolio cash balance.

benchmarking techniques, could estimate sustainable returns for each competitor—since they knew their competitive positions, and the markets in which they sold. Since competitors used similar technology it was easy to make good estimates of their capital base and productivity. Given this knowledge, it was clear that some had cash drains in nylon, and also cash generators in polyester.

From this knowledge of ICI's strategic benchmarks, and those of competitors, it was relatively easy to chart the potential for industry restructuring. In the 5 years which followed there was substantial rationalization; ICI disposed of its polyester capability, Montefibre and Montedison ceased production of nylon, while Akzo/Enka gave up its operations in textile fibres. A new competitive structure emerged which permitted most European producers to invest and grow. Without the new structure, the operational improvements which ICI brought about would not have led to the years of profitable innovation which lasted through to 1989.

Globalization in Fibres: 1990–1991

Between 1988 and 1990 underlying changes took place in market structures both in textile fibres, under increasing pressure from Asian competition, and in the important market for tyre reinforcement fibre. Global purchasing in the automotive industry changed the tyre market, increasing buyer power and destroying market boundaries. Within 5 years, a dozen major world tyre manufacturers merged to form five.

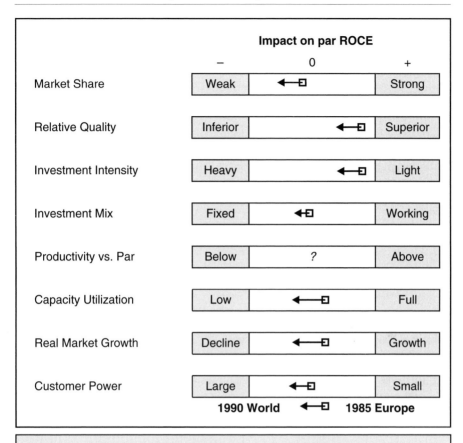

Figure 7. How industrial fibres changed.

Increased concentration in the tyre business coincided with DuPont's decision to joint-venture a fibre plant in Turkey, and with collapse of the market in Europe and North America. With international customers, and now competition from the world market leader in supply, a global market had been created at the start of another downturn. World-wide oversupply, and the further collapse of market barriers had their inevitable effect. Margins vanished.

The change had a serious effect on ICI Fibres' position. The tyre cord business moved from having a strong share in Europe to a much weaker share position in the global market. Its quality advantage, which had been built on service, was less easy to realize over a wider geographic spread. To make matters worse, just before the downturn ICI had invested heavily in the part of its product range most vulnerable to competition from DuPont.

Profit benchmarks for the new competitive situation were not encouraging. Sustainable returns—expressed as Par ROCE—in the business were not high enough to justify continuing investment. But at least they were positive, which

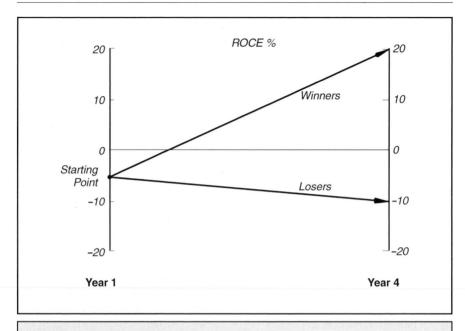

Figure 8. 'Winners' are worth a closer look.

was more than could be said for the two other European producers Enka and Rhone Poulenc. The problem was that these two were unlikely to be persuaded to quit the business—one was state owned and the other was central to its owner's broader strategy.

For DuPont, however, it was clear that the new market was an environment in which survival was possible. With a strong competitive position and good cost structure, DuPont had a 'Par ROCE' which was close to the cost of capital. It was attacking from a position where both strategic assets and the company's capabilities in cost control gave it considerable strength.

The approach which had worked in the 1980s, acquiring and divesting market positions, was no longer appropriate. A solution to keep ICI in the business would require changing Fibres from within. Were there any 'traceable' cases to show how businesses like this could transform themselves from loss to worthwhile profits within 3 years—without the stimulus of market growth? PIMS' time series database of business experience was used in a search for examples.

Finding Successful Role Models

The process required agreement with the business team on the important characteristics of the business—and the specific starting conditions. We looked for businesses in the PIMS database like ICI technical fibres in its new market

—with weak market positions, no market growth, diminished differentiation, selling direct to a few powerful buyers, etc. Having established that there were turnaround cases like this, comparisons were drawn between businesses which managed their way back to profit against those which failed, in order to identify common strategic benchmarks for recovery. Finally the business team identified how much of the transformation could be done in ICI Fibres.

Analysis showed at least a dozen similar businesses among the 3000 which PIMS have tracked over time which achieved the turnaround Fibres were looking for. It was clearly worth benchmarking how they did it, and what distinguished turnaround 'winners' from businesses which lost the battle for recovery.

Results of the benchmarking process presented the management team with a big challenge. The businesses which had achieved these remarkable turnarounds had made major strategic shifts, which looked hard to follow. Within a 4 year period they had:

■   cut costs dramatically, in manufacturing, overheads, R & D, and marketing;
■   almost doubled labour productivity, without increasing capital employed;
■   developed a differentiated quality position, with a focused product range;
■   taken initiatives on innovation aimed at two or three major customers; and
■   gained share and forced competitors to exit.

The benchmark comparisons made it very clear that the actions could not be treated as alternatives, that change on all fronts was needed if the business was to earn its keep, and that other management teams had successfully executed such a strategy on several fronts at once.

Having established the overall direction of a possible strategy, the next step was to establish what could be done on the ground. Workshops with the business teams, and more research, showed that plans to tackle each of these issues could be developed. The targets were not out of reach. Direct benchmarking of the production process at the main Doncaster factory against industry best practice demonstrated that the productivity improvements indicated as necessary by PIMS benchmarks could be met. It was also clear that overhead cost reduction through consolidating the business headquarters with other ICI Materials operations in Brussels would allow major savings. Discussions began with one of the Asian tyre majors to exploit the special advantages of ICI technology in an important market niche.

Rather than shut the plant, managers set out to develop and implement the strategy. ICI Technical Fibres was formed, based in Doncaster, with as much autonomy as possible. Target production and overhead cost savings were achieved faster than in the benchmark businesses.

But other aspects of the strategic shift proved harder to execute. By 1992 it was clear that progress towards targets for innovation and for industry rationalization was too slow. This shortfall against strategic benchmarks made the shape of the future very clear. Profitable investment would only be possible in conjunction with DuPont. In July 1993, after satisfying EC competition authorities on the merits of the move, ICI completed the sale of its fibres business world-wide to DuPont, in exchange for a cash sum, and for DuPont's interests in acrylic materials.

Lessons from ICI Fibres

Effective benchmarking starts with a good understanding of business units' strengths and weaknesses via strategic and 'macro' benchmarks. Only in this way can you gain full benefit from process benchmarking at the 'micro' level. While 'micro' focus on discrete processes can provide a deep understanding of what is needed to create superior performance, it presents practical problems. Heading the list is that it can be costly and time consuming—there are literally thousands of 'micro' benchmarks that apply to the many processes constituting a business, e.g. cost per invoice, 'best practice time' for tool changeover, marketing cost per customer order, etc. Many processes a business could benchmark will be unimportant, redundant or in need of major 're-engineering'.

At ICI Fibres, for example, micro benchmarking of the polyester business in the late 1970s would have done nothing to address the strategic problem facing ICI, which was a combination of scale, quality and productivity weaknesses in its polyester positions. To be effective, micro benchmarks must be linked with the broader strategic considerations.

The same is true of intermediate benchmarks of cost or performance. In the 1980s IBM put a great deal of effort into its 'best of breed' comparisons of products against competitive offerings, essentially benchmarking technical quality. The company failed to capitalize on its technical advantages because its market strategies were not designed to cope with customer and competitor fragmentation. There is no right way to do the wrong thing.

To avoid this type of mistake, the hierarchy of benchmarks is extremely helpful. Start at the business unit level with 'strategic' benchmarks for business direction, and 'macro' benchmarking for broad functional areas, then use the insight gained to focus on the processes vital to competitive success.

Moving directly from the 'strategic' level to 'micro' benchmarking processes may, in some cases, be appropriate. In others it is useful to look at 'macro' business measures to help establish operational targets. Such benchmarks will, in most businesses, contribute to the strategic planning process. They did so in the assessment of the strategic role of innovation at ICI Fibres in 1980–1981.

Operational benchmarking can measure business inputs, as well as outputs, for functional activities. PIMS research proves that functional costs (marketing, administration, R & D) are driven by specific parameters. For example, sales and marketing expenditures are influenced by 30+ factors that define customer, product and competitive characteristics. These factors are the ones to match in finding comparable businesses against which to benchmark, to set norms and 'best practice' cost targets.

Another example of this type of comparison is our work for the UK government on British Coal. As part of a review of overhead cost effectiveness, PIMS was able to provide matched comparisons against which marketing and administrative costs could be judged.[7] In addition to international norms for such costs, it was possible to find best practice targets in similar situations in primary industries and to identify some of the reasons behind the best performers' achievements.

Many managers find matched comparisons like this helpful in diagnosing problem areas and suggesting possible solutions. They were certainly an important element in target definition for ICI Fibres in 1991.

The final outcome in this case illustrates the importance of a hierarchy in benchmark setting. Having identified—at a strategic level—a proven way forward for the business, ICI's managers were spectacularly successful in following through one leg of the strategy. Cost reduction benchmarks, set at the 'macro' level for overheads and productivity, and at the 'micro' level for operating processes, drove major business changes. But without the other two legs of the strategy-focused innovation and competitor exit—it was not enough. The company could no doubt have identified other areas to benchmark, at a functional or process level. However, the chances that these would have contributed to a successful competitive strategy were small. Attempts like this might have been regarded by shareholders as courageous, but not as a particularly effective way of developing the business.

A benchmarking hierarchy helps keep the view of managers at all levels in a business focused on the ultimate necessity—a successful competitive strategy. Operational or process benchmarking without such a vision may help a business long term—or more probably it may not. To quote Sir John Harvey-Jones in his commentary on the events at ICI Fibres, *you may have a brilliant tactical win and through failure to appreciate the strategic significance and what is going on, throw away the game.*

Acknowledgements

We would like to acknowledge the help of Scot Davidson, former Managing Director of ICI Fibres and now at ICI Acrylics, and of colleagues Keith Roberts and Lourde Cadden in preparing this account.

Thanks are also due to PIMS member companies, including Shell, Xerox, Rover, Lucas, and Hydro Aluminium, whose ideas have influenced our own.

References

1. Y. K. Shetty, Competitive Benchmarking for Superior Performance, *Long Range Planning*, **26** (1993); Robert C. Camp, *Benchmarking*, Quality Press, (1989); Michael

J. Spendolini, *The Benchmarking Book*, AMACON (1992); A. Steven Walleck, J. David O'Halloran and Charles A. Leader, Benchmarking World-Class Performance, *The McKinsey Quarterly*, No. 1 (1991).

2. For a brief history of benchmarking at Xerox and David Kearns views, see Competitive Benchmarking: The Path to a Leadership Position, Xerox Corporate Quality Office (1987).

3. Robert Eccles, The Business Performance Manifesto, *Harvard Business Review*, January–February (1991).

4. PIMS letter 47, How to think about the shape of your business, PIMS Associates, London (1992); and R. Buzzel and B. Gale, *The PIMS Principles*, Free Press, New York (1987).

5 John Kay, *Foundations of Corporate Success*, Oxford University Press (1993).

6. Sir John Harvey-Jones, *Making it Happen*, Guild Publishing, London (1988). He describes decisions at ICI Fibres in chapter 3. Sir John was appointed to the Board of ICI in 1972, became Chairman in 1982, and retired in 1987. His TV series *The Trouble Shooter* promoted good management in UK industry.

7. PIMS Associates, *Benchmarking Overheads and Productivity—input to DTI Coal Review Team*, HMSO, London (1993).

13

Parenting Strategies for the Mature Business

Michael Goold

The mature businesses in the corporate portfolio are often seen as a problem. They do not have the growth potential of other businesses, and as a result they may receive less attention and fewer resources from the corporate parent. Managers in the mature businesses then feel neglected and demotivated, leading to a downward spiral of performance. This article shows how the corporate parent can avoid these pitfalls and develop a more constructive, added-value relationship with the mature businesses in the portfolio. It identifies the sorts of opportunities which the corporate parent should target and gives examples of companies such as BTR and Courtauld which have successfully nurtured their mature businesses..

In most multibusiness companies, mature businesses make up the bulk of the corporate portfolio. Yet chief executives and their corporate colleagues often seem unenthusiastic and even uncomfortable with such businesses. The emphasis is placed on opportunities in the company's growth businesses and diversifications are sought to shift the balance of the portfolio away from more mature businesses. The mature businesses may even be regarded as something of an embarrassment, which may inhibit the achievement of corporate targets. In such situations there is usually friction in the relationship between the corporate parent and the mature businesses.

Michael Goold is a Director of the Ashridge Strategic Management Centre. His publications include *Corporate-level Strategy: Creating Value in the Multibusiness Company* (Wiley Inc.) and *Strategic Control: Milestones for Long-term Performance* (Financial Times/Pitman).

Some companies, however, such as BTR, Cooper Industries, Emerson Electric and Hanson, regard mature businesses as prime opportunities for the corporate parent to add value. This article, which is based on extensive research with a cross-section of leading multibusiness companies (see Appendix), will identify the opportunities and the pitfalls involved in parenting mature businesses, and will draw conclusions about how corporate parents can improve relationships with their mature businesses.

What is a Mature Business?

The term 'mature business' is widely used by managers and academics in discussions of corporate strategy.[1] The primary defining criterion for describing a business as mature is usually slow growth in the market being served by the business. However, while some companies regard any business whose markets are growing at the rate of the GNP or less as mature, others reserve the term for growth rates of 0% or less. Other criteria used to identify maturity include the amount of technical change impinging on the business, the stability of the customer and competitor set, and the position in the product life cycle. Thus a startup business with aspirations to gain market share rapidly through products or services which rely on new technology, or through targeting the needs of a specific segment of customers, would not usually be regarded as mature, even if it was operating in an overall low growth market. The degree of self-sufficiency of a business, in terms of possessing sufficient resources to survive and prosper without help from its corporate parent, is also seen by some managers as relevant in judging the maturity of the business. Although the concept of maturity is universally recognized, there is evidently some lack of precision in its definition.

There are, therefore, different sorts of mature businesses:

■ slow growth versus declining served markets;
■ cyclically depressed versus secularly low growth served markets;
■ more versus less stable technologies, customers and competitors;
■ more versus less resource self-sufficiency.

There are also important differences between competitively strong, profitable 'cash cow' mature businesses and competitively weak, struggling 'dog' mature businesses; and between generally mature businesses which still have some growing markets, e.g. in particular countries or segments, and mature businesses with no real growth markets. The blanket label of maturity consequently disguises differences which are important to recognize for the corporate parent, since they may indicate different parenting opportunities and pitfalls.

Whatever definition of maturity is adopted, mature businesses represent an important component of most companies' portfolios. For many companies, well over 50% of sales, and often an even higher proportion of profits, come from businesses whose markets are growing at GNP levels or less. Even against the more restrictive criterion of zero growth or declining markets, there are significant numbers of companies in which a large fraction of the portfolio is mature. For all these companies, it is essential to understand how to be a good corporate parent for mature businesses.

Parenting Opportunities in Mature Businesses

The purpose of any corporate parent should be to add value to its businesses. In other words, the businesses should perform better as a result of the influence of the parent than they would as independent entities.*

Good corporate parents therefore constantly search for ways in which they can improve the performance of their businesses. We refer to situations in which there is an opportunity for a business to improve its performance and a particular role for the parent in bringing about the improvement as 'parenting opportunities'. We have found that unless the corporate parent is able to identify and focus on specific parenting opportunities in its businesses, it is liable to damage, rather than enhance, the performance of its businesses.[2] In our research we therefore attempted to list the main sorts of parenting opportunities which companies had most commonly found in mature businesses.

Lean Operations

In mature, stable businesses, there is sometimes a temptation for business-level managers to devote too little time and effort to productivity improvements and cost control. Managers may be seduced by unrealistic growth or new technology ambitions for their businesses, rather than buckling down to the hard grind of ensuring that day-to-day operations are as tightly managed as possible. Alternatively, business managers may become set in their ways and willing to accept a level of profitability that is lower than could be achieved with a real push for lean operations. In these circumstances, there is a role for the corporate parent to establish influence mechanisms and control processes which motivate business managers to stretch for the best possible productivity performance from their businesses. By pushing up productivity, profits can be kept moving ahead for long periods, even if underlying sales and market growth is low.

BTR illustrates the role of the parent in promoting lean operations. Through its renowned profit planning process, it exerts strong pressure on every one of its 1000 or more business units to maintain tight control of costs and search for continuous productivity improvements. Rather as KKR and other leveraged buy-out specialists have found, BTR has discovered that there are often oppor-

---

* It is possible that some businesses may perform individually worse, but that they may contribute so much to other businesses in the portfolio that the aggregate result is improved. The requirement is that the collective performance of all the businesses should be better, not that each individual business should perform better.

tunities to squeeze extra performance out of mature businesses through strict financial disciplines and ambitious targets. BTR targets a return on sales of 15% or better in businesses where most other competitors are content with 5–10%.

The value of concentrating on lean operations was stressed by almost all the companies with extensive experience of parenting mature businesses, ranging from Emerson to GE and from Philips to Hanson. Companies in more capital-intensive businesses, such as ABB, ICI, DSM and RTZ, however, also brought out the need to balance tight control of operations with selective investment to maintain the competitive position of the businesses.

Capacity Closure and Industry Rationalization

In slow growing and, particularly, declining businesses, there can be opportunities to improve performance through capacity closure and rationalization. There is often a role for the parent in encouraging timely capacity closure, since managers in the business may otherwise be inclined to protect their established empires for too long. More aggressively, it may be possible to acquire competitors, or swap capacity with them, in order to allow the closure of surplus capacity and bring about a more competitively stable and profitable industry structure. Such restructuring initiatives call for a breadth of vision and a level of financial resources which may not be available within the business itself.

Thus, although Courtaulds faces declining markets in several of its film and fibre businesses such as cellophane and acetate yarns, it has been able to maintain profitability in these businesses by leading an orderly industry-wide capacity reduction. In acetate yarns, for example, it has achieved this by establishing a joint venture with a major competitor, which now commands well over half of the total European market. ICI has also been involved in major asset swaps to allow rationalization in several sectors of the European chemical industry. The corporate parent has encouraged and helped the businesses to take the initiative in these capacity rationalizations.

Preventing Peripheral Investment and Diversification

There can also be temptations for business managers in mature businesses to indulge in peripheral investments and diversifications. Particularly in profitable cash cow businesses, there may be a desire to reinvest free cash flow rather than make funds available for the shareholders or for investment elsewhere. These investments provide a new challenge and an enlarged scope of responsibilities for the business, as well as the potential for incremental growth. But such investments seldom pay off, and a corporate parent can help to avoid frivolous, wasteful or unjustified investment by applying strict controls.

During the 1980s Champion, the spark plug manufacturer, diversified extensively into businesses which were only loosely related to its automotive component heartland, but which were expected to benefit from use of the

Champion brand. Most of these diversifications were unprofitable and diverted attention from the base business. In 1989 Cooper Industries acquired Champion and immediately set about reversing the diversification drive. Businesses such as oil additives, hand cleaners, automotive tools and even a car wash chain in Mexico were sold, and the focus was placed back on ignition systems for automobiles and aircraft. Hanson is another company from our research which has improved performance in many of its acquisitions through realizing parenting opportunities of this type.

Investing Through the Cycle

Many mature businesses are also cyclical in nature. Bulk chemicals, steel, aluminium, construction and banking are all examples. In cyclical businesses, the timing of investment (and of cut-backs) has a major impact on results. Ideally, the time to invest is at the trough, when current profitability is lowest, and the time to rein back is at the peak, when profitability is strongest. In practice, business managers are liable to be overly influenced by current results and to behave in precisely the reverse manner. A parent with experience of cyclical businesses and sufficient resources to invest in a counter-cyclical manner can help to offset these tendencies. If, moreover, the parent has skills in forecasting turning points, there is the potential to greatly enhance performance.

DSM and RTZ are both companies which operate in mature businesses which typically pass through pronounced price and profit cycles. Both companies have recognized that investment plans must not be unduly influenced by short-term cyclical fluctuations, and manage their finances to have funds available for good investments during depressed years as well as in stronger times. Neither company would claim to have a crystal ball for forecasting the ups and downs of the cycle, but in both cases the corporate parent is sensitive to the need to invest through the cycle and accustomed to taking a view on the timing of upswings and downturns.

Opportunistic moves to invest or make acquisitions at the trough of the cycle may be easier for smaller, family owned companies than for larger, more established corporations. Huntsman Corporation, now a $5 billion privately owned chemical company based in Salt Lake City, was built up from scratch by its founder, Jon Huntsman, through a combination of well-timed acquisitions at the trough of cycles with strenuous attention to lean operations subsequently.

Price and Margin, not Volume and Market Share

In stable mature businesses, the trade-off between pushing for higher prices and going for volume should be weighted more towards margin than market share. Holding prices down to gain market share may well upset the competitive equilibrium in a slow growth or declining market, and it is far from certain that the cost of gaining share will ever be recouped. But many business managers find it difficult to take a firm line on price and to risk volume loss, especially in low growth markets. A corporate parent with a depth of experience in judging the price/volume trade-offs in mature businesses can stiffen the resolve of business managers not to compromise on margins.

A second essential component of BTR's profit planning process is the emphasis it places on maintaining or raising margins, even if this means loss of volume. The importance of a firm resolve on price is reinforced by BTR's corporate price audit team which carries out spot checks to see that prices are being moved ahead through the year as planned. In BTR's philosophy, mature businesses should be managed for profit, not volume, since there is little point in looking for a long-term pay-off when the business is already mature.

Achieving Best Practice

Mature businesses can easily become staid, resistant to change, and ruled by bureaucratic procedures. Where maturity has led to corporate arthritis of this sort, the parent can help to loosen up the joints by pushing for the adoption of best practices from elsewhere, by refusing to accept second best performance, and by eliminating bureaucracy.

Many of GE's largest businesses, e.g. domestic appliances, lighting and electric motors, are mature and Jack Welch has set particular store by GE's ability to encourage them to share best practice across businesses and to root out bureaucracy in all its manifestations. GE's efforts to promote 'boundaryless' behaviour and well-known 'work-out' programme have been designed specifically to achieve these ends. It is through these means that GE adds value to a portfolio of businesses which is evidently highly diverse.

Achieving best practice standards is not a parenting opportunity which is peculiar to mature businesses only. Nevertheless, many corporate parents with largely mature portfolios, e.g. Emerson and Unilever, place particular emphasis on it. Indeed, as businesses mature, success often depends on fine-tuning operations and picking up new ideas rapidly, in order to remain ahead of the competition.

Appointing Tough Operating Managers

There is a widespread belief amongst nearly all the companies in our research that the sorts of managers who thrive in mature businesses have different skills and personality types from those who prefer growth businesses. Older, harder, more experienced operators, who derive satisfaction from squeezing the maximum possible performance from a business, are needed in mature businesses, and strategic thinkers, business builders and risk takers are liable to be frustrated by the task. Academic research generally supports this conclusion.[3]

Most corporate parents feel that the characteristics needed to succeed in mature businesses tend to be innate or gained through front-line experience.

Few management development programmes stress them, or succeed in building them. But companies such as Hanson, with many mature businesses in the portfolio, can offer managers plenty of experience of the right kind, and can identify those managers best suited to the task. Corporate parents that are able to develop a pool of managers that thrive on the challenges of mature businesses can add real value through the appointments they make to senior positions. Companies such as Courtaulds and Philips believe that they have become much better at recognizing the sorts of managers needed in mature businesses, and that this has been the key to improving performance in them. The role of the corporate parent is to identify people with the right skills and attitudes for mature businesses, and to encourage other managers with the potential to develop them. It is a matter of understanding what it takes to succeed in these businesses, and managing human resource development and succession planning accordingly.

Rejuvenation

In some mature sectors there are opportunities to achieve spectacular success by challenging conventional mind-sets and ways of doing business. By focusing on new or growing segments of demand, by adopting fresh approaches to the value chain or by exploiting innovative technologies, organizations such as Benetton in textiles and Swatch in watches have grown rapidly and profitably in basically mature businesses.[4] Successful rejuvenation strategies of this kind usually depend much more on innovative business practices than on heavy or sustained financial investment. In principle, there should, therefore, be opportunities for a parent to stimulate rejuvenation at the business level by encouraging entrepreneurial attitudes, and by pushing for and supporting ambitious and unconventional plans.

In our research, however, we found no corporate parents which specialize in promoting rejuvenation of their mature businesses. Many corporate parents accept that rejuvenation strategies can in some cases be highly rewarding, but believe that the large majority of rejuvenation initiatives in fact fail. Furthermore, they find it hard to distinguish, *ex ante*, between those mature businesses which contain genuine rejuvenation opportunities and those which are unlikely to respond well to such strategies. In addition they find it difficult to attract, retain and develop the sort of unorthodox, entrepreneurial managers which are needed for rejuvenation. For all these reasons, very few, if any, corporate parents regard rejuvenation as a parenting opportunity to focus on. It may well be that corporate parents, at one or more remove from the front-line of their businesses, are poorly placed to judge whether rejuvenation is a possibility, and that corporate structures are inimical to the sort of managers required. If so, rejuvenation parenting opportunities are likely to remain more attractive in theory than in practice.

'Horses for Courses'

The types of parenting opportunities which are most important will depend on the specific characteristics of each mature business. Figure 1 lists the parenting opportunities which have just been discussed and shows in which sorts of mature businesses they are typically most important. Thus, for example, capacity closure and rationalization is most likely to be a source of value creation in declining businesses, and will be less relevant in slow growth businesses. Equally, rejuvenation opportunities are more likely to be found in mature businesses which include some growing segments of demand and not in businesses with highly stable technologies, customers and competitors. The importance of appointing the right sorts of tough operating managers runs across all types of mature

Parenting Opportunities	Mature Business Characteristics					
	Slow Growth	Declining	Cyclical	Stable	Profitable & Cash Rich	Growing Segments
Lean Operations	✓	✓		✓	✓	
Capacity Closure and Rationalization		✓				
Preventing Peripheral Investments				✓	✓	
Investing through the Cycle			✓			
Price & Margin, not Volume & Share				✓		
Achieving Best Practice	✓					✓
Appointing Tough Operating Managers	✓	✓	✓	✓	✓	✓
Rejuvenation				✗		✓

Figure 1. Parenting opportunities in mature businesses.

businesses, and is effectively a pre-condition for successfully realizing all the other parenting opportunities.

Review

"We have some difficulty with what our added value is in mature businesses, and the mature businesses themselves tend to be restive about it too", stated the corporate strategy director of one of ASMC's member companies. This honest assessment reflected the fact that, as in many companies, not much thought had been given to what the nature of parenting opportunities are in mature businesses, and how they can best be realized. If the primary focus of the corporate parent is on the growing businesses in the portfolio, it is not surprising that the mature businesses often feel they have little to gain from membership of the corporate family.

More positively, several of the companies in our research felt that, tempered by the experience of the recession of the early 1990s, they are now devoting more attention to their mature businesses and becoming better at adding value to them. Hard experience gained in a generally low growth environment has forced these corporate parents to acquire new skills, and to focus afresh on how the performance of more mature businesses can be raised. They have found that there is a wide array of parenting opportunities to go for in mature businesses, particularly if the businesses in question have lost their way or gone off the boil. It is in these circumstances that the corporate parent can add the most value.

Undoubtedly, the most successful companies in adding value to mature businesses are those, e.g. BTR, Emerson and Hanson, which specialize in the task. They intentionally build the skills and management processes to identify and seize the parenting opportunities which arise in mature businesses, and they select businesses for their portfolios which are typically mature. For these companies 'maturity' is an important criterion in defining their 'heartland' or 'core businesses', and is seen as indicating a prime opportunity for the parent to add value, not as a problem to be avoided or de-emphasized.

Parenting Pitfalls with Mature Businesses

In our research we encountered many situations in which the corporate parent not only failed to add any value for its mature businesses, but actually damaged their performance. Moreover, we found that there were characteristic pitfalls in parenting mature businesses which accounted for the prevalence of value destruction of this sort. The main pitfalls were demotivating the managers of mature businesses, holding back the development of mature businesses, unhelpful interference on issues best left to the business managers and, in consequence, causing mature businesses to become overly protective of their own territory and decision rights.

Demotivating Managers

Many managers naturally prefer growth to maturity or shrinkage. They enjoy the challenge of building a bigger business and they perceive wider personal career opportunities if they succeed in doing so. Conversely they find cutbacks, downsizing and tightening the screws create stresses and tensions which they would rather avoid. Such managers are liable to find working within a mature business unattractive. Corporate parents, however, tend to exacerbate the problem and actually demotivate managers in mature businesses through their policies and actions.

The root cause of demotivation very often stems from ambitious corporate growth targets. For example, in one company a corporate target of growth at 10% per annum in real terms was set. For most of the businesses in the portfolio this was not impossible, but for several more mature businesses there was no realistic prospect of meeting the corporate growth goal. As a result, the managers of these businesses felt like second-class citizens, unable to make a sufficient contribution to corporate results. Corporate views of what counts as 'good performance' condition the way that managers of mature businesses perceive their role.

The corporate parent's attitude to career development and to resource allocation can also contribute to demotivation of managers in mature businesses. If career prospects are seen to depend on having a track record of growing businesses, assignment to a mature business will be perceived as the kiss of death. Equally, if careers are largely confined within a single business rather than involving cross-business moves, individuals may feel imprisoned by the limited growth opportunities in a mature business. Gupta and Govindarajan's research shows that managers in businesses with harvest strategies believe that the more successfully they implement their strategies, the more their career prospects decline.[5] Resource allocation patterns can be a further source of demotivation if the managers of mature businesses feel that they are constantly providing the cash for investment in corporate 'black holes' elsewhere, but are denied reasonable investment requests in their own businesses.

For all these reasons, the managers of the mature businesses in a corporate portfolio are frequently disgruntled. Many of the companies in our research were able to give vivid illustrations of how and why the corporate parent was mainly responsible for this state of affairs.

Holding Back Development

By allocating resources away from mature businesses, corporate parents not only demotivate their managers, but also inhibit their development. If corporate resource allocation priorities lead to investments with rapid pay backs being rejected or to rationalization programmes necessary for cost effectiveness being stalled, the corporate parent is damaging the business. There also needs to be a balance between short-term performance pressure and necessary longer-term investment for the continuing development of the business. Striking this balance is specially difficult in cyclical businesses with the need to make large, long-term investments, such as bulk chemicals. An emphasis on lean operations can, in some circumstances, represent a parenting opportunity. But, if taken too far, it can instead prevent mature businesses from fulfilling their potential.

In several companies, we have found that businesses which were labelled as 'mature' were starved of resources and attention by the corporate parent. Even high return investments were turned down, rejuvenation proposals were dismissed without proper consideration and requests for assistance from the corporate staff received low priority. In these cases, the corporate parent's perception of a business as mature, with little growth potential, becomes a self-fulfilling prophecy.

'Non-core' is an even more damaging label for the corporate parent to place on a business than 'mature'. Non-core businesses, by definition, come at the bottom of the priority list for scarce resources; their managers feel unloved and unwanted; any sense of longer-term business development is stultified. Other corporate parents are likely to get more out of the non-core business. Hence there should be as little delay as possible in disposing of it. Non-core businesses which are retained in the portfolio for long periods of time inevitably become run down and dispirited.

Unhelpful Interference

As businesses mature, they often become more self sufficient, and have less to gain and more to lose from parental intervention.[6] For example, previously the corporate finance staff may have been genuinely helpful in advising on systems and suggesting policies and controls. Now, the more mature business may have its own experts and its own ways of doing things, attuned to the particular circumstances it faces. Corporate 'help' then becomes 'interference', which impedes the business and soaks up valuable management time which could be better spent elsewhere.

There is an analogy with the family setting here, in which parents all too often fail to recognize that, as their children grow up, their needs and wants change, thus calling for a different sort of relationship with the parent. Similarly, corporate parents continue to stress parenting opportunities that may have been valid in the past, but which now have more potential for subtracted than added value.

A number of companies cited positive results from spinning off mature businesses that were no longer in need of the parent's influence or central to the corporate strategy, and the recent spate of successful de-mergers in the US and the UK provides further support for considering such moves. There can also be good reasons for bringing in minority partners or outside investors, as Philips has with Polygram, if the business needs to be distanced from the influence of the parent. But spinning off, or reducing ownership in, large mature businesses is seldom easy since there will be strong emotional ties to the business. As one company put it: "We would never consider spinning off the business, since it is intrinsic to the identity, history and culture of the company." Though understandable, these sentiments need to be challenged if the parenting relationship has become intrusive and interfering and no longer adds any net value.

Mature businesses often react to what they see as unhelpful interference by attempting to exclude the parent as far as possible from any influence on their affairs. Corporate visitors are not welcomed, information about what is going on in the business is jealously guarded, links with other businesses in the corporate portfolio are strenuously resisted, staffs are built up within the business which duplicate what is available from the parent. Of course, such behaviour is itself sub-optimal, since protectiveness and turf defence rules out the potential benefits that could follow from the parenting relationship. But parents that complain of the defensiveness and recalcitrance of their subsidiaries must recognize that it is often a reaction to their own intrusiveness, and that the fault may lie as much with the parent as the subsidiary.

Ways of Overcoming Parenting Pitfalls

A number of measures seem to be helpful in overcoming the parenting pitfalls in mature businesses. These include:

- Avoid corporate-wide growth targets, whether explicitly or implicitly communicated. Tailor the mission and objectives of each business to its own circumstances.
- Communicate clearly that mature businesses have an important role within the corporate portfolio. Avoid the 'second-class citizen' syndrome by encouraging pride in the professionalism with which they are managed and in the achievement of the objectives that they are targeting.
- Appoint managers to mature businesses with suitable natural instincts and skills. Manage career development and compensation to provide good promotion prospects and rewards for managers who succeed in mature businesses. Be willing to move managers across businesses to achieve this and make bonus formulae relate to targeted absolute levels of sales, profitability or cash flow rather than to growth over previous years.[7]
- Avoid neglecting or starving mature businesses, both in reality and in the perception of business managers. Balance 'lean and mean' performance pressures with selective support for investments that will pay off rapidly or are necessary for the long-term development of the business.
- Avoid labels with negative connotations, especially 'non-core'. Divest any businesses that do not fit within the corporate strategy as rapidly as possible.
- As businesses mature, review the nature of the parenting relationship with them,[8] and be willing to pull back from influence on issues on which net

added value is no longer positive. If businesses are genuinely self-sufficient, with no further parenting opportunities of significance, consider a spin-off or divestment.

These lessons have been derived from the experiences of the companies in our research.[9] Though they are in many ways straightforward, they are often overlooked. As a result severe parenting problems result.

Even if companies avoid the more obvious pitfalls in parenting mature businesses, some intrinsically difficult issues remain. Striking the right balance between short-term performance pressure and longer term investment is never easy, especially in cyclical businesses. Finding, developing, motivating and rewarding managers that are good at downsizing and squeezing businesses, particularly in corporate contexts where most businesses are growing, will remain a challenge. The key to a productive parenting relationship is therefore to concentrate the parent's influence around some genuine parenting opportunities, since it is probable that even the best parents will be unable to avoid all of the pitfalls.

Mature Businesses and the Corporate Portfolio

So far we have focused on the relationship between the corporate parent and each mature business individually. Now we turn to the role that mature businesses collectively play within the overall corporate strategy and portfolio. We shall consider the contribution they make to corporate growth objectives and to corporate cash flow, and the trade-off between having a portfolio dedicated to mature businesses or mixed between mature and other sorts of businesses.

Corporate Growth Objectives

The main reason for most companies' discomfort with the mature businesses in the corporate portfolio is that they do not make a satisfactory contribution to the achievement of corporate growth objectives. Improvement in profitability ratios may allow profits to move ahead rapidly for a period of time and market share gains may in some cases be possible, but the slow underlying rate of growth in these businesses' markets and the stability of their competitive environments make it unrealistic to look for continuing long-term growth at rates much above GNP. If there is an overall corporate objective of 10% per annum real growth or more, the presence of a significant proportion of mature businesses in the corporate portfolio will make it hard to achieve the target.

Many companies with rapid growth aspirations have therefore sought to diversify away from their mature businesses. For example, BAT shifted the balance of its portfolio away from tobacco by acquiring new businesses in retailing, cosmetics, paper and financial services; and ICI acquired new businesses in specialties and advanced materials and de-emphasized its more mature commodity products. In our research we found that most companies that have diversified in this way described their experiences as 'mixed'—which basically seemed to mean disappointing.

The reasons for these disappointments were that, surprisingly frequently, the new 'growth' businesses turned out to have less growth potential than had been anticipated;* that the profitability of the new businesses was often below expectation, so that the acquisition prices paid were not justified; and that, most fundamentally, the ability of the corporate parent to understand and contribute to the new businesses was, in many cases, limited, at least for several years post entry. The generally poor record of such diversifications does not mean that there have been no successes. But as one corporate strategy director put it, "the key thing has been to learn from our failures".

The basic lesson concerning diversifications away from mature businesses concerns the need to have or build skills for managing the new business, both at the business level and within the corporate parent. Technical or operating skills are not enough, unless complemented by suitable marketing and general management skills. Philips, for example, has become more and more aware that technical competences alone do not provide a sufficient basis for a successful new business entry. Moreover, parenting skills are as important as business-level skills. Companies such as American Express, RTZ, BAT and Shell have all been unwinding earlier diversifications in recognition of this fact. Without relevant management skills, diversifications are usually disastrous.

For companies whose heartland has always been in more mature businesses, a move into a growth business will almost inevitably require an understanding of some new critical success factors and parenting opportunities. A programme of learning about the new business will therefore be needed, and the issue is whether the costs and risks associated with gaining this learning will be justifiable. Will initial problems give way, in due course, to a situation in which the new business fits well with the corporate strategy and the parent is able to add value to it? Or will the learning never be successfully accomplished, resulting in continuing frictions and poor performance? These difficult judgements demand a careful and honest assessment of what it will take to learn enough about the new business to become a good parent for it. Most companies that have been through such a transition recognize that it can take several years to accomplish: BAT, for example, accepts that it was 10 years before it became comfortable with its new businesses in financial services. If instead the parent chooses to leave the

---

*Conversely, aggressive management of mature businesses—less likely if a diversification programme is top of the corporate priority list—can maintain growth through market share gains, penetration of new segments of demand and profitability improvements for surprisingly long. Several companies in our research that had resigned themselves to the low growth prospects in some of their major mature businesses have found that, given sufficient attention, they yielded far more growth than had previously been hoped for.

new business alone, it may reduce value destruction in the short term. But such a course is not conducive to eventual parental learning.

An alternative to diversifying into new and unfamiliar businesses is to question the basic growth premise. Should growth at rates well in excess of GNP be a corporate objective and is it necessary to be in fast growth businesses to achieve rapid corporate growth?

Rapid growth enhances the value of a company if it has a level of profitability above the cost of capital.[10] A share in a highly profitable company that is growing fast is worth more than a share in an equally profitable but declining company. But rapid growth reduces the value of a company if its profitability is below the cost of capital, so that it is far from clear that a share in a highly profitable but declining company is worth less than a share in a less profitable but growing company.

If too much profitability is sacrificed to achieve growth, the value of the company will fall. Growth goals should, therefore, always be conditional upon profitability levels and diversifications that enhance growth but reduce profitability should be viewed with suspicion.

Furthermore, the experience of companies such as BTR and KKR shows that rapid corporate growth is possible with a portfolio focused on mature businesses. Through aggressive acquisitions of new mature businesses and through skilful parenting that raises their profitability, such companies have achieved exceptional growth in corporate sales and profits. As these companies grow bigger, they admittedly need to find larger and larger acquisitions to maintain their historic growth record. Some commentators have therefore claimed that growth by acquisition cannot be prolonged indefinitely. But this concern is only relevant to very large companies, and its impact can in any case be mitigated by a willingness to spin off businesses to which the parent no longer adds much value. With an active programme of divestments, earnings per share and value growth can be maintained without the need to take over the whole of the economy.*

We therefore believe that parents with a high proportion of mature businesses in their portfolios should usually concentrate more on becoming good parents for these businesses, and less on shifting the balance of their portfolios into new, less familiar, but more rapidly growing businesses. As ICI found prior to its demerger, simultaneously trying to become a better parent for mature businesses and learning to parent unfamiliar and rapidly growing new businesses may be too difficult.

---

*In order to maintain value growth, the receipts from spin-offs must be reinvested in businesses whose profitability can subsequently be improved by the parent. In practice, transaction costs, tax considerations, and the instability caused by constant deals set some limits to what can be achieved. But, in principle, value growth can be achieved without ever greater corporate size.

Contribution to Corporate Cash Flow

The other side of mature businesses' limited growth potential is their high cash generation. They should have relatively low investment needs, and hence, provided they are adequately profitable, they should throw off a cash surplus. Many companies in our research cited the substantial cash flow contributions of their mature businesses as essential for corporate security and survival, particularly in recent recessionary times.

Of course, not all mature businesses are consistently strongly cash positive. Competitive pressures, cyclical downturns, and environmental investment requirements were all quoted as reasons why some mature businesses were not highly profitable and cash generative. But, with good parenting, most mature businesses should be capable of producing cash.

For the corporate strategist, the issue then is how to use the cash surplus. The options include

- investment in other parts of the portfolio;
- diversification;
- increased payout;
- share buy-backs.

Investment in other businesses may be worthwhile if they have return opportunities at better than the cost of capital. However, a perennial complaint of mature business managers is that the cash flow they generate is wasted on 'strategic investments' in other businesses that never pay off. These corporate black holes soak up the hard-earned cash from the profitable mature businesses, but do not build corporate value. Diversifications into businesses to which the parent can add value may be attractive, but diversifications into new growth businesses are fraught with difficulties, as we have already argued.

Increasing the dividend pay-out to shareholders or share buy-backs are, on the face of it, logical means of dealing with any surplus cash flow generated by the mature businesses. In most companies in our research, however, these options were not popular with senior management. Increasing the dividend payout and share buy-backs were felt to give dangerous signals about the performance, prospects and management of the company. They could suggest that current prices and profits were 'unnecessarily' high. Of even more concern is the implication that the top management have run out of good ideas for further investment and development of the group: "management vanity means that our senior managers like to believe they can find good investment opportunities for any surplus cash", stated one strategy director. Lastly, a raised pay-out may set a new level of expectations for the future that could, in the event, prove difficult to meet, especially in cyclical businesses. In consequence, most companies are somewhat reluctant to return surplus cash to shareholders. Whether this attitude is in the best interests of shareholders or reflects their preferences is a matter that deserves careful attention.

Dedicated and Mixed Portfolios

For some companies, e.g. Hanson, the corporate portfolio is largely or exclusively made up of mature businesses. The corporate parent specializes in adding value to mature businesses, and mature businesses are regarded as the company's heartland.[11] In such cases the corporate portfolio is 'dedicated' to mature businesses. For many other companies, e.g. 3M, BT, Barclays and Philips, the corporate portfolio includes some mature businesses but is by no means dedicated to them. Newer, faster growing, less stable businesses are equally, if not more important in the portfolio. We shall refer to corporate portfolios of this sort as 'mixed' between mature and non-mature businesses. Our research indicates that it is easier to be a good parent of mature businesses with a dedicated portfolio than with a mixed portfolio.

Parents with dedicated portfolios can gain experience and fine tune their parenting skills for realizing the particular parenting opportunities that arise in mature businesses. Furthermore they can establish corporate objectives, career structures, bonus formulae, resource allocation processes and decentralization contracts that are designed to minimize the parenting pitfalls in mature businesses. Companies such as BTR, Hanson, Cooper Industries and Emerson Electric seek out acquisitions in more mature sectors and have well-established processes for adding value to such businesses. In these companies there is no question of managers of mature businesses feeling that they are doing a less worthwhile job, or lack career opportunities; indeed, the road to the top requires an ability to perform well in the mature business setting. Because the whole of the parenting activity in these companies has been geared to the needs and opportunities of mature businesses, the parenting relationship with the mature businesses is constructive, positive and value-creating.

Parents with mixed portfolios face a harder task. They cannot and should not focus all their parenting around the particular needs and opportunities of mature businesses. But they do need to be able to identify and realize genuine parenting opportunities and avoid parenting pitfalls in their mature businesses. The best way forward depends upon the reasons why the mixed portfolio has been assembled.

In some companies a mixed portfolio follows from the absence of any clear corporate strategy for adding value to the businesses. A collection of businesses has been brought together by historical accident, by piecemeal development, or to achieve a balance across different sectors or geographies. But no serious attention has been given to the role of the parent in adding value to the businesses. The first essential step for these companies is to think afresh about how they can add value to their businesses, and to start to focus the portfolio on the sorts of businesses that have the most promise.[12] This in turn may alter the mix of mature and less mature businesses.

Mixed portfolios can also arise for life-cycle reasons. Over time, businesses which were once fast growing tend to slow down and eventually mature. A corporate parent that retains ownership through the life cycle will end up with businesses in different stages of maturity. But the sources of value creation that were powerful in the early stages of the life cycle may subsequently reduce in impact. 3M, for example, adds most value through facilitating technological advances and new product development. As businesses mature, these sources of value added tend to diminish in importance. In such cases there is a danger that currently relevant parenting opportunities for the mature businesses will be overlooked and that parenting pitfalls will be encountered, since the mature businesses lie outside the mainstream preoccupations of the parent. For 3M to graft a strong emphasis on lean operations or preventing peripheral diversifications onto its concern for new product development would not be easy, and might even undermine its basic technology-driven strategy. For these reasons it is worth considering spinning-off businesses as they mature, unless the parent is convinced that its sources of value creation remain (or can be made) substantial in the later stages of the life cycle.

If the sources of parental value added apply in both mature and non-mature businesses, the case for a spin-off is much weaker. RTZ, for example, majors on technical and project appraisal skills that are valid both for new mine developments and for much more mature mines, and expects to add value throughout a mine's life cycle. Parents that can add value to both more and less mature businesses can more readily justify a mixed portfolio.

Nevertheless, with a mixed portfolio the dangers of overlooking parenting opportunities and pitfalls that are specific to the mature businesses remain, and, if the critical success factors in the mature businesses are too different from the other businesses, it may still be best to consider a spin-off. In any case, the parent must be alert to the special parenting needs of the mature businesses and should make a conscious effort to meet them. In some cases it may be worth establishing an organizational grouping that brings together more mature businesses to create a focus on their needs.

Perhaps the most common type of value creation that cuts across mature and non-mature businesses concerns the parenting of linkages between businesses. Thus in companies such as BT or Barclays, the mature businesses have important connections with other, less mature businesses. The links can involve managing common customers (in Barclays both corporate and individual customers may buy a range of different financial services), drawing on a common resource (in BT the basic telecommunications network supports a number of products and services) or, most commonly, sharing best practice, as in Unilever or GE. Such linkages argue strongly against spinning-off businesses and for retaining a mixed portfolio.

Companies that decide to retain mixed portfolios need to recognize that the parenting relationship with the mature businesses in the portfolio will bring special opportunities and problems. They need to search for 'mature business' parenting opportunities as well as other, more general parenting opportunities. They must decide whether they will be able to realize these parenting opportunities, what changes in parenting would be needed to do so and whether the changes could be introduced without undermining other valuable aspects of their parenting. Last but by no means least, they should recognize the parenting pitfalls with mature businesses and, as far as possible, take steps to avoid them.

Summary

Mature businesses present particular opportunities and pitfalls for the corporate parent. By focusing on these opportunities and taking measures to avoid or overcome the pitfalls, corporate parents can establish positive, value-creating relationships with the mature businesses in their portfolios.

The root cause of many of the problems that corporate parents face with their mature businesses is often an inappropriate desire to shift the balance of the portfolio into fast growing businesses and away from more mature businesses. Growth in value for the shareholders is usually more likely to follow from concentrating on becoming a good parent for the mature businesses in the portfolio and accepting that any surplus cash should be returned to shareholders via share buy-backs or increased dividends, than from diversification into new and unfamiliar businesses in pursuit of faster growth.

Corporate parents with portfolios that are dedicated to mature businesses face an easier task than those with portfolios that are mixed between mature and less mature businesses. Mixed portfolios should only be retained if the parent has clearly identified sources of value creation that apply in both the mature and less mature businesses. Even then, the parent must be careful to take account of the special opportunities and pitfalls faced with the mature businesses in the portfolio.

Acknowledgements

I would like to thank my colleagues at the Ashridge Strategic Management Centre, Marcus Alexander and Andrew Campbell, for helpful comments on earlier drafts of this paper. I would also like to thank Professor Charles Baden-Fuller of City University Business School for stimulating my thinking about the rejuvenation of mature businesses.

References

1. See e.g. Kathryn Rudie Harrigan, *Managing Maturing Businesses*, Lexington Books, New York (1988); Charles Baden-Fuller and John M. Stopford, *Rejuvenating the Mature Business*, Routledge, London (1992) and Harvard Business School Press, Cambridge, MA (1994). While the problems of managing mature businesses have been

quite extensively discussed, the challenges for corporate parents in relating to their mature businesses have received far less attention.

2. See Michael Goold, Andrew Campbell and Marcus Alexander, *Corporate-level Strategy: Creating Value in the Multibusiness Company*, Wiley, New York (1994).

3. The best study of this issue has been carried out by Anil Gupta and V. Govindarajan, Build, hold, harvest: converting strategic intentions into reality, *Journal of Business Strategy* **4** (3) 34–47 (1984). There has, however, been surprisingly little empirical research focused on the question of what sorts of managers are most successful in mature businesses.

4. See Charles Baden-Fuller and John M. Stopford, *Rejuvenating the Mature Business*, Routledge, London (1992) and Harvard Business School Press, Cambridge, MA (1994) for further discussion of companies that have successfully pursued rejuvenation strategies.

5. See Gupta and Govindarajan, *op cit*, p. 36.

6. See the discussion of so-called 'ballast' businesses in *Corporate-level Strategy, op cit*, chap.14.

7. In companies such as BTR and Courtaulds, for example, managers can enjoy maximum bonuses even if their businesses show declining sales levels. See also Gupta and Govindarajan, *op cit*, p. 43.

8. See the discussion of decentralization contracts in *Corporate-level Strategy, op cit*, especially pp. 370–373.

9. Some similar points are made in a useful article by Richard G. Hamermesh and Steven B. Silk, How to compete in stagnant industries, *Harvard Business Review*, September–October, 161–168 (1979).

10. Research carried out by advocates of value-based management show that, both in theory and in practice, a company's value depends upon the discounted value of the future cash flows it will generate. It follows that growth only enhances value if the profitability of the growing businesses is above the cost of capital. See e.g. James M. McTaggart, Peter W. Kontes and Michael C. Mankins, *Managing for Superior Shareholder Returns: the Value Imperative*, Free Press, New York (1994); Tom Copeland, Tim Koller and Jack Murrin, McKinsey and Company Inc., *Valuation: Measuring and Managing the Value of Companies*, Wiley, New York (1990).

11. See *Corporate-level Strategy, op cit*, chap. 14, for a definition and description of the concept of a 'heartland' business.

12. See *Corporate-level Strategy, op cit*, Part III for a full description of a process designed to achieve this purpose.

13. Michael Goold, Andrew Campbell and Marcus Alexander, *Corporate-level Strategy: Creating Value in the Multibusiness Company*, Wiley, New York (1994).

Appendix

The Research Base

The research base for this article has two main sources. Firstly, it draws on the research carried out for the book, *Corporate-level Strategy*.[13] The main companies covered in this research were:

ABB	GrandMet
American Express	Hanson
Banc One	KKR
BTR	Motorola
Canon	RTZ
Cooper Industries	Sharp
Dover	Shell
Electrolux	3M
Emerson	TI
GE	Unilever

Many other companies were, however, interviewed in the course of this 4-year research project which took place in the period 1990–1993.

Secondly, a series of interviews and discussions were carried out with the member companies of the Ashridge Strategic Management Centre during 1994. These companies were:

Barclays Bank	Pearson
BAT Industries	Philips
British Petroleum	RTZ
BT	Shell
Courtaulds	Whitbread
DSM	Zeneca
ICI	

In both groups of companies there is a mix of those with higher and lower proportions of mature businesses in their portfolios. However, almost all the companies had at least some mature businesses in their portfolios and were able to cast valuable light on ways in which they felt that, as corporate parents, they added or subtracted value.

14

Linking the Balanced Scorecard to Strategy

Alan Butler, Steve R. Letza and Bill Neale

Kaplan and Norton's concept of the balanced scorecard has received wide acceptance from both academics and practitioners. The design and construction of balanced scorecards has not, however, been well documented. This article reports on a study undertaken for Rexam Custom Europe to determine, develop and implement a 'balanced scorecard' for top-level use. This article briefly reviews the theoretical background to the development of integrated performance measures, describes the performance measures currently in use at Rexam Custom Europe and the proposed measures based on a two-part balanced scorecard tailored to suit the particular requirements of the company.

"Effective measurement must be an integral part of the management process."[1]

"What you measure is what you get."[2]

These two edicts by Kaplan and Norton encapsulate the philosophy which is the driving force behind many companies' attempts to overhaul their performance measurement systems. Of course, it is a truism to say that effective management depends on the effective measurement of performance and results. However, it

Alan Butler is a project engineer for PLM Redfern Glass Ltd., Barnsley, UK.
Steve R. Letza is lecturer in Accounting & Finance at the University of Bradford Management Centre, UK.
Bill Neale is lecturer in Accounting & Finance at the University of Bradford Management Centre, UK.

is increasingly becoming accepted that 'traditional' measures centred on financial criteria are inadequate for the contemporary business environment.[3] Attention to a wider range of measures related to quality, market share, customer and employee satisfaction can yield a greater insight into the factors which drive financial performance. Most crucially, a shortfall in these non-financial performance measures may provide an early warning of an impending shortfall in financial performance and enable timely remedial action to be taken in order to moderate the damage to the financial results.

Yet the protection of short-term financial performance is by no means the main driver behind the search for a more complete set of performance measures. Broader performance measurement systems are increasingly seen as a device for delivering long-term strategic objectives.

The heightened interest among both academics and practitioners in performance measurement has stemmed from a confluence of factors.

First, the observation that successful companies both elsewhere in Europe and also in the Far East seem to place less reliance on narrow financial criteria than those in the so-called 'Anglo-Saxon' countries[4] and pay more attention to long-term strategic issues.[5]

Second, the rise of the Total Quality Management (TQM) movement[6] drew the attention of managers to the importance of focusing on the customer and to providing quality products and services as a means of maintaining competitive advantage. TQM, of course, has both an internal, or process, focus and also an external, or service, focus.[7, 8]

Third, Johnson and Kaplan's work[9] on the alleged failings of conventional management accounting drew attention to over-dependence on financial numbers by managers schooled in the DuPont and similar systems.

Fourth, the 'revolution' in information technology has facilitated the collection, access and interpretation of a vast amount and range of information.

It is not entirely clear why concentration on financial criteria should necessarily militate against success, yet observations that leading companies in the UK, allegedly the home of 'short-termism', feature among the leading European companies on financial criteria amidst continuing macro-economic underperformance does prompt a certain unease. For example, in the recent Financial Times 500,[10] 12 of the top 20 companies by Return on Equity (ROE) were British. In addition, among the top 25 giants by capitalization, six of the top 10 arranged by ROE were British.

As a result of the coalescence of these factors, senior managers now appear to appreciate that if they are to achieve their strategic plans, they should adopt a more balanced approach to measuring performance by considering financial and non-financial performance measures. Considerable attention is presently being given by academics and practitioners to developing a more comprehensive and integrated set of criteria for judging and guiding corporate and segmental performance, largely prompted by Kaplan and Norton's concept of the 'balanced scorecard'.

Kaplan and Norton have reported their experiences in designing scorecards for a variety of US companies. However, there is little evidence available of how companies are adopting and applying the Kaplan and Norton balanced scorecard model in the European environment.

This article reports how one UK organization, a subsidiary of a major quoted company, attempted to devise a balanced scorecard. The article is organized as follows: the next section describes the Kaplan and Norton balanced scorecard and the following section provides a brief 'pen picture' of the company and examines the process by which the scorecard was generated. Finally, the authors assess this process and also the concept of the Balanced Scorecard as it was worked out in practice.

The Balanced Scorecard

The Kaplan and Norton balanced scorecard, displayed in Figure 1, arose out of a research project with 12 companies which were judged to be at the 'leading edge' of performance measurement. The result of this was in Kaplan and Norton's words:

> "a set of measures that gives top managers a fast but comprehensive view of the business".

Kaplan and Norton[1] expanded this definition as follows:

> "The balanced scorecard allows managers to look at the business from four important perspectives. It provides the answer to four basic questions:

How do customers see us?	Customer perspective
What must we excel at?	Internal perspective
Can we continue to improve and create value?	Innovation and learning perspective
How do we look to shareholders?	Financial perspective

> While giving senior managers information from four different perspectives, the balanced scorecard minimizes information overload by limiting the number of measures used."

The scorecard has been adopted by many companies and its format and content appear to meet several management needs. Examples of users include, in the USA, Rockwater (part of Brown & Root) and Intel and Apple computers; in the UK, BP Chemicals, Milliken, the Nat West Group, Abbey National and Leeds Permanent Building Society.

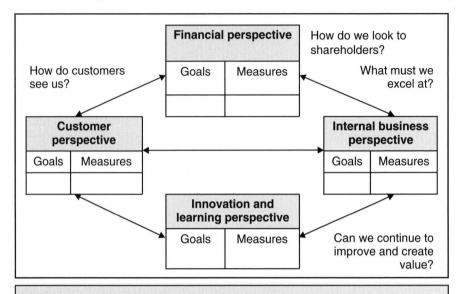

Figure 1. The segments of the balanced scorecard.

Kaplan and Norton[1] also state:

> "The scorecard brings together in a single report many of the disparate elements of the company's competitive agenda, e.g. becoming customer orientated, shortening response time, improving quality, emphasising team-work, reducing new product launch times and managing for the long term."

The scorecard guards against sub-optimization by forcing senior managers to consider all the important operational measures together. It alerts them to improvement in one area being achieved at the expense of another, or to an objective being badly met. The scorecard puts strategy and vision at the centre. Traditional measurement systems have a control bias, i.e. they specify the particular actions they want employees to take and then measure to see whether or not the employees have taken these actions—they try to control behaviour. The balanced scorecard, on the other hand, assumes that people will adopt whatever action is necessary to arrive at these goals. Senior managers know what the end result should be, but not necessarily how to arrive at that result. This can be a very powerful motivator for managers to perform to the best of their ability. As Mintzberg[11] says:

> "Performance control systems can serve two purposes, to *measure* and to *motivate*."

Rexam (Bowater) plc states in its annual report[12] that:

"Performance is closely monitored...We aim for a Bowater which is . . . well motivated and wanting to be stretched."

In summary, the scorecard is more than a performance measurement technique, it is a management system.

Calls for broader-based sets of performance indicators which may be more meaningful to operating managers, rather than financial criteria expressed at group or divisional level are by no means new, as Ezzamel[13] observes:

> "The call for non-financial quantifiable measures is not new; it has underlined much of the literature which has sought to expose the limitations of short-term financial measures of performance in divisionalised organisations."

So what is new? Like many 'new' ideas in management and accounting, the novelty lies in the emphasis. Kaplan and Norton's ideas express a dissatisfaction with the 'engineering' focus of performance measurement, as practised in the west for decades since the DuPont pyramid was devised. This embodies a negative feedback mechanism, driven by financial targets and precise task definition, designed to influence the behaviour of managers and their subordinates in order to achieve favourable financial results.

The widespread attention to strategic issues in management and accounting has sparked the realization that the 'old' performance measures overlook the importance of the firm's relationship with its environment, in particular with its customers. Hence, the need is apparent for a set of performance criteria more overtly oriented towards the firm's end-markets. The 'strategic focus' recognizes that a wide range of employee behaviours are compatible with favourable outcomes in terms of operating performance. Indeed, the essence of the balanced scorecard is the acceptance that some performance criteria are in conflict, and the task of management is to resolve these conflicts to achieve a balance of objectives.

Although offering a sample template, adopted by all of their collaborating firms, Kaplan and Norton[14] acknowledge that the balanced scorecard has to be tailored to each specific company. In particular, the resulting scorecard of indicators should be driven by the firm's strategy if it is not to consist merely of a listing of indicators:

> " . . . although there may be a potentially long list of non-financial indicators, individual firms have to be selective by linking explicitly their choice of indicators to their corporate strategy".[14]

A major task facing a company or division introducing a balanced scorecard is how to devise a set of measures explicitly linked to its strategy. Underlying this need is the essential condition that the strategy is widely understood and accepted within the organization, especially among those responsible for devising the scorecard itself.

The Organizational Context: Rexam Custom Europe

Rexam Custom Europe (RCE) is the European division of Rexam Custom, which in turn is part of Rexam plc, although RCE's reporting line is through Rexam Inc. based in North Carolina, USA. Until 1 June 1995, Rexam plc traded in the UK as Bowater plc. The organizational structure is shown in Figures 2 and 3.

RCE is a precision coater, laminater and converter of flexible materials to customers' special orders. This is a highly specialized contracting business which aims to:

" . . . emulate and supplement the technical strengths of key customers. We help customers speed products to market and offer them cost-effective alternatives to internal capital investments".[12]

RCE has three operational sites, Wrexham (Clwyd), Runcorn (Cheshire) and Kerkrade (The Netherlands). Its turnover in 1994 was 34 million, accounting for approximately 30% of Custom worldwide sales. Custom itself generates about 6% of the turnover of Rexam plc. Over the 4-year period from 1991, turnover has grown by just over 100%, i.e. an average annual growth rate of about 20%, as shown in Table 1. The 5-year financial record shows a smaller increase in net assets (41%), suggesting greater asset utilization over this period. The head count has risen by even less (35%), further indicative of on-going efficiency improvements.

RCE's overall strategy centres on 'extraordinary growth' and 'continuous improvement' with the aim of growing the business (turnover) organically by 20% plus each year. To achieve this, RCE must broaden its customer base and reduce development cycle times of new projects. In addition to the above broad objectives, other goals such as return on investment (Return on Net Assets) are set down as a part of the yearly budgeting process.

RCE has a well-established, mainly financial, reporting system. In addition to the reporting system, a number of non-financial performance measures exist at many levels but in no formalized, structured way, and the sheer volume of information prevents the measures being used effectively to drive the business.

Table 1. RCE's 5-year financial record.

	1995	1994	1993	1992	1991
Turnover (£'000)	38,300	34,200	22,400	19,600	19,000
Net Assets (£'000)	36,700	30,000	29,300	29,700	26,000
Number of employees	322	282	275	255	238

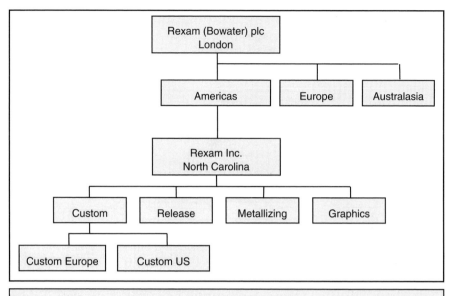

Figure 2. Organizational chart of Rexam plc.

We now look at the various stages in developing, establishing and implementing a balanced scorecard, which is designed to link measurement and strategy.

Scorecard Generation

Determining Key Performance Measures

The identification of the key performance measures was envisaged by Kaplan and Norton[1] as an iterative process in determining the balanced scorecard. The main stages in the process are shown in Figure 4.

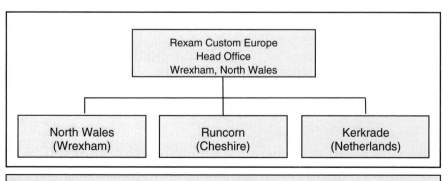

Figure 3. RCE's divisional organization.

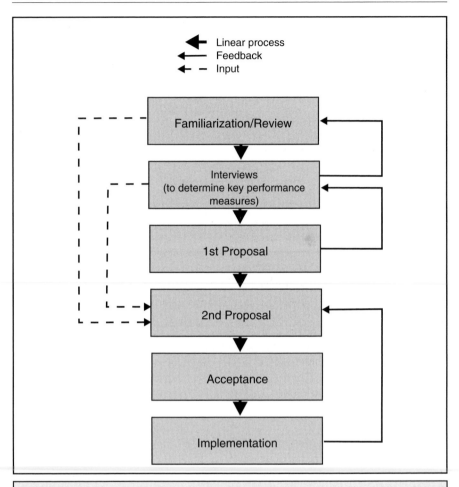

Figure 4. Identifying key performance measures.

The first stage in this process thus consisted of an assessment and review of the RCE measurement systems and data collection methods. This identified two main reasons why data was collected:

- Financial reporting to Rexam Inc/Rexam plc.
- Monitoring of continuous improvement for Total Quality Management/ World Class Manufacturing programmes.

Managers are conscious of the company strategy and attempt to work towards achieving the targets set, however, the first stage failed to identify a clear linkage between performance measures and strategy.

Rexam plc's corporate-wide vision is expressed in the Rexam 21 principles shown in Table 2. These principles focus on continuous improvement which is designed to propel Rexam plc into the 21st century.

Clearly, a balanced scorecard would have to be compatible with these corporate principles.

The next stage in the process was the determination of key performance measures. Senior managers (a representative total of 13 from the three operational sites, covering the functional areas of Operations, Finance and Human Resource Management) were circulated with an information pack about the

---

Table 2. The Rexam 21 Principles.

Customers	Our customers are the focus of all we do. Our customers' success is our success. We understand our customers, anticipating and exceeding their needs. We seek close and durable relationships, partnering for the long term, world-wide.
People	We believe that people make the difference. We insist on integrity and respect for personal values. Our success depends on incorporating different cultures and people who make learning a lifelong experience. We develop world-class people through training and education.
Innovation	We relish new ways to do things. We foster an environment where creativity and imagination are highly regarded and where problems become opportunities for innovative solutions.
Process	To achieve extraordinary growth we work together across titles, job responsibilities, organizational structure and geographic boundaries. We leverage our resources by sharing information and expertise. We encourage openness and initiative. We expect participation in decision-making and problem-solving across all functional areas and organizational levels.
Performance	We provide the best value and highest reliability. We apply appropriate methods to measure our continuous improvement. We expect personal commitment to our continuing improvement and change. We are never satisfied. What is done well today can be done better tomorrow.
Suppliers	We seek long-term suppliers who treat us as we treat our customers.
Community	We are responsible citizens involved in the communities in which we work. We strive to make our work-place and our world a safer, better and more enjoyable place.
	We benchmark ourselves against the world's best.

FINANCIAL PERSPECTIVE:

Goals	Measures	Unit	Current	Target
Extraordinary growth	Sales growth	%		
Profit growth	Operating profit	£		
Profitability	Return on sales (ROS)	%		
"Sweat the assets"	Return on net assets (RONA)	%		
Survive	Working capital %	%		
Survive	Cash generated (cash flow)	£		

CUSTOMER PERSPECTIVE:

Goals	Measures	Unit	Current	Target
Customer satisfaction	% On time delivery	%		
------------"-------------	Credit notes	No.		
------------"-------------	Complaints	No.		
	Customer satisfaction (?)	survey		
Extraordinary growth	% Sales from new customers	%		
	% Market share	%		
Partnership (customers)	% Sales with "partners"	%		
	Av order turnaround time	days		
Partnership (suppliers)	% of materials purchased from "partners"	%		

INTERNAL BUSINESS PERSPECTIVE:

Goals	Measures	Unit	Current	Target
Process improvement	% Waste	%		
------------"-------------	Av set up time	hrs		
------------"-------------	% Schedule achievement	%		
------------"-------------	Product cost yr/yr improvement	£		
------------"-------------	Av product lead time	weeks		
People	Employee satisfaction	survey		
------------"-------------	Training hours/employee	hours		
------------"-------------	Safety incidence/severity	No./?		
------------"-------------	Suggestion/employee	No.		
Waste/environment	Landfill tonnes/employ'/year	tonnes		
------------"-------------	% Waste recycled	%		

INNOVATION and LEARNING PERSPECTIVE:

Goals	Measures	Unit	Current	Target
Extraordinary growth	% of sales from new products	%		
------------"-------------	% R&D time on new products	%		
------------"-------------	No. of trials (new products)	No.		
------------"-------------	Av turnaround on sample req'	days		
------------"-------------	No. of enquiries	No.		
Reduction in development	No. of accepted projects	No.		
Cycle time	Av project cycle time	weeks		
------------"-------------	% of projects productive	%		
------------"-------------	No. of products changed after commercialized	No.		

Figure 5. RCE's first proposal.

CUSTOMERS:

Principle	Measures	Unit	Current	Target
Our customers are the focus of all we do. Our customers' success is our success. We understand our customers, anticipating and exceeding their needs. We seek close and durable relationships, partnering for the long term, world-wide.	Customer satisfaction index	Index		
	% Partners	%		

PEOPLE:

Principle	Measures	Unit	Current	Target
We believe that people make the difference. We insist on integrity and respect for personal valuos. Our success depends on incorporating different cultures and people who make learning a lifelong experience. We develop world-class people through training and education.	Employee satisfaction index	Index		
	Training hours/ employee	hr		

INNOVATION:

Principle	Measures	Unit	Current	Target
We relish new ways to do things. We foster an environment where creativity and imagination are highly regarded; where problems become opportunities for innovative solutions.	% Sales from new products	%		
	No. of "Spirit of innovation" awards	No.		

PROCESS:

Principle	Measures	Unit	Current	Target
To achieve extraordinary growth we work together across titles, job responsibilities, organizational structure and geographic boundaries. We leverage our resources by sharing information and expertise. We encourage openness and initiative. We expect participation in decision-making and problem-solving across all functional areas and organizational levels.	No. of "Spirit of Co-operation" awards	No.		
	No. of Commendations	No.		

Figure 6. RCE principles.

balanced scorecard, and then each was interviewed individually. Each interview was structured around a standard set of questions to gather information about the areas for which each senior manager was directly responsible and the key performance measures they used. Information was also gathered on any additional measures which senior managers would like to see and use in the future. From the results of these interviews, a first proposal for the scorecard (see Figure 5) was devised using Kaplan and Norton's 'four business perspectives' model.[1] The result was a scorecard that was essentially an aggregation of all senior managers' inputs.

A major problem encountered with this approach was how to limit the number of 'key measures' to just the 16–20 as recommended by Kaplan and Norton. The first proposal contained 35 measures, far too many to be monitored effectively. This large number of key measures led to a re-appraisal of the relationship between each of the performance measures and the company strategy. There seemed to be a fuzzy linkage along the sequence of:

$$\text{Strategy} \rightarrow \text{Obectives} \rightarrow \text{Measures} \rightarrow \text{Targets.}$$

Measures had been identified from the interviews but how these flowed from strategy and objectives was unclear. The key to unlocking this problem was found to be consideration of 'cause and effect'. Which were the key measures which 'caused' the business to grow and which were the 'effects', indicating that growth had taken place? Consideration of this relationship led to the scorecard being split up into two major sections:

- *Strategy* (Part A): Linking measures to key objectives and targets from strategy.
- *Principles* (Part B): Linking measures to the way that Rexam 'does its business' as outlined and articulated through the Rexam 21 Programme.

This revised approach was then presented to the senior management team and discussed both with the whole team and later with individual members.

Development of the Scorecard

The Principles section (Part B) of the scorecard was relatively straightforward and needed very little further development (see Figure 6). However the Strategy section (Part A) required considerable development to change it into a useful tool.

In the discussions which followed on from the presentation of the early draft scorecard, it became apparent to all the participants in this process that Kaplan and Norton's 'four perspectives' model was not the most appropriate model for RCE's culture. The various elements of RCE's strategy were discussed and an alternative approach for the Strategy section was developed.

Instead of Kaplan and Norton's 'four perspectives', three perspectives were adopted, focusing on:

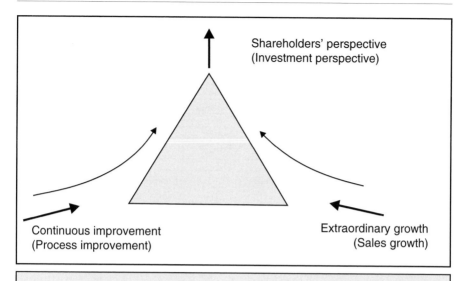

Shareholders' perspective
(Investment perspective)

Continuous improvement
(Process improvement)

Extraordinary growth
(Sales growth)

Figure 7. The Rexam Custom model.

- shareholders' (or financial) perspective;
- extraordinary growth perspective;
- continuous improvement perspective.

These are shown in diagrammatic form in Figure 7.

The Rexam Custom model shows the sales growth and process improvement, the *forward-looking* measures, driving the financial performance, the *backward-looking* measures. The second proposal (tabular format) for the RCE scorecard was as shown in Figure 8.

This second draft scorecard was again reviewed and discussed at top level. Some minor modifications were made before it was accepted as the finalized scorecard for implementation.

The Role of New Project Development

One of the critical factors in achieving the strategy of 'extraordinary growth' is the speed with which new projects are developed ('project' is the RCE terminology for a new product). However, unlike a conventional manufacturing company which can develop new products in response to a recognized need in the market place, RCE depends greatly on its customers' needs and ideas, involving a close liaison with those customers (this, of course, is inherent in the division's name).

As the process of identifying the key performance measures and development of the balanced scorecard proceeded, strong pressure was exerted by some senior managers for the scorecard to be used to monitor the development of new

SHAREHOLDERS' PERSPECTIVE:

Objective	Measures	Unit	Current	Target	Benchmark
Return on Net Assets (RONA) improvement *[target >XX% by 1997]*	Gross margin	%			
	Overhead, % of sales	%			
	Working capital	%			

EXTRAORDINARY GROWTH:

Objective	Measures	Unit	Current	Target	Benchmark
Sales Growth/broader base of customers *[target XX% /yr compound]*	% Sales growth yr/yr	%			
	% Sales from new projects	%			
	% Sales from top "4" customers	%			
	Factored sales of new projects sanctioned	£			
	Market share in markets where RCE No.1 or No.2	%			

CONTINUOUS IMPROVEMENT:

Objective	Measures	Unit	Current	Target	Benchmark
Profit Improvement *[target , Return on Sales (ROS) > XX% by 1999]*	Capacity utilization	%			
	Contribution/ productive machine hr	£			
	Waste	%			
	Production cost yr/yr improvement	%			
	Gross margin for new project development	%			
	Customer returns	%			
Cycle time reduction *[target , reduce cycle time by XX% by 1997]*	Av turnaround sample requests	days			
	Projects, sanctioned/ commercialized (over period)	%			
	R&D time on new projects	%			
	% Projects productive	%			
	No. projects changed after commercialized	No.			
	On time delivery (CLIP)	%			

Figure 8. The RCE strategy.

projects. Subsequent discussions revealed that performance in this area is, for a number of reasons, difficult to measure, monitor and control. Investigations were carried out into new project development and certain measures were incorporated into the cycle time reduction section of the final scorecard. However, it also became clear that the whole area of monitoring new project development was a separate wider management issue which needed to be tackled independently of the production of the balanced scorecard, with the role of the balanced scorecard being limited to performance measurement and management.

Development Finalizing, Applying and Using the Scorecard

In many ways, this phase was the most difficult part of setting up the balanced scorecard for RCE. This was because, in all the earlier stages, information was being drawn out of the company, whereas in this final stage, the balanced scorecard was being imposed upon RCE. The interview, discussion and other iterative processes in determining the scorecard should have minimized this sense of imposition to emphasize that the scorecard which finally evolved was the result of a partnership.

The development process was as follows:

- acceptance of the 2nd draft of the scorecard;
- preparation of draft metrics and method of calculation;
- discussion of definitions;
- finalization of definitions;
- identification of sources of data;
- finalization of format of scorecard for reporting;
- establishment of a procedure for regular reporting.

The crux of the development was determining (and agreeing) the definitions of the different metrics. As Figure 9 shows, this was also closely related to data collection, in the sense that individual metrics were only viable if the required data were easily available. Definitions of each of the measures were developed and sources of data were successfully identified. Each step was verified as practicable to establish the viability of the implementation phase.

Commentary

Having described the mechanism for establishing the balanced scorecard at RCE, we now examine some important issues arising from this process.

The Rexam Custom Europe exercise was neither imposed by the centre nor could it have been totally independent of it. To be viable, it had to conform to group strategic imperatives. At the time, Bowater/Rexam was suffering low asset utilization and was looking to strong growth performance in order to soak up

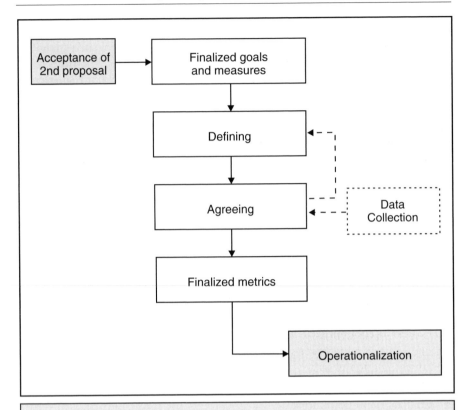

Figure 9. Stages in implementation.

that spare capacity to achieve a higher return on net assets—the rationale behind the 'Extra-ordinary Growth' objective of 20%. While some group members were rapid growers, there were several poor performers absorbing the cash flow from the strong areas. In this respect, while the growth objective was the primary aim, at least in the relatively short term, cash flow was beginning to be problematic at the group level.

This dissemination of corporate strategy was similar to the 'catchball' concept employed by many organizations, in particular Rank Xerox. Overall strategy is established by senior managers and then cascaded or deployed throughout the organization by means of the 'catchball'. Lower levels of management in effect 'catch' and take ownership of the strategy from the management level above. However, as at Rexam, there is usually substantial management autonomy in developing their own performance measures.

RCE had developed a set of somewhat *ad hoc* performance measures centred on profit, working capital ratios, control of overheads and sales by customer. Many of the supposed key measures were of little operational use but were thought to be regarded as important by management at higher levels of the organization. However, the management information system delivered a substantial volume of additional financial and operating performance data, much of which went unread.

Like so many innovations, the introduction of the balanced scorecard at RCE was driven by the initiative and perception of a newly-arrived senior executive. Each of the three sites had its own MD and Financial Director, although responsibility for cost control in the traditional sense had been transferred to local Operations Directors, essentially production and logistics controllers. Finding that the financial management functions were being competently performed, the new arrival recognized the inadequacy of the performance data being supplied to senior managers perceiving the need to 'add value at the strategic level' and generally to 'inject strategic thinking'. Any new performance criteria should identify the key growth drivers and to generate a reporting instrument which pinpointed areas of success and under-achievement. In his words, "RCE was good at financial numbers but unsure what were the key numbers which made the ship cruise along nicely".

In particular, developing a simplified set of performance criteria was an appealing device for provoking discussion on strategy drivers, and for sharpening focus on the critical role of project development with customers and how success could be identified in this area. In addition, the concept of 'putting it all on one piece of paper' seemed to offer considerable economy in the collection and dissemination of data.

Yet new performance criteria could not simply be imposed. Senior RCE managers believed that it was essential to ensure that all relevant staff understood and had confidence in the set of performance measures displayed in the final scorecard. The iterative process, pioneered by Kaplan and Norton, involving consultation, interviews and discussion, while time-consuming, enhanced involvement and participation. In addition, facilitation of the process by an external consultant probably encouraged more openness and frankness of expression. As a result, the scorecard which eventually emerged was more likely to incorporate the views of the managers concerned and, being owned by them, to secure their support and commitment.

It was clear that performance measurement and the linkages with strategy were important issues at RCE. It was easy to obtain acceptance of the principle of the Balanced Scorecard due to widespread dissatisfaction with the type and value of the data provided on a regular basis. As noted, this was plentiful, but not always suitable for the needs of senior managers. At the same time, there seemed to be general acceptance and strong support for the Rexam 21 Principles. Indeed, adherence to these became an important issue in the generation of the scorecard. The constraint imposed on the whole process by the need not to conflict with the principles provided testimony to the skill with which they had already been internally marketed within Rexam.

The commitment to the 21 principles and the special role of product development jointly explain why the scorecard deviated considerably from the template proposed by Kaplan and Norton and reported in their series of papers. However, they do acknowledge that each of the four specified categories require 'translation' into the special operating conditions and needs of individual companies:

> "The balanced scorecard is not a template that can be applied to businesses in general or even industry-wide. Different market situations, product strategies and competitive environments require different scorecards. Business units devise customised scorecards to fit their mission, strategy, technology and culture. In fact, a critical test of a scorecard's success is its transparency: from 15 to 20 scorecard measures, an observer should be able to see through to the business unit's competitive strategy."

However, the RCE template represents a radical departure from Kaplan and Norton's quadripartite representation which they regard as generic and to be used in all cases. Moreover, their quadripartite representation implies parity among the four sections although they do admit that good strategic results can still bring poor financial performance. In our view, very few UK firms will accept (for whatever reason) that financial results are of secondary or even equal importance to the drivers of strategy. To UK managers the danger with the Kaplan and Norton representation is that it may downplay the importance of financial results. Clearly, RCE executives appreciated the importance of financial criteria set by the group as a constraint on the development of their scorecard.

The Kaplan and Norton template was firmly rejected by RCE managers also on the grounds of its inadequate fit to RCE culture and business language. Quite simply, they believed it did not suit their needs, felt uncomfortable with it and sought instead a scorecard which conformed to the 21 principles. Perhaps this is the most important aspect of this study—Kaplan and Norton have devised an approach which seems to have overlooked the importance of the corporate mission. If staff generally accept that mission, then it seems preferable to build the scorecard around the mission, rather than to adopt a template developed in other corporate contexts. Not only is the RCE scorecard different in structure to that proposed by Kaplan and Norton, not only is it more extensive in its two-tier, strategy-cum-principles format, but more importantly, it operationalizes the corporate mission. Not every company can claim this.

References

1. R. S. Kaplan and D. P. Norton, The balanced scorecard—measures that drive performance, *Harvard Business Review*, January–February, 71–79 (1992).
2. R. S. Kaplan and D. P. Norton, Putting the balanced scorecard to work, *Harvard Business Review*, September–October, 134–142 (1993).
3. D. M. Brown and S. Laverick, Measuring corporate performance, *Long Range Planning* **27** (4), 89–98 (1994).

4. R. H. Hayes and D. A. Garvin, Managing as if tomorrow mattered, *Harvard Business Review* **60** (3),70–79 (1982).
5. M. Porter, *Corporate Strategy*, Free Press, New York (1980).
6. W. Edwards Deming, *Out of the Crisis, Quality, Productivity and Competitive Position*, Cambridge University Press, Cambridge (1986).
7. L. C. Hawkes and M. B. Adams, Total quality management: implications for internal audit, *Managerial Auditing Journal* **9** (4), 11–18 (1994).
8. L. C. Hawkes and M. B. Adams, Total quality management and the internal audit: empirical evidence, *Managerial Auditing Journal* **10** (1), 31–36 (1995).
9. H. T. Johnson and R. S. Kaplan, *Relevance Lost—The Rise and Fall of Management Accounting*, Harvard Business School Press, Boston, MA (1987).
10. *The Financial Times* 500, *The Financial Times*, 25 January (1996).
11. H. Mintzberg, *The Structure of Organisations*, Prentice-Hall, Englewood Cliffs, NJ (1979).
12. Bowater PLC, Annual Report (1994).
13. M. Ezzamel, *Business Unit and Divisional Performance Measurement*, Academic Press, London (1992).
14. R. S. Kaplan and D. P. Norton, Using the balanced scorecard as a strategic management system, *Harvard Business Review*, January–February, 75–85 (1996).

15

The Return of Strategic Planning—Once More with Feeling

Bernard Taylor

This article assesses the changes which are currently taking place in the Strategy Process. The author reviews recent thinking on Business Transformation and Strategic Leadership and considers how business unit teams are attempting to take charge of Strategy in organizations where Strategic Planning departments have been closed, and how the Strategy Process is being redesigned to suit the needs of fast-moving markets. Finally the article discusses how some companies are trying to involve the whole work force in implementing their strategies.

"Strategic Planning is Back—with a Difference"

In the past 30 years Strategic Planning has appeared in many guises. We can trace its development as it has moved from Long Range Planning to Strategic Planning in the 1960s, from Strategic Planning to Strategic Management in the 1980s and from Strategic Management to Strategic Leadership in the 1990s[1] (see Figure 1).

In 1994 Henry Mintzberg heralded the fall of Strategic Planning in its traditional form as a heavy bureaucratic system organized by large planning departments. But, to paraphrase Mark Twain, the rumours of its death were

---

Bernard Taylor is Emeritus Professor at Henley Management College, Executive Director of its Centre for Board Effectiveness and Editor of *Long Range Planning*.

exaggerated. In September 1996—*Business Week* reported that " Strategic Planning is back with a vengeance—but with a difference",[2] and the changes are the kind that Mintzberg would have wanted; less bureaucracy, more emphasis on implementation and innovation, fewer staff planners, more involvement of line managers and teams of employees. To quote *Business Week*:

> At one company after another, strategy is again a major focus in the quest for higher revenues and profits... Some companies are even recreating strategic planning groups... Mainstream consulting firms say their strategy business is booming, meanwhile a new wave of gurus and consulting farms has emerged... A recent study by the Association of Management Consulting Firms found that executives, consultants and business school professors all agree that strategy is now the single most important management issue and will remain so for the next five years.

This article examines how Strategic Planning has changed and how the Strategy Process is being adapted to provide an effective mode of navigation in the highly competitive, fast-moving, globalized markets of the late 1990s.

After the heavy pruning which occurred during the severe recession of the early 1990s, most major corporations have emerged leaner and fitter. The large planning departments and the other central staff groups have been cut back, but this has left a communications gap which top management in progressive companies are now trying to bridge through exercising personal leadership and by introducing more participative, team-based management styles. This means "democratizing" the strategy process to involve large groups of people along the lines of the General Electric Work-out process.

The annual planning round is being replaced by management debates on strategic issues. In innovative companies like 3M the planning system frequently consists of templates 'on the screen' which can be used and changed as required, and management teams are making greater use of strategy software.[3] More and more they are moving to "Real-Time Strategy".

Another major challenge is the need to develop and implement strategies for alliances or joint ventures, and for partnerships with major suppliers and key customers. Executives who are used to the rigours of market competition will need to acquire new skills and develop new strategy processes to manage collaborations and alliances.

Turbulence and the Need for Transformation

One of the major reasons for management's dissatisfaction with the conventional bureaucratic approach to strategy was the increasing speed of change in the business environment. During the last decade business leaders have had to respond to the 'reconfiguration' of entire industries due to three main trends:

Phase 1	**Long Range Planning**
	Extensive budgeting
	Extrapolative forecasting
Phase 2	**Strategic Planning**
	Two-phase process
	Corporate and business unit strategies
	Operational plans and budgets
Phase 3	**Strategic Management**
	Management takes charge of strategy
	Transformation of structure, culture, process and HRM
	Increasing employee participation
	Greater use of strategy software
Phase 4	**Strategic Alliances and Partnerships**
	Partnerships and networks with suppliers and distributors
	Alliances to access new markets and technologies

Source: B. Taylor, Henley Management College (1997)

Figure 1. Phases in the development of corporate planning.

- the *deregulation and privatization* of financial services, airlines, telecommunications, energy and water companies, railways and road transport;
- the *convergence of technologies* e.g. in multi-media (telecommunications, computers, television, media and entertainment) and in pharmaceuticals (biochemistry, genetics, bioinformatics and robotics);
- the *globalization* of industries like financial services, computers, automobiles and airlines, and the opening up of demand and supply markets in Central and Eastern Europe and in the Asia Pacific region.

One response from academics and business leaders has been to assert that industrialists should be more entrepreneurial and proactive in *transforming* their companies and in *re-inventing* their industries.

In *Competing for the Future*,[4] Gary Hamel, and C. K. Prahalad challenged executives to "stop the unrewarding and ultimately dead-end process of down-sizing and enter the dynamic realm of industry transformation and strategy regeneration".

Hamel and Prahalad recommended a number of approaches which managers may use to construct the shortest possible 'migration paths' to "get to the future first" (see Figure 2). A common requirement which underpins many of these techniques is that companies must develop the ability to *collaborate in order to compete*.

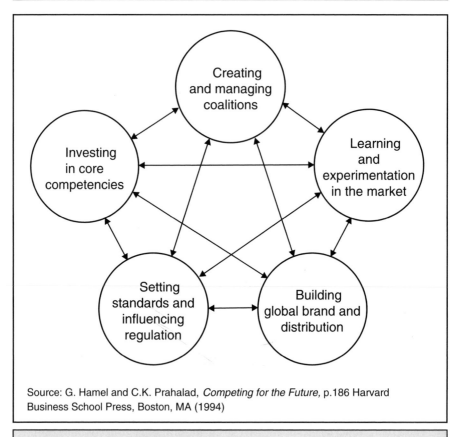

Source: G. Hamel and C.K. Prahalad, *Competing for the Future,* p.186 Harvard Business School Press, Boston, MA (1994)

Figure 2. Managing migration paths.

The transformation process is neatly summarized n a recent book by two Gemini consultants, Francis Gouillart and James Kelly.[5] Gemini are known for the help they have given to Philips in their Centurion turnaround programme, and the authors incorporate case studies from a wide range of companies in their book. Their framework suggests that divestments, closures and downsizing are important in the first two phases of the transformation process. But if a company is to survive and prosper in growing markets and to take advantage of new technologies, management must also lead their organizations through the later phases of *Revitalization* and *Renewal* (see Box 1).

Strategy as a Continuous Dialogue

Figure 3 provides a framework for analysing a company's strategic options in this rapidly changing environment. In some ways the process is simpler—less concerned with detailed planning and more focused on essentials. Also, it is no

---

Box 1

Transforming the Organization

- *Reframing* the company's conception of what it is and what it can achieve
- *Restructuring* the corporate body to bring it to a competitive level of performance
- *Revitalizing* the company's relationship with the competitive environment, igniting growth in existing businesses and inventing new ones
- *Renewing* individuals and the organization, enabling them to become integral parts of a connected and responsible world community.

---

longer thought of in terms of an annual discussion about the Strategic Plan, involving just the top teams. Rather it is a continuous dialogue about the future of the company which goes on throughout the year and involves management and teams of employees in all parts of the business.

There are three main areas for debate:

1. Strategy Formulation

This involves setting objectives and goals, appraising the company's performance compared with its main competitors, assessing the driving forces in the

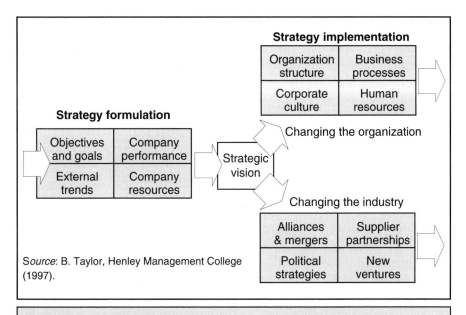

Figure 3. The strategic leadership process.

business environment and evaluating the company's financial, technical and human resources.

This is an iterative process: the resources may turn out to be too small to achieve the objectives, or the analysis of the environment may reveal unexpected threats. However, these discussions should produce a broad *strategic vision* of the shape of the company in the future.

2. Strategic Vision

The company vision should express in a few well-chosen words the business opportunity which the management is trying to sell to the shareholders, the customers, the employees and the other 'stakeholders'.

3. Strategy Implementation

All too often strategies remain "on the page" and are not implemented. A series of breakthroughs occurred in the 1980s and early 1990s as, with the help of consultants, companies learned to turn their strategies into action programmes.

(a) Changing the organization. Internal changes occur in four main areas:

- *Restructuring the Organization*—making it leaner, fitter and simpler.
- *Re-engineering Business Processes*—simplifying and speeding up the company's key processes such as product development, delivery, etc.
- *Company Culture*—making the company's mission, values and beliefs more explicit and emphasizing the need to produce value for customers, shareholders and other stakeholders.
- *Human Resource Management*—revising the contract with the employees, e.g. to allow more flexible working, to hold staff more accountable and to link rewards more directly to performance.

(b) Changing the industry. The 1990s have seen a crucial change in company structures 'from hierarchies to networks', with the emergence of the Boundaryless Organization.[6] Companies are forming closer partnerships with their major customers and preferred suppliers. They are entering new markets in Eastern Europe and Asia Pacific using joint ventures, and they are gaining access to the latest technologies by outsourcing or forming strategic alliances. In some cases where international standards are required, they are working on joint research projects with their direct competitors, just as Sony and Philips collaborated to develop the Compact Disk, and ICL and Fujitsu co-operated to promote open computer systems.

Using these new approaches, companies can in fact change the rules of the game in their industry. They can open up new markets, bring forward new products and process technologies and pioneer new distribution systems. The main ways to change the rules of the game are through:

■ *Alliances and Mergers*—alliances and joint ventures are designed to give a company access to an asset, typically a new technology, a range of products, a production system or a number of sales outlets, by offering to supply complementary resources in exchange. Mergers and acquisitions achieve the same ends and can change the structure of an industry in a more dramatic way.

■ *Customer–Supplier Partnerships*—many Western companies are now reducing the number of their suppliers and forming closer partnerships with them. This often results in lower unit costs, higher quality and faster delivery.

■ *Political Strategies*—companies also work in coalitions when they need to influence government agencies on social, regulatory or environmental issues.

■ *New Ventures*—the fourth way to change the industry is by pioneering new technologies, new distribution channels and new marketing approaches.

This is the kind of strategic framework which managers need to use to deal with today's complex business environment.

Mobilizing the Whole Organization to Deliver the Strategy

The essential problem which managers must address is, "How can we get all our employees involved in implementing our strategy?" But in the current situation—after downsizing, re-engineering and outsourcing—this is not likely to be the main problem that Western managers are thinking about. To quote Akio Morita, the former chairman and chief executive of Sony:

> People in the West are always talking about human rights, but when the recession hits them they don't hesitate to cut down their workforce. We believe if you have a family you can't just eliminate certain members of that family because profits are down. Recession isn't the fault of the workers. If management take the risk of hiring them, we have to take responsibility for them.[7]

Many leaders of Japanese companies regard the way they treat their employees as a major source of competitive advantage in relation to Western companies. To quote Konosuke Matsushita, the founder of Matsushita Electric:

> We are going to win, and the industrial West is going to lose out, there's not much you can do about it because the reasons for your failure are within yourselves. With your bosses doing the thinking while the workers wield the screwdrivers, you're convinced deep down that this is the way to run your businesses. For you the essence of management is getting the ideas out of the heads of the bosses and into the hands of labour. We are beyond your mindset. Business, we know, is now so complex and difficult, the survival of firms so hazardous in an environment increasingly unpredictable, competitive and fraught with danger, that their continued existence depends on the day-to-day mobilization of every ounce of intelligence.[8]

Chris Argyris recently made the same point:

> Twenty-first century corporations will find it hard to survive, let alone flourish, unless they get better work from their employees [this means] employees who have learned to take active responsibility for their own behaviour, develop and share first-rate information about their jobs and make good use of genuine empowerment to shape lasting solutions to fundamental problems.[9]

In recent years, some of the most important contributions to Strategic Leadership have been concerned with changing this "managerial mindset" and developing and testing business philosophies and managerial techniques which will enable business leaders to allow people at all levels to become involved in developing and implementing the company vision.

Developing Learning Companies

In his recent book *The Fifth Discipline*,[10] Peter Senge of MIT gave a new name and a new impetus to a movement which started over 20 years ago, with books like Donald Michael's *On Learning to Plan and Planning to Learn*.[11] The social learning school of writers has argued that Strategic Planning is based on an annual ritual and paper plans which are often out of date as soon as they are written. Instead visions and strategies should be used to give employees a general sense of direction and a set of values to understand and interpret these ideas so that strategies can be adapted to cope with continual change and uncertainty.

To quote J. Friedmann, an advocate of the social learning approach:

> If there are no ready-made 'solutions' and knowledge is revealed to us only in fragments and sequentially, the planner is not seen as a man having a superior knowledge in some field, but a superior ability to learn, with tools for exploring complex situations and models useful for strategic intervention. The planner must be able also to structure the learning experience of others, to be a teacher and a learner at the same time, with a willingness to explore alternative futures in search of new possibilities of action. In a situation of accelerated change this will require a tightening of feedback loops of information about change in both internal and external environmental states and a quickening of response times to new learning.[12]

How, then, can we build these learning organizations, and how can we train and develop this new type of planner or planning consultant? In their book *The Learning Edge*[13] Calhoun Wick and Lu Stanton Leon document the experiences of Rosenbluth Travel, Corning, Eastman Kodak, Motorola and I.P. Morgan in attempting to create 'a learning organization'.

Rosenbluth Travel

The approaches which companies use have certain common features. One is that learning organizations value their employees, treat them with respect and invest in their personal development. Hal Rosenbluth, the CEO of a successful independent travel business based in Philadelphia and co-author of *The Customer Comes Second, and Other Secrets of Exceptional Service*[14] describes his vision as a chain of people, service and profits. "We focus on our people, our people focus on service, and profits result". He goes on to say:

> One of the ways to create a positive effect on someone's life is through learning. I've heard others refer to their companies as life-long learning universities. It was key to me that we have the same kind of environment where learning would happen both consciously and sub-consciously on a daily basis.

J.P. Morgan

J.P. Morgan, one of the USA's leading financial institutions, stated in their annual report for 1991:

> Our combination of character and capabilities—the logic of J. P. Morgan—defines our competitive advantage in a complex world.

Anthony Beale, the partner in charge of Human Resources, explained:

> Our planning window is very short, and the cycle for creating resources from recruitment through training, through experience, is relatively long. You can say, 'Well, it's impossible to plan' or you can say 'I can't plan specifically, but what I can do is create pools of talent that give me the flexibility to absorb the volatility, hopefully at any pace and of any magnitude.'[13]

The "Morgan culture" is reflected in aggressive recruiting, in the sense of partnership between employees and the organization and in the expectation that everyone will always act for the good of everyone in the organization.

Corning Inc.

When James Houghton took over the job of chairman of Corning Inc. in New York State in 1983, he described his corporate vision for 1995. He wanted Corning "to become a world leader in quality; a champion of workforce diversity; and a better financial performer" and he said all of the company's 29,000 employees would be encouraged and expected to be active participants in the company's quest for improved performance.

In managing major changes, Edward O'Brien, the Vice President for Human Resources at Corning, has a "change formula" which he borrowed from Richard Beckhard.[15] He said:

Every individual you want to change must be dissatisfied with the way things are now. They have to see a desired future. Then they have to agree that the first steps for them make sense, and they have to believe it enough to do it. All this has to be greater than the normal resistance that everybody has to change. The only way to get them there is by their involvement, their meaningful participation.

When they had important changes to discuss, in order to involve employees and to answer their individual concerns like "What's in it for me?", "Will it affect my pay?" and "What's going to happen to my career?", he organized large-scale interactive workshops for 400 people at a time over 2 or 3 days. A division manager would present his vision, then the meeting would break into groups to discuss their reaction to it. Finally the manager would respond to their concerns.

Motorola Inc.

Specific targets are indispensable if people are going to learn, change their behaviour and improve their performance. Motorola Inc. of Schaumburg, Illinois, has a specific goal:

> to provide customers with what they want, when they want it, with Six Sigma quality and best-in-class cycle time.

In statistical terms, Six Sigma means 3.4 defects per million. Learning and Kaizen—continuous improvement—have been the foundation of Motorola's successful drive to improve quality, and the company won the first Malcolm Baldridge National Quality Award in 1988.

They have also been concerned to help senior managers in implementing change. George Fisher, Motorola's CEO, said he was concerned about the quality of the company's leadership—in particular he said "They can't get things implemented on time." Instead of holding their annual executive development seminar, Motorola asked top management to identify a number of critical problems facing the company. Then they formed two teams of senior executives and gave them each a problem to tackle, first to propose a solution and second to implement the solution on a pilot basis. The teams stayed together for 3–4 years which shows the kind of commitment Motorola has to becoming a Learning Company.

Adopting Participative Management as a Company Style

Other common themes of companies which are involved in an attempt "to deliver strategy through people" are Employee Involvement and Participative Management, which are opposite sides of the same coin.

Clearly, most organizations have some executives and supervisors who use a participative management style. However, some firms have taken a corporate decision *to adopt a participative management style as a corporate policy* (see Box 2).

Box 2

Employee Involvement: Some Key Elements

- an 'internal marketing' campaign to introduce employee inviolvement or employee empowerment as a programme with a recognizable brand name;
- a programme of training for managers to help them to change their approach from 'command and control' to 'coaching and supporting';
- the elimination of a number of first-line supervisors and their replacement by self-managed work teams or 'cells' who can agree goals and time scales with other groups, schedule their own work, allocate tasks within the group and measure their own performance;
- there is also a good deal of team training required in areas such as quality assurance, productivity improvement, cost control, customer service and innovation;
- promotion is commonly restricted to managers who achieve 'role model' ratings both in terms of performance and management style;
- pay and bonuses are usually related to the performance of the team as well as the individual;
- executives are appraised on a '360 degree basis' including 'upward feedback' from subordinates plus information from employee surveys and comments from colleagues as well as the usual interviews with superiors; this feedback is frequently mediated through an independent consultant;
- the elimination of some levels of management and the delegation of more authority to lower levels 'where the work is done'.

Ford Motor Company

Donald Peterson, the former president and chairman of the Ford Motor Company, led one of the most radical changes in the history of the company. By turning Ford's pyramid upside down, encouraging employee involvement, participative management and teamwork he brought about remarkable improvements in morale, product quality and profits. Ford managed one of the biggest turnarounds known in the motor industry. During the 1980s when Peterson was at the helm, Ford moved from last place to first place in quality among the Big Three. The company gained seven percentage points in market share, despite continued market penetration by the Japanese. Also there was a steep improvement in profits. In 1986 and 1987 Ford profits were ahead of General Motors despite their difference in size.[16]

General Electric

At General Electric one main thrust behind employee involvement is the "workout" programme. This process is designed to identify and eliminate practices and processes which are preventing the company's vision or the business's strategy from being implemented. Work-out appears to be one of the most effective management techniques available for eliminating barriers to the implementation of a company's strategies.

Jack Welch, the chairman and CEO, says the objectives of work-out are to get rid of thousands of bad habits collected over the years and to put the leaders of each business in front of a hundred of their people 8–10 times each year to hear their opinions about the company. He wants to encourage employees to confront their bosses in public.

The work-out programme which initially involved only the top three layers of management is now being expanded to include the whole organization.[17] (see Box 3).

Enabling Operating Managers to Take Charge of Strategy

Before the downsizing of the early 1990s, as part of the strategic planning process in a large divisionalized company the Corporate Planning department would prepare planning guidelines—including economic and market forecasts, corporate objectives and policies, and management priorities for investment. The Business Planning team in the division would review their market sector, benchmark the company's products and services against the competition and analyse relevant political, technological and economic trends. The Finance department would prepare risk and sensitivity analyses, and the Personnel department would produce forecasts of wage levels and manpower requirements and assess the implications of new legislation.

Now, after "downsizing", Corporate Planning teams have been removed and the central staff groups have been cut back in marketing, manufacturing, information technology and human resources. Some of these services have been "outsourced" to independent companies whose contracts may not include giving advice to divisions. In some companies divisional offices have disappeared. Business unit teams are being asked to take responsibility for the day-to-day management of their profit centres as well as for developing and implementing a strategy for the longer term. To enable business unit teams to take charge of strategy, companies are using three approaches:

Corporate-level Strategy[18]

The first requirement for an integrated divisionalized company is that there must be an excellent understanding between the corporate-level management and the managers of the business units.

■   The board and the top management must understand the nature of the business in each of their operating units, for example they should agree what role

---

Box 3

The General Electric Work-out Process[17]

Step 1 Review the Business Strategy
This describes the company's main business opportunities, assesses its performance compared with competitors and describes the programmes designed to bridge any gaps.

Step 2 Involvement in Work-out
The second step is to ask, "how much more effective would you be in achieving this strategy if all impediments were removed?", Also, "how do we identify and eliminate wasteful work practices?"

Step 3 Listing Wasteful Work Practices
Groups of 5 or 6 managers generate detailed lists of wasteful work practices. These lists are then put together and the entire group reviews the practices targeted for streamlining or elimination. They ask three questions: "What is our objective?" "Who should be involved?" and "What information do we need?"

Step 4 Functional Groups
They then break into functional groups to identify what they experience in their own work and what delays they impose on other groups. Their conclusions are presented to the whole group and reviewed as in Step 3.

Step 5 Cross-functional Groups

The participants then meet in cross-functional teams to identify work processes, procedures and controls that hinder *teamwork* across functions. These problems are then allocated on flip charts which bear the names of specific functions or departments.

Step 6 Contracts and Recommendations
Contracts are written to eliminate or streamline each work practice and achieving specific goals. Within two months each function must report back to the whole group making its recommendations. The business unit head chairs the session and agrees or declines the proposals giving clear reasons. The recommendations are then summarized for the major business in a report.

---

the division will play in the company's portfolio of businesses, e.g. does the top management want to 'invest for growth' or 'harvest for cash'?

- The corporate team and the divisional managers should also share common values and priorities—about the need for product innovation, product quality, customer service and employee participation.
- They should share a common sense of purpose, common objectives and policies. It is necessary for the corporate team to make clear to the divisional management their ambitions for the company as a whole—their purpose, their broad strategy and their specific goals.

■ The corporate team should also make clear what resources can be made available—not just money, but manpower, technology and facilities.

Strategic Contracts

Once this mutual understanding has been established, a 'contract' should be agreed between the management at the centre and each business unit team, stating what resources and services the centre will provide and what the business unit will deliver. Consultants are currently offering two approaches which provide a practical framework for this 'Strategic Contract': Shareholder Value and the Balanced Business Scorecard. Both these approaches offer a philosophy, a well developed framework and measurements which can form the basis of an agreement between the Centre and a division or business unit. In Britain, Lloyds Bank, BP, ICI and ICL are using the shareholder value approach. NatWest Group and United Parcel Services (UPS) are equally committed to the Balanced Scorecard.[19]

Team-based Planning

If operating managers are going to take charge of strategy they will need to use a practical, team-based approach. They will require a number of readily understood team-based processes which will deliver results in terms of alternative scenarios, core competences, mission statements, strategic options, project plans, etc.

One book which deals in practical terms with the shift from strategic planning involving large central staff groups to team-based planning which "empowers" profit centre teams is *Real-Time Strategy: Improvising Team-Based Planning for a Fast Changing World* by a team of academics and consultants based at Brigham Young University.[20] Their model uses the concept of 'Strategic Alignment', i.e. harnessing the organization and the people in it to implement the strategy (see Figure 4). They also provide a tool kit of techniques which are designed to help managers to analyse their company's activities into various categories in order to focus their efforts on "competitive advantage work" (i.e. work which creates a competitive advantage in the market) and outsource or eliminate work of less strategic importance.

A 'Grass Roots' Approach

The extent to which staff at all levels can be involved in developing and implementing business strategy will depend upon the type of organization and the kinds of products or services which are being offered upon the extent to which *confidentiality* must be preserved and what *specialist knowledge and skills* are required. However participative the management wish to be, they are still likely

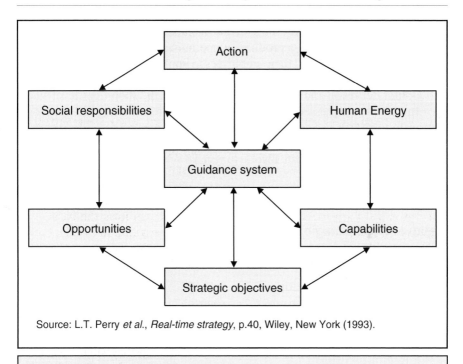

Source: L.T. Perry *et al.*, *Real-time strategy*, p.40, Wiley, New York (1993).

Figure 4. The strategic improvising model.

to require the skills of strategy consultants and financial specialists to arrange mergers and acquisitions, alliances and joint ventures, and customer–supplier partnerships.

In professional service organizations which have highly trained personnel (e.g. management consultancies, schools and colleges, scientific and engineering research establishments) it is vital to engage all the staff who can make a contribution. An illuminating Harvard Business School study of strategy-making on Wall Street found that many investment banks were adopting a 'grass roots' approach to strategy. Tom Strauss, the president of Salomon Brothers, explained the process as a 'reverse funnel' effect.

> We let ideas percolate up and most get discarded. Sometimes ideas even start with senior management [but] we have to plant them in the middle of the firm since we need the organization behind them. If people want something to happen it will happen.[21]

As a senior executive at Goldman Sachs put it:

> You need a mechanism to push the ideas upstairs, since the best ones come from the trenches

Leading Japanese companies like Toyota, Honda and Canon even apply this grass roots approach to mass production operations. It is remarkable how they have been able to involve all their employees in implementing their strategies. It is normal for them to publish their Corporate Philosophy, Corporate Principles and Corporate Vision and to take the ideas down to the shop floor level where the principles are expressed in practical, operational terms which the work force can relate to.[22] This also seems to be the direction which some western corporations like General Electric and British Airways have chosen, but few of these companies could claim, as can Toyota, to receive a million suggestions each year from their workforce.

Re-inventing Strategic Planning

Strategic planning declined for a number of reasons:

- *Large central planning teams were found to be costly and ineffective.* To quote one chief executive: "I've never seen so much talent so misused." They were too preoccupied with sophisticated analysis to provide the strategic radar which companies so badly needed to enable them to adapt to the massive changes which were occurring around them. In a turbulent and highly competitive environment a successful company can go into decline very quickly, as one management after another discovered. This happened not just to IBM but to airlines, utilities, banks, insurance companies, construction and property businesses. Following deregulation, the privatization of public companies or the introduction of new lower-cost technologies, new companies entered the market, prices fell and the established businesses became unprofitable. The major players had to find a new cost base and new markets or go out of business.
- *The annual planning round proved to be too cumbersome and inflexible to cope with fast-moving high technology markets.* In personal computers, mobile telecommunications, computer games or multi-media, it is not unknown for a product to go through a complete life cycle in one or two years. While the Business Plan is still going around the company, the real decisions are being taken elsewhere.
- *The strategic planners, along with other central staff groups, were putting a break on the line managers.* Operational managers found that their plans were being reviewed by corporate planners who often did not understand what was happening in the market. The planners were removed "to allow the managers to manage".
- *When the plans were finally approved, the business unit teams did not 'own' them,* consequently the plans were not implemented and stayed in the file.
- *Planning as a bureaucratic process did not produce innovative thinking.* In general the plans were simply an extension of "business as usual".

Now, after the great purge of restructuring, downsizing and business process re-engineering, companies still desperately need strategic thinking, and Strategic Planning has returned in the form of Strategic Leadership. We can identify a number of separate but converging trends:

- Strategy is not regarded as an annual event but as a *continuous dialogue* which takes place throughout the year.
- Strategy discussions are not focused on operational plans but around a few *strategic issues*.
- The place of the large strategic planning teams has been taken by directors of corporate development who work on *corporate projects* such as strategic alliances and joint ventures, entry into new markets in Eastern Europe and South East Asia, etc. They have a small staff who work closely with senior executives at headquarters and in the divisions; if they need more manpower they use external consultants. This has resulted in a boom in strategy consulting.
- We have also seen the emergence of the *profit-accountable organization*. The top executive team is increasingly working to targets which have been agreed with the board of directors, and the divisional or business unit teams are working to targets which they have agreed with the group chief executive. Group services work to targets and budgets which have been agreed with the executive committee and the divisions.
- Strategy consultants earn their fees by working with the top management team to benchmark the company's performance, collect evidence of major external trends, do some 'blue-sky thinking' about the future and formulate a *corporate vision*. The key strategic issues should emerge as management identify the *gaps* between the corporate vision and the strategies which are being suggested by the various businesses.
- Management then face the task of *aligning the organization behind the strategy*—the policies and processes, the organization structure, the information systems and the people.
- The focus is now mainly on *implementing strategy* through:
  - management training in the shareholder value or balanced business scorecard approach;
  - developing learning companies which focus on the development of their human assets;
  - adopting participative management and employee empowerment as a company-wide management style;
  - techniques which are designed to encourage 'honest upward feedback' from the employees to the management, individually and in groups.

Like other key business processes, strategy-making is being re-engineered. To make a success of this changeover in organizations which have been "downsized", and in many cases demoralized by closures and redundancies, will require a major effort of leadership by top management. Otherwise the 'Fall' of Strategic

Planning which occurred in the 1980s and early 1990s will be followed not by a transition to Strategic Management or Business Transformation but by a regression to 'muddling through'. To quote Sir James Goldsmith:

> Muddling through is a euphemism for failing to plan forward. It means acting tactically and without a strategy; it means confusing the means with the end... If we continue to avoid facing the facts... the epitaph on the grave of our democracy will be: 'They sacrificed the long-term for the short-term, and the long term finally arrived'.

References

1. Bernard Taylor, Strategy without planners: getting organised for strategic leadership, In *Business: The Essential Factfile*, Prentice Hall, Englewood Cliffs, NJ (1997).
2. John A. Byrne, Strategic planning, *Business Week*, 2 September (1996).
3. Mahen Tampoe and Bernard Taylor, Strategy software: exploring its potential, *Long Range Planning*, **29** (2), 239–245 (1996).
4. Gary Hamel and C.K. Prahalad, *Competing for the Future*, Harvard Business School Press, Boston, MA (1994).
5. Francis J. Gouillart and James N. Kelly, *Transforming the Organisation*, McGraw-Hill, New York (1995).
6. Ron Ashkenas *et al.*, *The Boundaryless Organisation*, Jossey Bass, San Francisco (1995); and William H. Davidow and Michael S. Malone, *The Virtual Corporation*, Harper Collins, New York (1992).
7. *International Management*, April (1988).
8. Richard Pascale, *Managing on the Edge*, p.279, Penguin, Harmondsworth (1991).
9. Chris Argyris, *Good Communication That Blocks Learning*, Harvard Business Review, July/August, 77–85, (1994).
10. Peter Senge, The Fifth Discipline: *The Art and Practice of the Learning Organisation*, Doubleday, New York (1990).
11. Donald Michael, *On Learning to Plan and Planning to Learn*, Jossey Bass, San Francisco, CA (1973).
12. J. Friedmann, The future of comprehensive urban planning: a critique, *Public Administration Review*, **31** (3), 326.
13. Calhoun W. Wick and Lu Stanton Leon, *The Learning Edge: How Smart Managers and Smart Companies Stay Ahead*, McGraw-Hill, New York (1993).
14. Hal Rosenbluth, *The Customer Comes Second, and Other Secrets of Successful Service*, Marrow (1992).
15. Calhoun W. Wick and Lu Stanton Leon, *op.cit.*
16. Donald Peterson and John Hilkirk, *Teamwork New Management Ideas for the Nineties*, Victor Gollancz, London (1991).
17. For full details see Noel M. Tichy and Stratford Sherman, *Control Your Destiny or Someone Else Will*, Harper Collins, New York (1994).
18. Michael Goold, Andrew Campbell and Marcus Alexander, *Corporate Level Strategy*, John Wiley, New York (1994).

19. For further information on the Shareholder Value approach see: Alfred Rappaport, *Creating Shareholder Value*, Free Press, London (1986); Roger W. Mills, *Finance, Strategy and Strategic Value Analysis*, Mars Business Associates, Lechlade, Glos., (1994). For an introduction to the Balanced Scorecard read Robert S. Kaplan and David P. Norton, Using the balanced scorecard as a strategic management systems, *Harvard Business Review*, **74** (1), Jan/Feb, 75–85 (1996).

20. Lee Tom Perry, Randall G. Stott and W. Norman Smallwood, *Real-Time Strategy: Improvising Team-Based Planning for a Fast-Changing World*, John Wiley, New York (1993).

21. Robert G. Eccles and Dwight B. Crane, *Doing Deals: Investment Banks at Work*, Harvard Business School, Boston, p. 122 (1988).

22. See Toyohiro Kono (ed.), *Strategic Management in Japanese Companies*, Pergamon, Oxford (1992).

Index